© 2009 Aboriginal Healing Foundation

Published by:
Aboriginal Healing Foundation
75 Albert Street, Suite 801, Ottawa, Ontario K1P 5E7
Phone: (613) 237-4441
Toll-free: (888) 725-8886
Fax: (613) 237-4442
Email: research@ahf.ca
Website: www.ahf.ca

Design & Production:
Aboriginal Healing Foundation

Printed by:
Dollco Printing
Ottawa, Ontario

Printed version:
ISBN 978-1-897285-72-5

Electronic version:
ISBN 978-1-897285-73-2

This project was funded by the Aboriginal Healing Foundation (AHF), but the views expressed in this report
are the personal views of the author(s).

Ce document est aussi disponible en français.

Response, Responsibility, and Renewal

Canada's Truth and Reconciliation Journey

Edited for

the Aboriginal Healing Foundation

By

Gregory Younging
Jonathan Dewar
Mike DeGagné

2009

TABLE OF CONTENTS

PREFACE

This is the second installment in a two-volume set produced by the Aboriginal Healing Foundation. This volume contains personal reflections on the opportunities and challenges posed by the truth and reconciliation process, which was constituted in the 2006 *Indian Residential Schools Settlement Agreement*, to aid in the deliberation of work facing Canada's Truth and Reconciliation Commission.

The work of truth and reconciliation has at its core human relationships. The Indian residential school system, and the policies that informed it, has shaped not only the past, but the present. It has shaped relationships between the Canadian government and Aboriginal peoples, between the abused and their abusers, and between individuals within families and communities. Indeed, as we set out on this unique voyage, every wrinkle in the territory may be understood as a relationship.

The residential school system itself came about as the consequence of human relationships. Through the treaty negotiations of the late 1800s, Aboriginal people agreed to allow use of their traditional territories in exchange for (among other things) training of their children in the skills of agriculture and animal husbandry. This training was not to supplant Aboriginal cultures, but to enhance and sustain them into the future. The churches had long sought government support for their efforts to Christianize Indians and saw their opportunity in the treaty provision. The government, eager to divest itself of its obligations, entered into a formal relationship with the churches. The government was optimistic that the forcible assimilation of Indians into Canadian society would solve "the Indian problem" and open the land fully to settlement within a single generation.

In other words, a relationship of ostensible good faith and mutual respect between peoples yielded to a political relationship of convenience, coercion, and advantage. Displaced by the nineteenth-century project of "nation building" were the concerns, interests, and humanity of Aboriginal people. The partnership of church and state in the fashioning of a colonizing residential school system constituted a crass and painful betrayal when viewed from the perspective of human relationships.

Whatever ways, if anything, to improve the future must be informed by an awareness of past relationships and a commitment to the principle of mutual respect. Although the residential schools' systemic bigotry and racism are repudiated today, there are many reminders that not all is well in the relationship between Canada and Aboriginal people. Nor is all well in the relationships among Aboriginal people themselves, relationships that have been maligned across the generations by institutions such as the Indian residential school system, the criminal justice system, and the child welfare system. Addictions, domestic abuse, suicide, and poverty are all "relationship indicators" suggesting that the deep wounds of the past require a comprehensive response informed by an understanding of human relationships impacted by historic trauma.

Truth and reconciliation, separately, are but steps along the path of healing this and many other subsequent betrayals. None is a fixed target; they are grounded in relationships and, like a conversation, do not move in straight and predictable lines. What truth, reconciliation, and healing require, at minimum, are human presence and commitment. Beyond this is uncharted territory.

Masi,

Georges Erasmus
President
Aboriginal Healing Foundation

Photographer: Allen Deleary

RESPONSE, RESPONSIBILITY, AND RENEWAL:
CANADA'S TRUTH AND RECONCILIATION JOURNEY

INTRODUCTION

In the spring of 2008, the Aboriginal Healing Foundation (AHF) released *From Truth to Reconciliation: Transforming the Legacy of Residential Schools*. It was released to coincide with "Remembering the Children: An Aboriginal and Church Leaders' Tour to Prepare for Truth and Reconciliation."[1] This initiative, led by the National Chief of the Assembly of First Nations and, along with representatives of the Roman Catholic Church, the spiritual leaders of the Anglican, Presbyterian, and United churches sought to promote the work of the upcoming Indian Residential Schools Truth and Reconciliation Commission. In announcing the tour, organizers said the following:

> We believe it is essential that Canadians pay close attention to this process of truth telling ... This is the opportunity for all of us to hear the voices of the children who attended residential schools, to listen to their stories, and to learn, maybe for the first time, of the impact that residential schools have had on Canada's First Nations, Inuit and Métis communities.[2]

The release goes on to say that the Aboriginal and church leaders hope the tour would raise awareness about the work of the Truth and Reconciliation Commission and help to educate both church members and other Canadians about the legacy of residential schools and the impacts of colonization on Aboriginal people and their communities. "We see this tour as an opportunity to model what a new and positive relationship between Aboriginal and non-Aboriginal people might look like."[3]

The tour and the AHF's publication *From Truth to Reconciliation* were neither conceived together nor designed for the other's benefit. They were coincidentally conceived and came about through processes germane to the respective parties involved. *From Truth to Reconciliation* began in the summer of 2007 as an AHF Research initiative designed to address the AHF's stated commitments to reconciliation:

We see our role as facilitators in the healing process by helping Aboriginal people help themselves, by providing resources for healing initiatives, by promoting awareness of healing issues and needs, and by nurturing a supportive public environment. We also work to engage Canadians in this healing process by encouraging them to walk with us on the path of reconciliation.

Ours is a holistic approach. Our goal is to help create, reinforce and sustain conditions conducive to healing, reconciliation and self determination ...

We emphasize approaches that address the needs of Aboriginal individuals, families and the broader community. We view prevention of future abuse, and the process of reconciliation between victims and offenders, and between Aboriginal people and Canadians as vital elements in building healthy, sustainable communities.[4]

As the editors of *From Truth to Reconciliation* pointed out in their introduction to the volume, the AHF "has encountered many gifted individuals whose life and work have been dedicated to promoting justice and reconciliation in individual, community, and societal relationships here in Canada and abroad."[5] A compelling cross-section of such individuals were invited to offer their personal perspectives on truth and reconciliation as the many interested parties awaited with anticipation the final approval of the *Indian Residential Schools Settlement Agreement*, which would include what many considered to be its flagship component, the Indian Residential Schools Truth and Reconciliation Commission (TRC).

As copy rolled in that summer and fall, the editorial committee noted the significant, but expected, passing of these key milestones, notably 17 September 2007, the day the *Agreement* came into effect and the Government of Canada began receiving applications for the common experience payment, another core component of the *Agreement*. But there was one surprise in store.

In her Speech from the Throne on 16 October 2007, Her Excellency the Right Honourable Michaëlle Jean, the Governor General of Canada, said, "Our government recently concluded a final settlement on Indian

Residential Schools and will launch a commission for truth and reconciliation. The Prime Minister, on behalf of our Government, will use this occasion to make a statement of apology to close this sad chapter in our history."[6]

The editorial committee had certainly expected contributors to tackle the subject of apologies, discuss the nature of "this sad chapter," and offer opinions on what appropriate action would be required to address the legacy of residential schools. Contributors to the first volume did not disappoint. Several articles detail the power, possibilities, challenges, and failings of apologies specific to residential schools in Canada—notably those proffered by the churches and the Government of Canada's 1998 *Statement of Reconciliation*—and to others more generally.

With the Governor General's words, the emotional tenor in communities across Canada did seem to rise, even in an already charged atmosphere. This was exacerbated by the fact that no further details were offered in the speech or in the media buzz that followed. There was a clamouring for details, even for insights into basic procedural matters, and a sense that people wanted to begin to debate the big issues of apology and forgiveness. Instead, the conversation—in the form, primarily, of media coverage—was focused on past efforts at government apology and statements made by the government about the relationship between apology and the work of the TRC, with the need for that process to play out first and foremost.

Then, on 13 February 2008, Canadians watched as Australian Prime Minister Kevin Rudd made a formal apology for past wrongs committed by successive Australian governments on its Indigenous population. Prime Minister Rudd apologized in Parliament to all Aborigines for laws and policies that "inflicted profound grief, suffering and loss."[7] He singled out the Stolen Generations of thousands of children forcibly removed from their families. Canadians watched as Australia's Aboriginal peoples responded, some with mixed reaction. Absent, these detractors noted, was any commitment to compensation.

In Canada, meanwhile, compensation was being administered in the form of the common experience payment and information was circulating about the subsequent individual compensation component, the independent assessment process for physical and sexual abuse claims. To some, though, there was a void. There were varying degrees of awareness of the *Agreement* and its components. Many felt the TRC, in particular, had a low profile outside of the parties to the *Agreement* and partner organizations involved in related issues, through no fault of the TRC itself, which was only just beginning to staff an office in preparation for the incoming chair and two commissioners. The organizers of the "Remembering the Children" initiative stepped into this void, and while *From Truth to Reconciliation* was well along in its development, the editorial committee did note the synergistic possibilities of these recent developments. In short order, the tour, an initiative independent from the government and TRC, welcomed the Aboriginal Healing Foundation's contribution to the truth and reconciliation discourse and included the volume as part of its multi-city tour. And so, on Sunday, 2 March 2008, the Aboriginal Healing Foundation launched *From Truth to Reconciliation*.

There are numerous ways one may read that title. One titular concept—a sense of movement from truth (or from more than one truth) to and through reconciliation—was nicely articulated in Jennifer Llewellyn's article, "Bridging the Gap between Truth and Reconciliation: Restorative Justice and the Indian Residential Schools Truth and Reconciliation Commission," which highlighted a key challenge faced by the South African Truth and Reconciliation Commission, one likely to be replicated in Canada: "As the TRC begins its journey, it must figure out how to navigate the complex and difficult road of 'truth' and map a course toward reconciliation. In doing so, it will face the substantial challenge that others who have travelled this path before have encountered: bridging the gap between truth and reconciliation."[8] To date, over 10,000 copies of *From Truth to Reconciliation* in both official languages have been distributed across Canada and internationally, and response to the volume has been overwhelmingly positive.

Issues related to the TRC and its mandate continued to percolate, and perceptions continued to be varied as all parties awaited the major milestones of the TRC launch and delivery of the apology. Eventually, an announcement was made that the Government of Canada's official apology would be made on 11 June 2008, but details, again, were scarce. Would the Prime Minister deliver the apology in the House of Commons? What role would residential school Survivors, their families, communities, friends, and supporters play in the development, delivery, and reception of the apology? How would Canadians receive and perceive the apology?

That auspicious occasion answered many of those questions, but as one may well have expected, of course, it was now open season on response and opinion. So, in the summer of 2008, the AHF decided to commission a second set of articles from Aboriginal and non-Aboriginal individuals in Canada and abroad to continue to promote the truth and reconciliation discourse, particularly the many challenging issues being raised given the significant developments in the few short, intervening months between the release of the first volume and the decision to embark on a new round of commentary. The first volume was intended as an opportunity to float some big ideas concerning truth and reconciliation, targeted, in part, for incoming commissioners who would doubtlessly be bogged down, at least for a short while, with the practicalities of leading a new commission. Others, meanwhile, concentrated on promoting the TRC itself and the work it was expected to do.

This second volume was initially seen as an opportunity for new authors to continue to probe, promote, or put forth big ideas about truth and reconciliation and to respond to those ideas already out there; yet again, unexpected developments occurred. On 20 October 2008, mere months after the TRC was launched and its leaders appointed with great fanfare, Justice Harry LaForme resigned as chair of the TRC, followed shortly thereafter by commissioners Jane Brewin Morley and Claudette Dumont-Smith. Subsequently, the TRC entered what may be called a holding pattern. A new void was, to some, palpable. Many noted that some Survivors have passed on from this world in the months since the launch of the TRC on 1 June 2008, the government apology that followed ten days later, and these announcements. This new void also forced communities to wait, yet again, for answers to questions large and small, philosophical and practical.

This void, like others before it, was pierced by action. As with the "Remembering the Children" initiative—itself a response to questions about how, when, and where the TRC would begin to act—there have been grassroots truth and reconciliation initiatives. Gregory Younging, a member of the editorial committee for this volume, was part of the University of British Columbia Okanagan and Ki-Low-Na Friendship

Society's 20 March 2009 "Reconciliation: History and Future in Our Midst" event. Like other events that have been held during the months since the TRC was announced, the community was inspired to begin the truth and reconciliation discourse in its own backyard with friends and neighbours—with or without a formal connection to the TRC. Several of the authors featured in this volume have been similarly involved in their communities at the community level, sometimes promoting, sometimes challenging the work ahead of all parties to reconciliation. That commitment to identifying the issues, sharing ideas, making recommendations, meeting challenges, and challenging the status quo is evident throughout this volume.

And here we are, yet again, putting forth a volume into an arena of waiting hands and, hopefully, open minds. We hope to reach many—those involved in the discourse already and those coming to concepts of truth and reconciliation in this historic Canadian context for the first time. The incoming Truth and Reconciliation Commission chair and commissioners, whose appointments are expected to be announced as we go to print, will meet similar circumstances but with vastly heightened expectations. This context is important; but, it is the ideas like those expressed in the following pages that should carry the most weight with the newly constituted TRC. As with the first volume, we see movement and momentum, possibilities and potential, but also challenges. As such, we have titled this volume *Response, Responsibility, and Renewal: Canada's Truth and Reconciliation Journey*.

This volume, like the first, presents each paper with a short biography of the author. The editorial committee has edited with a light hand, as our intent was to offer authors an opportunity to share their thoughts and opinions. The articles are grouped thematically within three sections; however, we acknowledge and, in fact, delight in the way many of these pieces overlap and intersect with others. To that end, the section titles reflect these possibilities, and we invite readers to journey through yesterday's, today's, and tomorrow's challenges and achievements.

Section 1: History in Our Midst has a strong historical component with an emphasis on its place within our lives today. Jose Kusugak offers a vividly descriptive account of his and his brother's residential school experiences, of being "taken" and of returning home, and concludes with a thoughtful take on the good times and bad times. In the wake of the 2008 apology, Rene Dussault reminds the reader that "it remains just as urgent that Canada re-examine the very foundations of its relationship with Aboriginal peoples" and revisits the report of the Royal Commission on Aboriginal Peoples (RCAP) and the detailed 20-year strategy it proposed to restore the social, economic, and political health of Aboriginal peoples in redefining their relationship with the rest of Canada.

Sophie Pierre tells the story of the St. Eugene Mission Resort and a community's determination to change the legacy of residential schools, at least one school in particular, into something positive that would benefit the community for generations to come. James Igloliorte tells the story of Labrador Inuit and a different, less well-known apology, and he places their experiences within the larger reconciliation discourse.

Susan Crean writes about the need to take ownership of our history to truly participate in reconciliation efforts. She highlights her friendship with Métis writer Howard Adams and her own Anglo-Canadian identity and connection to the Northwest Rebellion when her great-uncle went to fight against Louis Riel at Duck Lake. She does this to underscore the personal-within history. Rita Flamand writes about growing up Michif by recounting her day school experience, highlighting the important similarities and distinctions between the Métis experience with residential schools and church and government influences. She calls for a telling of the "true history of Métis people."

Ian MacKenzie writes "Now is the time to heal" from his position as a founding member of the Centre for Indian Scholars, promoting the interface of Christianity and First Nations traditional religions. For Drew Hayden Taylor, satire is good medicine. He takes a humourous approach to the Prime Minister's apology, but asks us to consider some complex questions about apologies and forgiveness and where we all go from here. Mick Dodson offers an Aboriginal Australian perspective on that country's experience with apology. He, too, asks where one goes next— post-apology—noting that not only was it "a marginally transformative experience for Australia," but "a fundamental step in building a respectful relationship between Indigenous and non-Indigenous citizens." He highlights the need to address unfinished business and closes with a most recent development that may well be yet another fundamental step forward.

Readers will notice that the title of the following section—*Section 2: Reconciliation, Restitution, Rhetoric*—bears at least an alliterative resemblance to the volume's title, with its three *Rs*. As with *Response, Responsibility, and Renewal*, there is a sense of promise in recent words and deeds. There are also processes and problems to consider.

Heather Igloliorte writes about Inuit art and artists and the "power of visual art to speak across linguistic, cultural, and generational divides." She claims that this presents "an opportunity for artists to tell these stories to a broad audience and to support the continued strengthening and revitalization of the national reconciliation process." Richard Wagamese writes about his experience with the child welfare system and the intergenerational effects of residential schools. He stresses the importance of personal reconciliation, the experiences of "people who fought against the resentment, hatred, and anger and found a sense of peace," and the need for the Commission to hear these truths.

Peter Harrison writes about the major challenge facing the TRC, which is coping with ignorance at its most basic levels by dispelling myths about both the history of the policies and the present landscape of settlement agreements and compensation. Scott Serson, like Dussault in *Section 1*, revisits the RCAP report, but focuses on Canada's response, *Gathering Strength—Canada's Aboriginal Action Plan*, highlighting its four objectives: renewing partnerships; strengthening governance; developing a new fiscal relationship; and supporting strong communities, people, and economies. He asks the reader to first consider Canada's words and actions since 1998 and then to consider reconciliation and fiscal fairness.

Taiaiake Alfred pulls no punches, calling reconciliation "an emasculating concept, weak-kneed and easily accepting of half-hearted measures of a notion of justice that does nothing to help Indigenous peoples regain their dignity and strength," and argues for a restitution discourse to address the crime of colonialism. Waziyatawin, too, places residential schools within the larger colonial project and calls for bigger solutions. She offers practical steps for addressing "the crimes of land theft, genocide, ethnic cleansing, and colonization" in the Dakota homeland of *Minisota Makoce*.

David Hollinsworth looks critically at Australia's apology and calls for Australia to act to ensure genuine reparations and healing for all those damaged by past policies and practices. Roland Chrisjohn and Tanya Wasacase tackle the rhetoric of Canada's apology and of the TRC mandate, arguing that "truth and reconciliation are not justice, and the Commission will not produce justice even if successful in its mandate."

Section 3: Tomorrow's History opens with the remarks made by the Most Reverend Fred Hiltz, Primate of the Anglican Church of Canada, in Ottawa, Ontario, on 2 March 2008 during "Remembering the Children: An Aboriginal and Church Leaders' Tour to Prepare for Truth and Reconciliation," saying "As churches we have *so much* for which to be *so sorry*" and pledging to live the words of apology.

Valerie Galley argues that a commitment to reconciliation must include a commitment to revitalize and protect Aboriginal languages. Mari Tanaka presents her perspective as a new immigrant to Canada and writes of learning about residential schools and the impact it had on her as she sought to develop her own identity as both Canadian and Japanese.

Erin Wolski offers the Native Women's Association of Canada's culturally relevant gender-based analysis framework as a tool the TRC should consider and use as it seeks to serve the needs of Aboriginal women and to represent their unique experiences. Natalie A. Chambers reflects on her experiences as an immigrant woman living on-reserve. She urges other settler peoples to engage in critical self-examination as a first step in the process of working through their roles as colonizers in the past so that all may imagine a better future for generations.

John Ralston Saul writes, "Reconciliation can only begin when the people of Canada collectively wish it." He details the optimism he has encountered across the country, building towards a "new consensus," but identifies four barriers that still stand in the way. Finally, Gregory Younging describes his own intergenerational experience with residential schools and his connection to this experience through his mother and her work as well as his own academic and activist work.

The conclusion by the editorial team, without attempting to summarize or reiterate the insights, recommendations, and personal experiences so ably articulated by the authors, considers the concept of history that is past, present, and future in light of the very particular context of recent events.

NOTES

[1] *See the website*: Remembering the Children: An Aboriginal and Church Leaders' Tour to Prepare for Truth and Reconciliation. Retrieved 21 April 2009 from: www.rememberingthechildren.ca

[2] David MacDonald cited in "Remembering the Children: An Aboriginal and Church Leaders' tour to prepare for Truth and Reconciliation," press release, Toronto, ON. Retrieved 21 April 2009 from: http://www.rememberingthechildren.ca/press/2008-02-15.htm

[3] *Cited in* Remembering the Children: An Aboriginal and Church Leaders' Tour to Prepare for Truth and Reconciliation, see note #2.

[4] Aboriginal Healing Foundation (2001:9). *Aboriginal Healing Foundation Program Handbook, Third Edition.* Ottawa, ON: Aboriginal Healing Foundation. The vision, mission, and values can also be found on the AHF website at: http://www.ahf.ca/about-us/mission

[5] Castellano, Marlene Brant, Linda Archibald, and Mike DeGagné (2008:4). Introduction. In Marlene Brant Castellano, Linda Archibald, and Mike DeGagné (eds.), *From Truth to Reconciliation: Transforming the Legacy of Residential Schools.* Ottawa, ON: Aboriginal Healing Foundation:1–8.

[6] Jean, The Honourable Michaëlle (2007). Governor General's Speech from the Throne to open the second session, thirty-ninth Parliament of Canada on 16 October 2007. Retrieved 21 April 21 2009 from: http://www2.parl.gc.ca/Parlinfo/Documents/ThroneSpeech/39-2-e.html

[7] Rudd, The Honourable Kevin (2008). Prime Minister of Australia Speech - Apology to Australia's Indigenous Peoples. House of Representatives, Parliament House, 13 February 2008. Canberra, AU: Prime Minister of Australia. Retrieved 21 August 2008 from: http://www.pm.gov.au/media/Speech/2008/speech_0073.cfm

[8] Llewellyn, Jennifer (2008:186). Bridging the Gap Between Truth and Reconciliation: Restorative Justice and the Indian Residential Schools Truth and Reconciliation Commission. In Marlene Brant Castellano, Linda Archibald, and Mike DeGagné (eds.), *From Truth to Reconciliation: Transforming the Legacy of Residential Schools.* Ottawa, ON: Aboriginal Healing Foundation: 183–201.

Section 1

History in Our Midst

Coming out ceremony for
Cassandra Bisson, Kyleigh Biedermann, and Hanako Hubbard-Radulovich
M'Chigeeng, Ontario
Photographer: Allen Deleary

JOSE AMAUJAQ KUSUGAK
(E3-917)*

Jose Amaujaq Kusugak was born in 1950, in an igloo in Naujaat (then Repulse Bay) located on the Arctic Circle. He is the second oldest of 12 children. Both of his parents had worked for the Hudson's Bay Company; his father was a handyman and his mother worked as a cleaner and fur washer. Jose went to school in Chesterfield Inlet, Nunavut, and Churchill, Manitoba. He attended high school in Saskatoon, Saskatchewan. After graduation, he returned to Rankin Inlet, Nunavut, to work at the Eskimo Language School, a branch of the University of Saskatchewan. Later, he taught Inuktitut and Inuit history at Churchill Vocational Centre.

Jose has been active in Inuit politics since 1971, shortly after the founding of the Inuit Tapiriit Kanatami (ITK) (then Inuit Tapirisat of Canada). He persuaded the new organization of the critical need to standardize the written Inuit language, which is primarily an oral language. However, funding for this project had been delayed, so Jose worked as an assistant to Tagak Curley, the first president of ITK, and introduced the concept of land claims to Inuit in the Arctic. In 1974, he went to Alaska to study how the land claims process worked there. From 1980 to 1990, Jose worked as the area manager of CBC in the Kivalliq (Keewatin) region. He served as president of Nunavut Tunngavik Incorporated, one of four regional organizations that make up ITK, from 1994 to 2000. He was elected president of ITK in June 2000. He describes the relationship of the Inuit to Canada as First Canadians, Canadians First. Jose and his wife Nellie live in Rankin Inlet, Nunavut, and they have four grown children.

* *This was Jose's number when he went to residential school.*

ON THE SIDE OF THE ANGELS

THE BAYS

The Hudson's Bay Company (HBC) or "The Bay" was incorporated on 2 May 1670,[1] making it the oldest incorporated company in the world. Two hundred and eighty years later, on 2 May 1950, I was born into the "Bay" in Naujaat (Repulse Bay) where mother and father both worked for the HBC. On my birthdays, the trader would point to the HBC insignia on their main store and give me a present, which was often a sucker candy. I would slurp it with pride to make all around me jealous with envy. The HBC, with all its own problems, was not in the Arctic to change Inuit people. It was there because of the furs it wanted to obtain from Inuit hunters, who were master hunters of Arctic animals.

Healthy hunters brought in more furs, so the HBC gave their traders minimal training on meeting the medical needs of the Inuit hunters. I have even seen them pulling teeth and giving shots when necessary. Inuit and "The Bay" had a good partnership. Inuit wanted the goods and the Bay wanted the furs. The Bay boys learned Inuktitut, the language of Inuit, so there was very little assimilation of Inuit toward the *Qablunaaq* (white people) world. *Qablunaaq* HBC boys wrote several books[2] praising Inuit knowledge, culture, and perseverance. This was not from the goodness of their hearts necessarily, it was but an acknowledgement of what the HBC employees needed and wanted to learn from Inuit on Arctic survival.

Even the churches, who were appalled at the shamanistic rituals of Inuit in some regions, only wanted to save souls and not necessarily change culture. They were not necessarily anti-Inuit, but were just not Inuit. Many Inuit became Christians because the churches had what Inuit wanted: biscuits, beans, prunes, hope, and gifts of clothing from other Christians from the south. I remember there was always a strong smell of mothballs in the clothing, which is one of the first *Qablunaaq* smells we encountered.

My mother did not like the HBC's practice of stockpiling the furs of bear, fox, seal, and other fur commodities throughout the winter. But

> Many Inuit became Christians because the churches had what Inuit wanted: biscuits, beans, prunes, hope, and gifts of clothing from other Christians from the south.

in the spring, at the first sign of break up of the creeks and rivers, she would then start cleaning the furs with sunlight soap, brisk floor brush, ulu, and flour. She would do this work until the ship came in to collect her pressed and sewn bales of fur.

An Arctic Childhood

Life as children at that time was pretty carefree. For all we knew there were at least two kinds of *Qablunaat* in this world: traders and priests. There would be an occasional airplane that came in to bring groceries and magazines. When the traders were done with the magazines, they would give them to my mother and she would then redo the wallpaper in our sod house with new pictures from the magazines with a flour-and-water paste. Sometimes, lemmings would be just on the other side of the wallpaper eating the flour. (When someone needed boils and other skin ailments tended to, my father would sometimes harvest lemmings and use them as gauzes.) A capital "H" is shaped like *aqsaaraq*, an Inuit finger-pulling game of strength. So my siblings and I would play *aqsaaraqtaaqpunga*, a game of finding capital *H*s in the magazine text on the walls. When we got tired of *aqsaaraqtaaqpunga*, we would play *nimiriaqtaaqpunga* or finding capital *S*s, because they were shaped like snakes or worms.

As Roman Catholics, we would go to catechism where we were taught about the "earth maker" *Nunaliuqti* (God), who was the almighty. We were taught that when His son comes down from heaven to gather believers, the ones going to heaven would go to his right side and the ones going to hell would go to his left side. It dawned on me one day that the HBC side of Naujaat would be on the left side of Jesus when he descends onto the sea, so my younger brother Cyril and I used to practice running to the church side so we would be ready when His son does come down. After one of these exercises, we came into the sod house where my mother was re-wallpapering and father was skinning foxes and smoking his corncob pipe. Mother asked why we were out of breath and, after I explained, she asked father to tell us "the truth." Father stood up slowly with his bloodied hands, messed up long hair, and, with a drag from his pipe, made a halo shape with his hair around his head. With his hands to his side dripping blood, he looked like Jesus Christ himself and he said, "My sons, Jesus would come down from the land side, which would put us on the right hand of God." Mother mumbled something like, "Husband!!" but that was good enough of an answer for me and my younger brother Cyril, and off we went knowing we were safe.

We were all taught from birth our roles in life on this world. Boys were promised to girls sometimes at birth; their relationship to each other depended on their given names. Rules of life were taught, and this was communicated orally, since Inuit had no written language, history, folklore, sciences, music, rites of passage, and so on. During hardships of any kind, great care was given to having at least one survivor pass on the history. Just like the *Qablunaat*, Inuit had hypotheses and did experiments to get to the scientific conclusion. As they could not write the conclusion down, for memory, they would make it into a taboo like, "If you do not follow it you will die within a year." Sometimes, messages were given in pictographs, but mostly they depicted the environment like weather, ice conditions, fatness of caribou, husky dog behaviour, seasons, and wind directions. Anything to do with the necessities of life, we were taught to read through pictographs.

Since Inuit have an oral history and communication, lying was a "deadly sin," because it could lead to the death of someone. The number one commandment was, "Obey your father and mother and your uncles and aunts without verifiable evidence, but understand everyone or anyone else could be lying to you." The number two commandment was, "Respect the environment for you are part of it." Inuit look at themselves as part of the ecosystem. This is not to say that Inuit were a perfect race, they were not. Society control was harsh. Most people were paired off as *iviriit* or "ratters" to each other. If Inuit found you cheating, stealing, or doing unmentionables they did not approach you directly; instead, they tell your *iviq*, your "ratter." Your ratter would wait until there was a large gathering, and then put your "sins" to music and publicize your sins that way. It was a real shame to be put into a song publicly.

Inuit were socialists but kept their own implements. They could ante their things when gambling, but had to share their harvest of animals to the point that it was possible for a successful hunter *not* to get anything from his hunt, which would be a source of pride for the hunter. Until the hunter shared his harvest, his cache of meat would be stored, but it was never to be disturbed by someone else, even when found by people

Inuit who have been infected with tuberculosis have exceeded all reported rates worldwide. Their rates are reportedly among the highest in any human population. As an example, the C.D. Howe medical ship had brought approximately 1,600 Inuit who were infected with the disease to sanatoriums across southern Canada in the 1950s, and many never returned home.[3]

who were starving. This was not a law, but the people had such pride in respecting other people's "things" that they would rather starve. This did not include everyone, of course, but most people.

The whole basis of learning was through observation and through bettering what had been observed while respecting the environment. We were taught the neuroplasticity of the brain: the use of the brain is infinite. Our brain can communicate with spirits. We can transcend to check on our relatives' situation by meditating. We can become shamans by befriending spirits. This was not a religion, but a science of the brain that was achievable. The spirit world, being real of course, also had its own rules, and shamans had to follow and obey them. These are known as *tirigusungniq* or "not to hurt or break the rules of the spirits." Inuit Christians followed these rules and knew they were not breaking the commandments of the Holy Bible. Commandment number three says, "Do not serve other gods before me." It does not say do not have other gods or spirits so long as you put Almighty God first.

Michael, my older brother, was already going to residential school in Chesterfield Inlet when I really started to remember things. There is little I do not remember after he came home after his first year. It was about the same time that my father also came home from spending time at a sanatorium in Manitoba for tuberculosis. They both had amazing stories from the "south." From his experience down there, my father told us about plugging wires or ropes into walls to make lights work, of record players, and of other implements. He also spoke of tokens people had in their pockets and that they could trade these tokens at any store. Michael told us of the language he was learning in school and of the huge buildings he shared with many other Inuit of many different dialects. In this dawn of change, my younger brother and I were still just trying to figure out why the trader had brown stool and not black like the rest of us.

Ours was a strange world full of wonder. It seemed as if it could not get any better because we had everything a child could ever want. I was about seven years old and had a promised wife whom I was very shy with, but I followed the rules and gave her everything from soap to oranges. We had many dogs each with a name. We had freedom and rules to enjoy our freedom, and, as children, we were encouraged to be playful and have fun. We had a child's language, which we were to use until we became old enough to use a more mature Inuit language. We only heard innocent stories as we were asked to go outside to play when the adults were discussing mature subjects. We had chores such as getting water and training puppies. We observed as much as we were allowed to. There were rituals to keep us safe and keep us from sickness. Cyril and I were inseparable. We did everything together. We sometimes thought we were the only two people in the whole world.

BEING TAKEN

Then one day a "flyable" took me away from our world through the sky to a dark and desolate place. I do not remember having time to say goodbye to Cyril, my soul mate. I do not remember saying goodbye to the puppies or the bright environment before we boarded the RCMP Single Otter to go to Chesterfield Inlet Residential School. I seem to remember playing with Cyril and then seeing the Union Jack put up the flagpole that signified a plane was going to come in, which was always a fun time. Perhaps, as always, the pilot would have a sucker for us, but this time the sucker was me. Michael was on the plane with me. He was my older brother but he was not Cyril. Perhaps we were close at one time, but his time in the residential school had alienated us somewhat. Still, because he was a sibling and of blood, I hung on to him. I did everything he did. When he looked out the window of the plane, I searched to see what he was looking at. When he closed his eyes, I did too, but opened mine often to see if he had opened his. I observed everything he did as I was taught to observe and do. I was on my own now, still a child with Inuit child language, not old enough to be on my own. But now, my childhood was behind me. I was on my own. I thought perhaps Judgment Day had come and we were going to a very happy place, but then again the plane landed on the sea.

I remember fish swimming under the pontoons of the plane. I remember being carried by one of the pilots to the beach, whimpering and thinking we were going to be left behind. The pilots smiled and spoke gibberish to us, and, before sunset, we took off again to finish our trip, which I had hoped would never end. The unknown was numbing to think about. Because time must elapse, it did, and too soon we landed in the dark on a lake somewhere. I do not know about the other children, but I was now

There were 25 hostels across Nunavut and the Northwest Territories. "From 1955 to 1970, the Department of Northern Affairs ran the federal government's northern education system. After 1970, control of education was handed over to the new Northwest Territories government. The First federal hostel (Turquetil Hall) was opened in Chesterfield Inlet in 1951 as a missionary school, which was transferred to federal authority in 1954. The last federal hostel (Churchill Vocational Centre in Manitoba) was opened in 1964."[4]

following my brother and not focusing on anything else. He was all I had left. He probably talked to me, but the fear was overwhelming so I tried not to see or focus on anything else. I would then hang on to my older brother for the rest of the trip. Everyone else and everything was black.

THE SCHOOL

Entering "the hostel," it was impossible to ignore all your senses. Strange voices and languages could be heard in the distance, strange new smells permeated the air at the doorway, and everything was painted in white, in contrast to the people in black. My brother and I were immediately separated, as we were seemingly separated by size. Now, I was alone, alone as I had never been before. A cry was in my throat, but being there with other children my size, it was not the right thing to do. I did not cry and did as little as possible so as to not attract attention from the Sisters (nuns). We were taken to the kitchen and mess hall and then given tea and "Roman Catholic" biscuits. In Repulse Bay, Roman Catholic biscuits were rare so we always ate them slowly to see who would have the last enviable mouthful. But in my new world, "*vite!!*" was the word being repeated. One of the nuns would put her hand under the children's chins, making them chew faster and repeating this word "*vite, vite …!!*" From that moment on, *vite* became a normal word, as we were to do most things in a hurry. When we did not *vite*, we were half lifted by the ear and made to *vite*.

After tea and biscuits, I had to pee, but had no way of knowing how to ask and dared not attract more attention than necessary. I thought surely they would take us outside to pee or maybe to a real toilet room like the HBC staff house. Instead, we were led into the bedroom—the biggest room I had seen in my life up to that time—and told to undress and put on a new set of soapy-smelling clothes. The nun mumbled many meaningless things, but I kept my head down like the huskies we controlled lest we yelled at them more. I eyed where they put my brother and, after what sounded like "Hail Mary," we were put to bed. The nun went to every bed and made sure that we all had our hands visible on top of the blankets (apparently, I later learned, so that we did not masturbate) and out went the lights. In Repulse Bay, I had shared a bed with my brother Cyril all my life, now I was sharing with a room full of seemingly countless children who spoke, cried, walked, and tossed and turned. I tried to not move in case one of the sleepwalkers came my way, and then sometime during the night, I fell asleep looking towards my brother's way.

I remember dreaming, not of family or of home, but about this kid who we were told about during catechism. He was trying to empty the ocean with a spoon. The point, apparently, was that it was impossible. I remember always thinking it was possible. Anyhow, he put out his hand holding a thimble and told me to pee in it. I told him I should not, but he was so peaceful and innocent and he was in our catechism, so I relented and peed in the thimble, at first holding back so I did not overflow it. Then, when it did not overflow, I let out a flood. To my surprise, I relieved myself without ever filling the thimble. When he proceeded to carefully pour the thimble into the spoon, I woke up to the nun doing her wake-up call. I saw then that everyone was wearing the kind of clothing I was given the night before, and the nun was holding the same kind of clothing herself. She made folding motions, which everyone else was doing, so I folded my dripping-with-pee clothes and put them under my pillow as instructed. I followed others in the procedure of washing, brushing teeth, and breakfast and then went to my first day of school.

The first morning of school was surprisingly nice, as the creatures of the night before were a distant memory now. We were even given hot chocolate, a rare drink in Repulse Bay, and then we took a nap. This is not so bad I thought. The morning ended too fast, it seemed, when we had to go back to the hostel for lunch. At least that was what they told us. At the hostel doorway, our supervisor was waiting and nudging everyone as they went by her in a single file. Since the morning went so well I had my head up to observe what other children were doing so I could do the same. I stepped up to the nun and waited for a nudge, but instead of a nudge, I got pulled by the ear and, nearly hanging in the air, I hopped alongside her while willing myself not to cry.

We stopped next to my bed with the sheets pulled out. She made it obvious that she wanted me to carry them, so I did. I could hardly see over the sheets, blanket, and pajamas in front of me, but I did not have to as my ear was leading me to my next stop, a washing tub. I washed the sheets and pajamas with a bar of soap and wrung them out as much as I could. The nun kept yelling gibberish to me throughout "lunchtime," and

As a people, we Inuit are still coming to grips with the most important event in our history, the arrival of the Canadian government during the 1950s ... Government policy has evolved from the pursuit of assimilation. Children were taught and encouraged deliberately to disown their own language and culture.

Billy Day
Vice-President
Inuvialuit Communications Society
Speaking at the public hearings of the Royal Commission on Aboriginal Peoples Inuvik, NWT
6 May 1992

by the time I was finished, it was time to go back to school. I asked what my school friends had for lunch and was told frozen fish, biscuits, and tea. Frozen fish? In the summer? How do you freeze fish in the summer? Their answer was, "I do not know." School was fun though. We learned many things we never knew existed. All the trees had apples or oranges. There were bears of different colours. We counted numbers that went beyond twenty.

There was a *Qablunaaq* boy named Dick who had a funny-looking dog. Singing, art, and science were my favourite subjects. One day our teacher told us that plants grow because of water and that if we water plants we can help them grow. During recess I found fall flowers and watered them daily, and sure enough, they seemed to be growing. When freeze-up time came I made a little snow shelter for them and continued to water them. Then one day a blizzard came and I could not find them anymore, but I thought about them throughout the year and the following spring I found them again. The ice buildup had protected them.

They also taught us to play bingo. At my first bingo game I won cigarettes. I was so happy they asked me to give these to some older Inuk and, later, a teacher gave me a skunk figurine. We also played "mass" with child-size chalices, tabernacle, robes, and so on. One evening, when we were playing mass, we heard this girl crying with all her might. Then we saw it was Amia, the oldest girl in the hostel, being dragged down the stairs by her long hair. She was holding her own hair with both hands so the nun would not pull it out by the roots. She was made to apologize for saying "bad things" to some boy. I felt some guilt as she was the girl the oldest boy used to have me deliver messages to about where to meet. I was the youngest child in the school at the time and getting picked on horribly by a gang of older children. Amongst other things, they would stick a knife into the snow with the blade up and I was forced into a push-up position over the knife. They would then take turns stepping on my back. One day the oldest boy said he would protect me from anyone if I would take messages to the oldest girl, which I gladly did for the protection. He kept his word and no one bothered me after that.

ABUSE

One day I heard there was "abuse" at the school. It reminded me of my mother, who had spent time at a nun convent, telling us before we left for the residential school that we should never be touched on certain parts of our body. I guess she knew "things" about certain priests or brothers. Later on, her words served well for me and, apparently, my older brother, as many of the unfortunate victims were terribly sexually abused. (I only learned of this as an adult after the residential schools issue started coming out.) These were some of the boys I went to school with and they never shared any of this as they were kept silent with threats. One of them told me they were made to sit side-by-side naked while they were waiting to be taken to the Brother's bed to service him one by one. When one was done, he would have to tell the next boy it was his turn and so on.

I have not heard these horrible stories about the nuns except from one boy, who I do not believe as he lied about too many things. He claims to have been sexually abused by nuns, but I think he is just ashamed to admit it was from the same Brother.

BAD TIMES, GOOD TIMES

For all the horrible stories, there are as many or more happy stories: Christmas plays, feasts, letters from home, bishop visits, anointings, learning new things, coming of spring, last days of school, and going home. Bishop visits were particularly happy occasions. All the rooms were transformed with colourful, silky coverings—light pink, yellow, and purple. All the beds were covered with these magical covers. High Mass was done royally with all the priests in their finest, with canes, hats, and fine jewellery. The Gay Pride parade in Toronto would be jealous of this. As fast as the magic appeared, it disappeared when the bishop left. Everything was dark and gloomy once again.

When spring was coming, things seemed to ease or perhaps our minds were preoccupied with thoughts of home. There were snowless patches of earth to play in, lemmings to kill, puddles to jump into, and punishments that did not seem to happen as often. The frozen fish, whale blubber (*maktaaq*), caribou, and other meats were not so frozen at suppertime.

Cleaning up classrooms and school things meant that the time of going home was coming soon. We just could not count the days, as we never knew until we were *vited* to the airplane.

GOING HOME

Going home after being away for ten months brought thoughts of puppies, little sister, mother and father, and of course Cyril. But the truth is that one can never really go home again. My family had grown more at home. Cyril had matured a year as an Inuk. His Inuit language had changed, his observations and doings were beyond mine as an Inuk. Yes, I had learned some foreign knowledge, but I had not aged at home. The puppies grew up, my sister was no longer a baby, and my parents acted differently towards me as they were not quite sure how to address me or how I would react. My language and mannerisms were still so childish after a year and being away. But after some minor tweaking adjustments, Cyril and I had two months to be who we were and are: two free spirits with much to learn from each other. We laugh heartily because we now have brown stool just like the white folk.

YEAR OF THE APOLOGY

For many years I had argued within myself over the good and the bad of going to residential schools. I always sided with the government and the churches as I thought they were on the side of angels. They were only following a curriculum that had no Inuit cultural content at all. They could only teach what they knew and, of course, they could not teach what they did not know. I knew there were exercises where students were not allowed to speak their mother tongue, but in linguistic terms, this is known as a "full immersion" language course. I had not learned about hunting, skinning, and igloo building because I had not had the opportunity. I heard this assimilation was intentional, but it could have been done so smoothly that I did not know that it happened to me. I am observant because I am Inuk and smart enough to know that, as an Inuk, I am way behind students who quit school or never went. I know less than them about Inuit culture and language, but that goes with the territory.

I was asked by Inuit Tapiriit Kanatami to join Mary Simon in attending Prime Minister Harper's "offer of full apology on behalf of Canadians for the Indian Residential Schools system."[5] Unfortunately, I was committed to going somewhere else, but on 11 June 2008, I listened to every word on the CBC Radio: "the federal government, partly in order to meet its obligation to educate aboriginal children, began to play a role."[6] That was why my mother blindly allowed us to be taken away year after year. The Prime Minister continued:

> Two primary objectives of the residential system were to remove and isolate children from the influence of their homes, families, traditions and cultures, and to assimilate them into the dominant culture. These objectives were based on the assumption aboriginal cultures and spiritual beliefs were inferior and unequal. Indeed, some sought, as it was infamously said, 'to kill the Indian in the child.'[7]

For some reason I missed my mother then. I was numb and had an uncontrollable urge to cry, but the residential school had taught me to keep my cry underground. I cry when I am alone. After *mamiattugut* (the apology) and "forging a new relationship between aboriginal peoples and other Canadians,"[8] I made a hard copy of the text and went to board my plane to deal with the Dene/Inuit Manitoba border issue.

Thank you all who made this happen. You have achieved no less than Mahatma Gandhi and Martin Luther King, Jr. achieved for their people. They have freed us through peace and persistence and that includes you, Prime Minister.

Merci, thank you, *masi cho, qujannamiik*!

Remember, though, we are all accountable for things we do and for things we do not do.

For many years I had argued within myself over the good and the bad of going to residential schools. I always sided with the government and the churches as I thought they were on the side of angels.

NOTES

[1] More information on the history of the Hudson's Bay Company can be found at: http://www.hbc.com/hbcheritage/history/

[2] Samples of these books can be found online at The Champlain Society Digital Collection website: http://link.library.utoronto.ca/champlain/search.cfm?lang=eng (There are 26 documents with digitized sample pages if one searches for key words "Inuit or Eskimo.")

[3] *See:* Clark, Michael and Peter Riben (1999). *Tuberculosis in First Nations Communities, 1999.* Ottawa, ON: Minister of Public Works and Government Services Canada (retrieved 1 April 2009 from: http://www.hc-sc.gc.ca/fniah-spnia/alt_formats/fnihb-dgspni/pdf/pubs/tuberculos/1999_commun-eng.pdf); and CBC (2007). Nunavut health group to commemorate Inuit TB victims, CBC News, Tuesday, September 11, 2007. Retrieved 1 April 2009 from: http://www.cbc.ca/canada/north/story/2007/09/11/nu-tb.html

[4] King, David (2006:1). *A Brief Report of The Federal Government of Canada's Residential School System for Inuit.* Ottawa, ON: Aboriginal Healing Foundation.

[5] Prime Minister Harper offers full apology on behalf of Canadians for the Indian Residential Schools system. June 11, 2008. Ottawa, ON: Office of the Prime Minister. Retrieved 4 September 2008 from: http://www.pm.gc.ca/eng/media.asp?id=2149

[6] Prime Minister Harper's statement of apology.

[7] Prime Minister Harper's statement of apology.

[8] Prime Minister Harper's statement of apology.

Inuit board the C.D. Howe for medical and eye check-ups
Kimmirut (formerly Lake Harbour), Nunavut, 1951
Photographer: Wilfred Doucette
Library and Archives Canada, PA-189646

(Courtesy of Legacy of Hope Foundation's
"We were so far away...": The Inuit Experience of Residential Schools exhibit)

René Dussault

René Dussault has led a distinguished legal career for some 45 years as a public administrator and lawyer. He obtained his doctorate from the London School of Economics and Political Science at the University of London in the United Kingdom. His areas of expertise in law include Aboriginal, administration and constitutional, regulatory and public, appellate litigation and judicial review, and human rights. René served as counsel to the Research Committee on Health Insurance, to the Federal-Provincial Affairs Department, and to the Québec Commission of Inquiry on Health and Social Welfare. He held several senior positions in the Québec provincial public service, including founding president of the Professions Board and Deputy Minister of Justice. In 1989, René was appointed to the bench and has served for nearly 20 years as Justice of the Court of Appeal of Québec. He was also co-chair of the Royal Commission on Aboriginal Peoples in Canada. René has also been actively involved in legal education. He was past director of the Graduate Studies Program and lectured at the *Université Laval* Faculty of Law. He was a professor at the *École nationale d'administration publique* and the first incumbent of the Bora Laskin Chair in Public Law at Osgoode Hall Law School. René now serves as counsel at Heenan Blaikie Aubut, a law firm in Québec.

René served as Associate Editor of the *Canadian Public Administration* journal and wrote and co-authored numerous articles and books, including the seminal *Traité de droit administratif*, subsequently translated into *Administrative Law: A Treatise*, which received the Walter Owen Award from the Canadian Bar Association's Foundation for Legal Research and the *prix du Concours juridique* from the Québec Bar Foundation in 1988.

René has been recognized throughout Canada for his achievements in the area of public administration and for his outstanding contributions to the advancement of law, the legal profession, and the promotion of equality. Among others, he was awarded the Québec Bar Medal, the Vanier Medal of the Institute of Public Administration of Canada, and the Touchstone Award of the Canadian Bar Association; was appointed Fellow of the Royal Society of Canada; and granted honorary Doctor of Laws degrees from York University and Dalhousie University.

RECONCILIATION:
THE ONLY WAY FORWARD TO FAIR AND ENDURING COEXISTENCE

On 11 June 2008, ten years after the *Statement of Reconciliation*[1] was issued, paving the way to a series of measures intended to right the wrongs of the past in relation to Aboriginal peoples in Canada under the residential school policy, a policy clearly aimed at assimilation, the Government of Canada finally presented an official apology.[2] In the formal setting of the House of Commons in the presence of representatives of all Aboriginal peoples of Canada and with the support of the opposition political parties, the apology and accompanying request for pardon can constitute, depending on the related follow-up action, a true turning point in Canada's relationship with Aboriginal peoples. Two factors seem to support this hope. First, the apology crowns a series of concrete steps already undertaken to reduce the repercussions of this erroneous policy, a policy aimed at alienating children from their families and separating them from their traditional culture, which leads us to believe that the apology is sincere. Second, to the extent that the apology can be seen as an undeniable expression of a profound change that will enable trust to be rebuilt, it can become a fundamental element, key to the potential success of the work undertaken by the Truth and Reconciliation Commission established in its wake. In order to succeed and thereby mark a turning point in the relationship, reconciliation first requires that trust be rebuilt.

There is no magical formula for resurrecting this trust. It nonetheless seems that the sought-after healing, especially in this case when it has a profound intercultural significance, starts with sincere apologies that recognize past injustices, signalling an authentic desire to right them and showing that a long-lasting commitment has been made. As worthy as they are, such apologies are not sufficient. They must be accompanied by a solid action plan that cannot otherwise limit itself to the single issue of residential schools. Regarding this, I recall that the report of the Royal Commission on Aboriginal Peoples (RCAP) proposed a detailed 20-year strategy to restore the social, economic, and political health of Aboriginal peoples and redefine their relationship with the rest of Canada. Still to this day a source of inspiration for change, this strategy included a dual pathway, namely an immediate, sustained effort aimed at restoring the health and capacity to act of individuals, families, groups, and nations and the gradual establishment of a new balance of political powers and economic resources.

> Twelve years after the publication of the RCAP report, it remains just as urgent that Canada re-examine the very foundations of its relationship with Aboriginal peoples.

According to the RCAP Commissioners, Canada had to commit itself to reducing by half the gap in social and economic conditions between Aboriginal and non-Aboriginal peoples within 20 years of the publication of the report.[3] They emphasized that Canada could no longer permit itself to maintain the current regime of dependency, of lost productivity and ever-increasing social expenses. Estimated at just over $13 billion in 1996, the amount spent by governments on Aboriginal peoples had to increase to over $17 billion annually by 2016, based solely on demographic growth.[4] In view of such a perspective, rooted in the unstable foundations of the relationship established between Aboriginal and non-Aboriginal people, a result of the uprooting and assimilation actions of our common history, the RCAP Commissioners pointed out that Canada could "no longer afford merely to 'manage' the continuing crisis in the relationship by mediating potential areas of conflict while leaving unaltered the foundation on which that conflict inevitably arises."[5]

Where does it stand today? Twelve years after the publication of the RCAP report, it remains just as urgent that Canada re-examine the very foundations of its relationship with Aboriginal peoples. The existence of conflicts created by this deficient relationship is undoubtedly not conducive to establishing the climate of trust needed to accomplish such an endeavour. Yet, this climate of trust is necessary to reviving a desire to build bridges among the partners that would enable them to move beyond prejudices to a common vision and to achieve a genuine reconciliation. To the extent that reconciliation appears to be the only reasonable way forward, every effort must be made, further to the official apology presented by the Government of Canada, to find grounds for agreement upon which a shared future can be built.

The success of this endeavour relies on our reciprocal capacity to give meaning to the fundamental, long-lasting relationship established by formal agreements between Canada and Aboriginal peoples, a meaning that respects not only the spirit of the agreements, but also provides for consideration of today's realities. In other words, in order to succeed, the partners have to envision the desired reconciliation, not only in terms of interdependence, but also of convergence and open-mindedness. This requires that they attach a lot of significance on a daily basis to everything that can foster constructive management of the relationship. For example, governments should assure themselves that there is a good degree of coherence between the positions they adopt in the statements of principle and arguments they present before the courts. Governments should also ensure that the changes they propose to make to social and economic policies represent the beginning of an authentic development of Aboriginal and regional reforms that can be seen and understood by all parties as being beneficial to all. For their part, Aboriginal leaders should clearly state, in the likelihood of an agreement, how they would like to implement the change and the extent of the effort they are prepared to devote to this task.

After some 500 years of a relationship that has moved from mutual respect and cooperation to one of paternalism and assimilation, it is in the interest of all Canadians for the federal and provincial governments and Aboriginal peoples finally to agree on the foundations of a fair and enduring coexistence. One of the most sensitive aspects of this endeavour, currently underway, concerns the conciliation of Aboriginal and treaty rights and Canadian sovereignty shared by the federal and provincial governments. It is, therefore, not surprising that in its 15 May 2000 issue, *Time Canada,* in "Getting Angry over Native Rights," described this endeavour as "the most sweeping social adjustment in Canada's history."[6] This conciliation, supported simultaneously by agreements between the parties and judicial decisions, raises a number of new and untested legal questions in terms of government function as well as land and resources. I would like to mention a few that I think the justice community should examine.

Government Function

+ As part of the current sharing of legislative jurisdictions, how can we make room for Aboriginal norms? Can the federal and provincial governments give up exercising their power in favour of Aboriginal governments as well as free up some of their current areas of jurisdiction?

- In the context of Aboriginal self-government, how and to what extent do we acknowledge their ability to implement community justice systems?

- How do we allow for non-Aboriginal people's participation in the decision-making process of Aboriginal governments vested with territorial jurisdiction?

- On the very real assumption that a constitutional right to self-governmental exists, does this right, like the right to self-determination, belong to the Aboriginal nations or to each of their respective bands?

LAND AND RESOURCES

- How do we conciliate Aboriginal title and the interests of all Canadians?

- Does Aboriginal title belong to the Aboriginal nations or to each of their respective bands?

- What happens when several Aboriginal nations lay historical claim to the same territory?

- In resolving territorial claims, how can we achieve goals of clarity and certainty without resorting to an extinguishment of rights clause?

In view of the real difficulties posed by these questions, some could be tempted to give up and conclude that conciliating rights is an impossible mission. It is therefore very important for the legal community and all Aboriginal and non-Aboriginal partners to address this endeavour in the spirit of seeking solutions, rather than submitting to failure. In my opinion, what is at stake is Canada's image as a respected member of the global community.

NOTES

[1] Indian and Northern Affairs Canada (1998). *Statement of Reconciliation* (*see* Appendix 1). Retrieved 23 January 2008 from: http://www.ainc-inac.ca/gs/rec_e.html

[2] *See* Appendix 2.

[3] Royal Commission on Aboriginal Peoples (1996). *Report of the Royal Commission on Aboriginal Peoples. Volume 5: Renewal: A Twenty-Year Commitment.* Ottawa, ON: Minister of Supply and Services Canada.

[4] RCAP (1996) Volume 5.

[5] Royal Commission on Aboriginal Peoples (1996:603). *Report of the Royal Commission on Aboriginal Peoples. Volume 1: Looking Forward, Looking Back.* Ottawa, ON: Minister of Supply and Services Canada.

[6] Time Canada (2000:16). Getting Angry Over Native Rights. *Time Canada* 155(20):16–24.

Sam Crow and his immediate family and some relatives outside the warehouse of the Hudson's Bay Company Outpost at Richmond Gulf, 1949, Richmond Gulf, Quebec [Tasiujaq (formerly Richmond Gulf), Quebec]
Credit: S.J. Bailey, Department of Indian and Northern Affairs collection
Library and Archives Canada, PA-110861

(Photo: Courtesy of Legacy of Hope Foundation's
"We were so far away...": The Inuit Experience of Residential Schools exhibit)

Sophie Pierre was born in Cranbrook, British Columbia. She obtained a business administration diploma from Camosun College in Victoria on Vancouver Island. Sophie has led her own band, St. Mary's, for 30 years, with 26 of those years as Chief. She no longer functions as chief, but still demonstrates her commitment to her community through her ongoing involvement in youth activities, women's advocacy, and Elders' support.

Sophie has always been a strong advocate of economic development as a means to achieve self-determination for Aboriginal peoples. With Sophie at the helm, she demonstrated this commitment through her dogged determination in making Ktunaxa/Kinbasket Tribal Council's St. Eugene Mission Resort a reality for her people. Her business savvy has made her one of the most recognized Aboriginal leaders in the country, and she is a frequent speaker at business and economic development conferences. In 2003, Sophie was honoured with the National Aboriginal Achievement Award in the business category for her leadership in the creation of the largest and most elegant destination resort/casino in Western Canada. "It's not a personal award," Sophie says, "It's an indication of what our bands have accomplished." In addition to this award, she was recognized as CANDO's 2002 Individual Economic Developer of the Year.

She is a past co-chair of the First Nations Summit and a recipient of the Order of British Columbia. In December 2002, Sophie received the Queen's Golden Jubilee commemorative medal, created by the Department of Canadian Heritage where recipients are nominated and selected by their hometown communities.

NÉE Eustace:
The Little Girl Who Would be Chief

On 22 January 2003, I stood on the front steps of the St. Eugene Mission Resort (now the St. Eugene Golf Resort & Casino), near Cranbrook, British Columbia, and proudly watched as my five year-old granddaughter, Samantha, helped cut the ribbon to officially open our hotel. As I had looked out across the snowy driveway, my mind had drifted back in time to 1956, and I saw another little girl coming up the same driveway, desperately holding on to her mother's hand and looking up towards the Sister standing on the same spot where, forty-seven years later, I stood in 2003. That little girl was me. My name is Sophie Pierre, née Eustace, a member of the Ktunaxa Nation. I am Chief of my community, *Aqam*, also known as St. Mary's Indian Reserve, and I am a Survivor of residential school. That little girl in 1956 would spend nine years at the Kootenay Indian Residential School and, forty-seven years later, would witness the opening of a five-star hotel at the same site. This is our story. It is a story of making the choice to turn something so negative in our history, as Ktunaxa living in our traditional territory, into something positive for our future generations. It is a story of courage, perseverance, and some might say stubborn determination, but mostly it is a story of vision and choices.

The Kootenay Indian Residential School, formerly known as the Industrial School, was built in 1910 and operated by the Catholic Church until 1970. Children from southern Alberta, the Okanagan and Shuswap, as well as from the local Ktunaxa area were brought to this school for ten months of each year. I am often asked what it was like in the school, and I reply that it was a very lonely place for a child to grow up. It did not matter if you were a local kid like me who could see my home from the top dormitory windows, but could not return there, or if you were an Okanagan or Shuswap kid who would not see their parents or their home for the whole ten months. When the school shut down in 1970, the Oblates, the priests who operated the school, made a deal with the federal government to turn over the school buildings and the land in trust to the five local bands. It seemed like a wonderful idea at the time, and the transfer was made. Before long, it became clear that what we had was, in fact, a huge white elephant. The building maintenance costs were prohibitive, and eventually the building was abandoned.

It would stand empty for the next twenty years, a constant reminder of the pain, failure, and abandonment that our people felt, until one day, at a band meeting in our community, which we call, *Aqam*, complaints were voiced about how much we had suffered and lost at the former residential school. One of our Elders, Mary Paul, very softly said, "If you think you lost so much in that building, it's not lost, you just need the courage to go back in there and get it. You only really lose something if you refuse to pick it up again." It would take a few more years of struggling with the aftermath of the residential school before we really understood what she said and then make the choice to follow her words.

Our Ktunaxa Nation Council, made up of five local bands, agreed that if we were going to do anything with the former school building it would have to be some type of a business venture, something that would generate money for its own maintenance costs. This eliminated any social program-type initiative in education or health, for example. So the idea of a hotel and golf course was born. We started talking to various people in government, like Indian and Northern Affairs Canada (INAC), in banks, and in the hospitality industry. Understandably, we were met with a fair amount of skepticism: Would anyone want to stay at a former residential school? How will we attract business being off the beaten track (meaning on the rez and away from a major highway)? How will financing be realized (again, because we are on the rez)? But we also had support right from the start by people who could see our vision, people like then premier of British Columbia, Mike Harcourt. At a business summit in London, England, Harcourt spoke of the growing business opportunities with First Nations and used our development plan as an example. Mike Harcourt remains one of our staunchest supporters to this day.

One of the first things we had to do was get the support of all our communities, since the lands where the resort was planned upon was Indian reserve lands held in common by our five bands. INAC's regulations require a referendum for any land-use development. We spent two years planning the development and bringing the plans to band meetings, to individual homes, and to any gathering we could to get as much input as possible from our nation members. This was not an easy process. There were many former students who strongly believed that we should just knock the building down—get it off the face of the earth—because they had suffered so much in that building. But slowly, primarily through the work of our youth, as they were the ones bringing the plans out to the communities, the words of Mary Paul started to come through. The referendum vote went through the five communities with no problem in 1996, and, more importantly, we had gained the approval and support of our people that would see us through the tough times ahead.

We ended up building a forty million dollar resort by creating partnerships between our tribal council and such entities as the Royal Bank, Columbia Basin Trust, Lake City Casinos, and Delta Hotels with the help of government programs like INAC's Aboriginal Business Canada Program and from Western Economic Diversification Canada and with the help of Human Resources and Social Development Canada, among others. But first we had to convince every one of these parties of our vision: to change something so negative for our people into something positive, something we could all be proud of and want to be a part of. We could only do that because we, the Ktunaxa, believed it ourselves.

In March of 2003, we had our initial nation meeting in our new hotel. This was very emotional for us as it was the first time for many of our members to re-enter the former school building. It was imperative that we were prepared for this. In the mid-nineties, our treatment centre had created an innovative program called the Residential School Trauma Training Program. This enabled members from our nation to understand the very deep-rooted effects of our residential school experience and that it was so powerful it created trauma in our lives and in the lives of all our families. I cannot possibly explain in full how critical the work was that these courageous people undertook. They first had to deal with their own pain by understanding where it came from and then they had to learn how to help themselves and then all the others out there who were still suffering. They became our Trauma Training Counsellors, and they were there to help us as we participated in our first meeting in our own hotel. The counsellors held talking circles to give everyone a chance to express their feelings and emotions. The one I participated in included many people that I had gone to school with. One woman's comments in

> There were many former students who strongly believed that we should just knock the building down—get it off the face of the earth—because they had suffered so much in that building.

particular stayed with me. She said, "I was really scared to come here and almost stayed home this morning, but then I remembered Mary's words and so I came. I'm so glad I did. When I came in the front door I was blown away by how beautiful the room was. It really is a hotel. It really is ours and I'm so proud of what we've done!" Both of us cried after she spoke.

The Trauma Training Counsellors did so much to make our dream a reality. While I have been given a lot of credit for the physical building of the resort, it was really these people who brought us through it safely, and they continue today to provide guidance to those still dealing with the residual effects. They also helped Survivors from other nations who came to the building while we were in the middle of the development to deal with their own ghosts. We held many cleansing ceremonies, including one with the Catholic Church—a bishop had participated. The ceremonies held both our own Ktunaxa cleansing as well as the other First Nations' cleansing ceremonies, and these were of major importance to all of us, particularly while we were doing the non-structural demolition. The majority of that work was done by our own people, and we had to ensure their safety in every sense of the word.

The 2003 year was a very challenging year, with huge ups and downs for us. With the tremendous high of seeing our dream come to fruition with the opening of the hotel came a very stressful summer of financial crisis. Even though we were in business, with the casino opening in 2002 and the golf course in its third year of operation, we were beyond broke. Every effort we made to refinance the development fell through, and by December 2003, we were seeking protection under the *Companies' Creditors Arrangement Act*,[1] one step away from bankruptcy. Because of all that we had gone through, failure was not an option. This is when our Elder's words really pulled us through; we needed courage and perseverance, especially since one of our own communities was now fighting us and insisting that we should give up and let someone else come in and take over the property. The rest of us knew we could not let that happen. So, with the full support of the other four communities, we were able to enter into a partnership with two other First Nations, Samson Cree from Alberta and Mnjikaning First Nation from Ontario. We signed our partnership agreement in November 2004. In September 2008, we celebrated our fourth year with a positive financial report given to our shareholders at our annual meeting. This partnership, which I believe is a first between three First Nations from different parts of our country, is truly something we can all be proud of.

We chose to maintain the history of the former residential school and share it with our guests through an interpretive centre and through the many pictures we have displayed throughout the resort of our life while at the school. One of those pictures is of six little girls in their first communion finery. Sometimes, when I walk past that picture I smile at those girls and tell them, "We did ok!" You see, one of those little girls was me.

Notes

[1] The *Companies' Creditors Arrangement Act* (commonly referred to as the "CCAA") is a federal Act that provides large corporations in financial trouble to restructure its financial affairs in order to avoid bankruptcy.

St. Eugene Golf Resort & Casino

Courtesy of Ktunaxa Nation Council

James Igloliorte was born in Hopedale, Labrador. As a young boy, he attended the Moravian-run grade school in his home community along with the Yale School in North West River. He then graduated with a Bachelor of Science and a Bachelor of Education from Memorial University (Newfoundland) in 1974. In 1980, his legal career began when he took up duties as a lay magistrate. In 1985, he graduated with a Bachelor of Law from Dalhousie University (Nova Scotia) and, later, returned to take up duties in Happy Valley-Goose Bay as a circuit judge. James has been a deputy judge of the Territorial Court of the Northwest Territories and was honorary colonel of 5 Wing Goose Bay for a year. He retired from provincial court in 2004.

James had taught a preliminary course in legal process with the Inuit-only Akitsiraq Law School, affiliated with the University of Victoria, in Iqualuit, Nunavut. He has been a Labrador director with the Innu Healing Foundation and was a commissioner with the Royal Commission on Renewing and Strengthening Our Place in Canada. He has also worked as Newfoundland and Labrador's Child and Youth Advocate. James is currently employed as sole Commissioner of Qikiqtani Truth Commission in Nunavut. He is also a director with the International Grenfell Association and was president of the St. John's Native Friendship Centre.

In 1999, James was awarded a National Aboriginal Achievement award in the field of law. He also received an honorary Doctor of Law from Memorial University in 2002.

The Labrador Inuit Experience
with Canadian Governance

Aboriginal people in Newfoundland were left out of the Terms of Union[1] with Canada in 1949. In this less-than-stellar national event, the lasting impacts of this singular omission for Labrador Inuit were only truly reconciled with the signing of the *Labrador Inuit Land Claims Agreement*[2] in 2005. This Agreement can pave the way for reconciliation, where self-governance and land ownership offer the hope of reversing the debilitating effects of suicide, loss of self-worth, and poverty affecting those people who were relocated from their northern territories in Labrador. The omission has yet another legacy that must be addressed by Canada, which is the common experience of Inuit children having been part of the residential school system, however characterized and however denied.

The Inuit of Labrador, located in the southernmost part of the Arctic and subarctic regions of the world of all the Inuit peoples, have much in common with their northern kin. Centuries of transitory migration had placed them in contact with the alternatively thawing and freezing salt seas, where *natsiq* (the little ringed seal) provided heat, shelter, food, and clothing to help sustain them. They lived exclusively on the Arctic tundra and among the freshwater lakes and rivers, where *tuktu* (the caribou) provided the necessities to also help sustain them. Their mastery over *kimmik* (the sled dog) allowed winter travel over the frozen land and sea, and this ingenious travel technology kept their culture alive and vibrant. Their exposure to the ways of *Qallunat* (the white man) transformed semi-nomadic ways into permanent communities, where incidents of transition resulted in personal and social upheaval.

As with other Inuit groups in Canada, Labrador Inuit are now beginning to define their own version of history, to shape the important elements of their own society, and to take control of their own governance in a new transitional phase, which is only one of many more to come. These changes do not occur in a vacuum, but rather in the living context of people and government policies with their unique regional and community histories.

Today's achievement assures us that understanding between distinct cultures is possible and that mutual respect and cooperation are attainable. This moment marks the start of our efforts to ratify the Agreement and make it law. The challenge now is to turn the work of our negotiators into a monumental achievement for the Inuit of Labrador, the people of this province and Canadian society as a whole. I believe that we can, and will achieve this, and I look forward to the ratification of the Agreement by the Labrador Inuit, the House of Assembly and Parliament.

William Anderson III
President
Labrador Inuit Association
On the initialling of the Labrador Inuit Land Claims Agreement
St. John's, Newfoundland
29 August 2003

Unless the histories are written and accepted by the people themselves, reconciliation for perceived inappropriate actions in the past will not occur.

The recent apology given to Survivors of the residential school system by the prime minister and the leaders of the Canadian parliamentary system, in the presence of representative Aboriginal groups, was a powerful symbol of the reconciliation process at work in this country, and this will encourage the less visible aspects of Canadian-Aboriginal relationships to be revealed. This article is intended to allow a small corner of the Canadian mosaic to express its truth, so that over time a more complete picture is portrayed of how reconciliation can overcome marginalization, even in circumstances that are remote from this country's centre.

THE CONFEDERATION STORY FOR LABRADOR INUIT

Dr. Maura Hanrahan, writing for the research component of the 2002/2003 Newfoundland and Labrador Royal Commission on Renewing and Strengthening Our Place in Canada, exposed what she referred to as an untold story in Confederation. Prophetically titled, *The Lasting Breach: The Omission of Aboriginal People From the Terms of Union Between Newfoundland and Canada and its Ongoing Impacts,*[3] Hanrahan's report relates the unprecedented actions by the premier, Joseph Smallwood, and the prime minister, Lester B. Pearson, to ignore the federal government's responsibility to exercise its fiduciary duty of legislative and administrative control over the Aboriginal population, as was the case in other provinces:

> After World War II the global map was being redrawn as Britain and other European powers disposed of their colonies and territories. Newfoundland became a province of Canada in 1949; the Terms of Union were the legal agreements that bound the two countries. While the Terms described everything from Canada's transportation obligations in the new province to the colour of margarine, they did not mention Aboriginal people. According to the 1945 Census, there was a significant Aboriginal population in this jurisdiction; there were 701 Eskimos, 527 Halfbreeds, and 431 Indians ... The presence of Indians was recognized in Newfoundland law, if only through

the ban of sale of liquor to Indians ... The omission appears to be a remarkable oversight, especially given the special status of Aboriginal people elsewhere in Canada. Recent historical research, mainly by First Nations lawyer Jerry Wetzel, describes the process through which this happened.[4]

In countering the federal and provincial justifications for the Newfoundland anomaly, she goes on to say:

> The claim that the province wanted to administer Aboriginal affairs is meaningless; no other province was ever given the option to do so, given Canada's fiduciary relationship to Aboriginal people and federal jurisdiction over Aboriginal issues. Whenever other territories had joined Canada, Ottawa had made treaties or other arrangements with the relevant Aboriginal nations, set aside reserves, enforced the *Indian Act*, and began providing programs and services. This did not happen in Newfoundland. According to one legal opinion, because of the omission from the Terms of Union, s. 91 (24) of the Canadian constitution makes Aboriginal matters in Newfoundland and Labrador federal jurisdiction – as in the rest of the country ... Further, S. 91 (24) of the Constitution articulates the fiduciary responsibility of the federal government for the First Nations, Metis, and Inuit peoples of Canada.[5]

Hanrahan relates that this omission had the consequence of Ottawa's program delivery in the various Canadian regions being applied to this province and covered under the aegis of Atlantic Canada, even though there might be no programs funded in Labrador:

> This province is considered as "covered off" whenever projects in the Atlantic region are funded. In other words, if projects or programs go ahead in Nova Scotia and/or New Brunswick, they are considered to cover the whole region – even though the Aboriginal people in Newfoundland and Labrador do not participate or benefit in any way.[6]

RECONCILIATION THROUGH LAND CLAIMS

Thankfully, at least for Inuit in Newfoundland and Labrador, this half century of constitutional oversight was addressed in the comprehensive *Labrador Inuit Land Claims Agreement*, which was formalized in 2005. The Agreement resulted in Inuit-owned and Inuit-controlled lands, including an offshore zone; Labrador Inuit lands where Inuit could exercise self-government control; the establishment of a national park; percentage shares in resource revenue from the province; wildlife and plant-harvesting rights; and a federal government compensation package. These tangible aspects of the Agreement strengthened a real sense of accomplishment and transition to greater autonomy in determining Inuit affairs and, over time, will result in self-governance and sovereignty that could reverse the unsettling negative consequences to Inuit families.

Following the formal signing ceremony, the province and the Labrador Inuit Association (LIA) negotiated an apology to be given to the survivors of the Hebron and Nutak relocations of 1959.[7] As a ten-year-old boy, I had witnessed the incidents of relocation in the late summer arrival of these northern strangers, many of whom became my school friends, as they were segregated to the back of the village and into their canvas tents. I remember the shy and quiet entrances by couples visiting our parents in the early days in an apparent attempt to combat homesickness and longing for their community as well as to get relief from the crowded conditions in what we called the Hebron side. The rigorous structure of the Moravian Church services and religious year clearly helped soften the cultural differences and offered some continuity, but alcohol abuse from homebrew and other liquor purchased from the American Distant Early Warning Line base on the hill near the village affected everyone's daily life.

In the next few years, before my departure for high school in central Labrador, you could see the influence of the Moravian missionaries waning as the pull of secular life combined with the natural tendency to rebel against strict religious practices grew. Upon my return to Labrador in 1981 as a lay magistrate and subsequently as a provincial court judge, I saw first-hand the full flowering of social destruction, as explained in the words of Carol-Brice Bennett:

Without a community and hunting places of their own, Hebron Inuit lost their social and economic security. Family networks were severed as married sons and daughters moved to different communities, and lived apart from their elderly parents and from aunts and uncles, cousins and childhood friends. Poverty, demoralization, and frustration led people to consume alcohol in excess which contributed to family violence, accidental deaths, criminal offences and the further breakdown of family relations. Elderly people are believed to have died sooner from the heartbreak of being exiled from their homeland, and from being humiliated in the communities where they ended up living. The last wish of many elders was to be buried at Hebron, but even this request could not be fulfilled.[8]

The apology was, for the Hebron and Nutak relocatees, as necessary and important as the land claims agreement for other members of the LIA. It was given on behalf of the province by newly-elected Premier Danny Williams, who appreciated the importance of the event because he ignored the bureaucratic fear of attracting negative and excessive attention to a highly charged emotional atmosphere. At the last minute, during a meeting with survivor Andrea Webb and me (I was master of ceremonies), we exchanged hugs in the centre of the school stage rather than remain at our respective microphones at opposite ends of the large stage. Both parties had thrown aside bureaucratic wisdom in favour of a genuine display of apology and forgiveness. The sincerity of the statements, including the Premier's agreement to a spontaneous private meeting by the assembled Hebron and Nutak survivors and the reciprocated display of respect for the Premier, demonstrated to me the power of reconciliation on a scale I had not thought possible.

A NEW CHALLENGE

Labrador Inuit accept that this country needed to express its apology to Survivors of the Indian residential school system, and they are happy for the acknowledgement by Canada that the truth has come out about this dark chapter of Canadian-Aboriginal history. Yet the impact of the Government of Canada's omission in the *Newfoundland Act*'s Terms of Union still haunts Labrador Inuit. The newly formed Nunatsiavut (translated: Our beautiful land) Government is now forced to make a case

> The sincerity of the statements, including the Premier's agreement to a spontaneous private meeting by the assembled Hebron and Nutak survivors and the reciprocated display of respect for the Premier, demonstrated to me the power of reconciliation on a scale I had not thought possible.

Canada acknowledges that First Nations children and some Inuit attended the narrowly defined residential school system. What is the bureaucratic fear that denies the impact on Inuit but precipitates the apology for all the others?

that Inuit families were affected by the common experience of removal from family, culture, and social structures in the same era that resulted in the undeniable truth of the Indian residential school system. Canada acknowledges that First Nations children and some Inuit attended the narrowly defined residential school system. What is the bureaucratic fear that denies the impact on Inuit but precipitates the apology for all the others? In the new truth and reconciliation process, which is about to start, there is little doubt that the overwhelming evidence will favour the inclusion of those Labrador Inuit survivors who were separated, by the best of intentions, from nurturing families and a distinct and vibrant culture. The inevitable reward of patience for Inuit is as certain as their knowledge in the healing power of the land.

NOTES

[1] *Newfoundland Act*, 1949, 12–13 Geo. VI, c. 22 (U.K.). An Act to confirm and give effect to Terms of Union agreed between Canada and Newfoundland. Retrieved 14 October 2008 from: http://www.exec.gov.nl.ca/royalcomm/resources/nf_act.htm

[2] Nunatsiavut Government (2005). *Labrador Inuit Land Claims Agreement*. Retrieved 14 October 2008 from: http://www.laa.gov.nl.ca/laa/liaclaims/pdf/January212005AgreementComplete.pdf

[3] Hanrahan, Maura (2003). *The Lasting Breach: The Omission of Aboriginal People From the Terms of Union Between Newfoundland and Canada and its Ongoing Impacts*. Nain, NL: Royal Commission on Renewing and Strengthening Our Place in Canada.

[4] Hanrahan (2003:235) [references removed].

[5] Hanrahan (2003:236) [reference removed].

[6] Hanrahan (2003:240).

[7] Williams, Danny (2005). Speaking Notes: Statement of Apology to the Inuit of Nutak and Hebron, January 21, 2005 [see Appendix 5 for a copy of the statement, including Andrea Webb's response to the apology on behalf of the Hebron Committee]. Retrieved 14 October 2008 from: http://www.nunatsiavut.com/pdfs/Hebron_Apology.pdf

[8] Brice-Bennett, Carol (2000:11, 13). *Reconciling With Memories: A Record of the Reunion at Hebron 40 Years After Relocation*. Nain, NL: Labrador Inuit Association.

1999 – The Hebron Reunion
2002, Heather Igloliorte
Oil on canvas

This photo is of a painting that forms part of a diptych, with the other half found on the cover of this volume. The people in the images were all residents of Hebron: the image of the children on the cover is from a photo taken inside the Moravian church months before the relocation was announced (the Inuit were taken by complete surprise), and the painting of the older group above is a compilation of photos of people who returned to Hebron for a three-day reunion in 1999, 40 years after the fact.

SUSAN CREAN

Susan Crean was born and raised in Toronto, Ontario and is of Scots/ Irish descent. She is a freelance writer and activist who has lived, besides Toronto and Paris, in Florence and New York City and in Vancouver and Gabriola Island in British Columbia.

Susan has worked as a current affairs producer for CBC-TV, an arts management consultant, a magazine editor (*This Magazine*), teacher, and broadcaster. Susan has two degrees in art history and a diploma in museology from the École du Louvre in Paris, and since her return to Canada in 1970 has had academic appointments at six Canadian universities. She was the first Maclean-Hunter Chair in Creative Non-Fiction at UBC in 1990 and taught at the School of Journalism at Ryerson University from 2000–2006. Susan is a former chair of the Writers' Union of Canada and a founding co-chair of the Creators' Rights Alliance/Alliance pour les droits des créateurs (CRA/ADC). She served on the Minister's Advisory Committee on the Status of the Artist in British Columbia from 1993–1994 and on the board of Access Copyright from 1992–1995. She has represented creators on copyright issues for over thirty years, latterly at the international level through the CRA/ADC, attending meetings at the World Trade Organization and the World Intellectual Property Organization in Geneva and Hong Kong.

She has written and lectured extensively on the subject of intellectual property. Her articles and essays have appeared in magazines and newspapers across Canada, and she is the author of seven books, the first, *Who's Afraid of Canadian Culture*, appearing in 1976. Her latest book, *The Laughing One – a Journey to Emily Carr*, was nominated for a Governor General's award and won a BC Book Prize in 2001. She serves on the board of Native Earth Performing Arts and, in 2007, was awarded a Chalmers Fellowship. She is currently based in Toronto.

BOTH SIDES NOW: DESIGNING WHITE MEN
AND THE OTHER SIDE OF HISTORY

Like a great many Anglo-Canadians, I was taught creation stories at school where the history books we studied celebrated the heroics of Champlain and Brébeuf while double-damning Louis Riel for betraying his non-Native ancestry as well as the State. The fact was that the only event involving Aboriginal peoples that conveyed any sense of the First Peoples' view on things was Riel's Rebellion. Even so, the Métis war of resistance was downplayed, and Riel, the feckless leader of the doomed uprising, was characterized as a cross between Rasputin and Bonnie Prince Charlie. At my school, an Anglican Church school for girls, we collected money for the missionaries teaching "the Indians up north," and we venerated Duncan Campbell Scott as a Confederation poet. We played lacrosse and basketball on teams called Iroquois, Cherokee, Sioux, and Ojibway though no one explained that the Iroquois are the Six Nations Confederacy, (one of the first structures in world history that resembles the United Nations) or that the Cherokee lived in the southeastern United States until 1838, when the American government forced them off their ancestral lands and marched them a thousand miles west to Oklahoma on what they called the Trail of Tears (*Nunna Daul Tsunny*).[1]

Along with the narrative about the founding of Canada by both the French and the English came the notion—preached by the likes of Emily Carr and Marius Barbeau, as well as D.C. Scott—of Aboriginal culture constituting Canada's ancient past, the prehistory upon which the modern nation could be built and with which an authentic Canadian culture could be fashioned. This was the idea of Canada embraced during the 1920s and 1930s by the emerging national elites who borrowed indiscriminately from Indigenous cultures while enacting the laws and policies that encouraged their extinction, all the while ignoring the existence of pre-existing Aboriginal title and rights. The story of Canada I was raised on, thus, denied the connection between assimilation and appropriation, between the past and the present. So, when my Great-Uncle John joined the Queen's Own Rifles and headed west in 1884 to fight Riel at Duck Lake, it apparently had nothing to do with the legacy of deprivation and death left to the Métis by the encounter—the "Prison

Emily Carr spoke "through a tradition that was already well established by 1928—the tradition of White people writing about Native peoples, representing their ideas, telling their stories, and speaking for them on the one had, using their technology and exploiting their art on the other."[2]

Charles Marius Barbeau (1883–1969) was an anthropologist who, although spending much time in fieldwork among many First Nations in Canada, held an attitude towards Aboriginal people as being tragic figures doomed to extinction.[3]

of Grass" that the late Métis author and leader Howard Adams would describe eighty-five years later.[4] By the same token, the beaded tobacco pouch Great-Uncle kept all his life has been passed down as a mute souvenir, with no story or provenance attached.

This de-personalization of history is one way to forget it. Psychologically, you can construct a moat around the nasty bits, declare immunity through distance: *It didn't concern me; it was someone else's fault; it happened way too long ago to matter now.* This is why truth and reconciliation requires proactive remembering. For white Canadians, for all non-Native Canadians, I think, this requires owning—not just owning up to and saying sorry, which is the easy part, but actually taking ownership of— the residential schools story. There is no requirement for us to have been there to be affected by it or to benefit from the arrangement of privilege that had my eight-year-old self collecting nickels for the enterprise. It is an old argument, but everyone *is* implicated when the State takes after one group of citizens or dispossesses one whole race of people, because it does so in the name of everyone. Moreover, at this stage in our collective history, simple fairness in the process of reconciliation demands that candour be offered on all sides; the disclosures of residential school Survivors need to be met with something more than *pro forma* apologies from churches knee-deep in lawyers, jail sentences for the few perpetrators who managed to get caught, and silence from a comfortable majority.

To my mind, ownership means understanding the how, who, and why of something like the residential school solution—how it was set up, who helped it function, and why the abuse was tolerated. Like other chapters in the saga of white/Aboriginal relations, we need to go deeper than just recognizing that Aboriginal peoples were betrayed and victimized. We need to acknowledge that such damage has been inflicted that it will indeed take seven generations to heal. We need a public reckoning with the fact that whole cultures were broken, children brutalized, and poverty and racism institutionalized by design. We need to acknowledge that all this was sanctioned by the prevailing value system, which is to say the race-based conventions of British imperialism, and that it required institutions and individuals to pull it off. It is true that D.C. Scott has ended up better known for his assertion that "Our object is to continue until there is not a single Indian in Canada that has not been absorbed into the body politic"[5] than any line of poetry he wrote. He has rightly been identified as the chief architect of the residential school system and of the policy of assimilation; he was also the man who devised a way to secure convictions under the potlatch laws and who came up with the concept of *involuntary* enfranchisement (which was actually on the books for two years, allowing the government to unilaterally remove a person's name from the band rolls and confer full citizenship and the right to vote without that person's consent).[6] As the Deputy Superintendent General of Indian Affairs for nineteen years who spent fifty-three years with the Department, he arguably has had a greater impact on the lives of Indigenous people than any other single individual. So it stands to reason that his legacy would be held up to the light first, but there were others and other incidents that require remembering.

Rarely do we connect the dots to see, for example, the pattern of governments resorting to the exclusion, discrimination, and exploitation of the disadvantaged and the racially other. It started with the *Indian Act*, which was followed by the *Chinese Head Tax*, the *Chinese Immigration Restriction Acts*, and the internment of Japanese Canadians. These are merely the highlights, for the list is long and the pattern is ingrained. Even with the *Charter of Rights*, equity laws could come and go, and no apology in the House of Commons, made to the sound of land claims stalling in the background, can atone for, much less change, the culture that produced the residential schools. That culture must take it upon itself to alter the stereotypes, correct the history, fill in the gaps, or re-educate the public. What is the public to make of it anyway, given the government's continuing refusal to sign the United Nations' *Declaration on the Rights of Indigenous Peoples*? This confusion is symptomatic. The mixed signals are a product of a lack leadership by non-Native elites and intellectuals and an absence of any real discourse in mainstream society.

I imagine it is hard for an Aboriginal person to know what to make of Trutch Street in Vancouver. I am not sure I know myself. I have often wondered if the residents there are aware of the man's claim to fame or of why Joseph Trutch would be so honoured in that area of Kitsilano where most of the streets are named after trees or famous British battles (such as Trafalgar, Waterloo, and Balaclava). Well, Trutch was lieutenant-governor of the province in the 1870s and the first commissioner of Lands and Works. He was instrumental in the imposition of a reserve system and dismissed the Aboriginal people as

The Douglas Creek Estates in Caledonia, Ontario, has become the focal point for tensions between local residents and members of the Six Nations of the Grand River after barricades were set up by Six Nations members in February 2006. The friction stems from claims by Six Nations that thousands of acres of the tract of land granted to them in 1784, in recognition of their loyalty to the Crown during the American Revolution, have been stolen or sold without fair compensation. There are charges of violence and of racial discrimination from both sides of the dispute.

"utter savages." He wrote, "I have not yet met with a single Indian of pure blood whom I consider to have attained to even the most glimmering perception of the [C]hristian creed ... the idiosyncrasy of the Indians of this country appears to incapacitate them from appreciating any abstract idea, nor do their languages contain words by which such a conception could be expressed."[8] Trutch was not carrying out orders; he was issuing them. He was part of a generation of white men, intent on having their way with the land. Not surprisingly, Trutch initiated the campaign for the removal of the Songhee people living in Victoria, using his office to encroach on their rights and to pressure them into leaving, which they eventually did in 1911.[9] Two years later, in 1913, the Squamish living on the south shore of Burrard Inlet were herded from their homes, loaded onto barges, and relocated to North Vancouver.[10]

In today's world you would have no compunction about identifying this behaviour as unjust, racist, and probably genocidal. But, there is something anachronistic about judging Trutch and his fellow zealots as extreme when their attitudes were perfectly acceptable at the time. To my mind, it is the juxtaposition that matters; the comparison of the old days with ours illustrates just how far democracy has travelled in Canadian society over 150 years. To remember Trutch is to remember that his perspective did *not* exactly prevail; Stephen Point of the Skowkale First Nation is now Lieutenant-Governor of British Columbia. To remember Trutch is to see his legacy at New Caledonia in 2008 and to realize how high and how barbed the cultural barriers still are and how limited the understanding and memory are in the non-Aboriginal community.

Dredging up detail serves to anchor the past to the present and allows history the colour and voice of personal experience. It introduces nuance and illuminates the sidelines where you can always find dissent. Indeed, in my travels through the archives researching the life of Emily Carr and the relationship of her career to the history of land claims, I came across letters-to-the-editor from individuals objecting to the potlatch laws. I also found information on the amazing Arthur O'Meara who made a reputation for himself as a meddlesome class traitor.[11] A one-time Ontario lawyer and Anglican lay-minister, O'Meara spearheaded a coalition of reform and labour groups in 1910 called the Conference of Friends of the Indians of British Columbia that supported land claims and Aboriginal title. Seventeen years later, he reappeared as

"From 1885 to 1923, approximately eight-two thousand Chinese immigrants were forced to pay a head tax to enter Canada ... In 1923, the Government of Canada enacted The Chinese Immigration Act ... which was tantamount to a complete prohibition on immigrants of Chinese origin or descent and lasted until 1947 ... Over twenty-two thousand Japanese Canadians were arrested, taken from their homes, separated from their families, and interned in prison camps during World War II."[7]

a key figure in the campaign of the Nisga'a chiefs who, after decades of foiled attempts to get their case heard in court, finally appealed to Parliament. Astonishingly, a joint Senate-House committee was set up. By April 1928, the politicians had rendered their report and, by summer, Parliament had passed amendments to the *Indian Act* to prohibit the raising of monies to pursue Aboriginal land claims.[12] It could be called the O'Meara provision, for as counsel to the Allied Indian Tribes of BC, O'Meara had appeared with Peter Kelly and Andrew Paull before the Committee. What had transpired has to be one of the most sustained and vicious attacks on a witness in the annals of Canadian politics. It was a very rare moment where an act of collective villainy was committed in public.

O'Meara was jeered and heckled all through his presentation, the worst of it coming from the Conservative MP from Vancouver Centre, H.H. Stevens. There was no restraining the man who accused O'Meara of manufacturing the evidence. Everyone went along with the attack, and O'Meara was eventually required to produce the document he was quoting from (the rare and precious compendium known as the *Papers Connected with the Indian Land Question*,[13] the authoritative record on the question between 1850 and 1875, although everyone in the room knew he did not possess it. The document appeared to have been deliberately withheld from Native leaders, and the villainy is in the revelation that there was actually a copy of it in the room. The Indian Commissioner for British Columbia, A.E. Ditchburn, was not prepared to surrender his own copy to the Committee, but D.C. Scott, who did have his copy with him, eventually allowed O'Meara to read passages from it, claiming that he was not aware that the document in question was, in fact, the one he had on hand. However, Stevens continued to pressure O'Meara for evidence, questioning him on every point.

The Committee report declared that there was no such thing as Aboriginal title and laid blame for the long and fruitless appeal of the Nisga'a on manipulative outsiders. It deplored those "designing white men" by whom "the Indians are deceived and led to expect benefits from claims more or less fictitious."[14] O'Meara, a lightening rod for the Committee's anger, also gave the Members of Parliament and Senators the scapegoat they needed. To the public, they could thus present themselves as saviours of Aboriginal integrity, fending off white men who would exploit and mislead the innocent Aboriginal people (who were, after all, wards of the state). As spin-doctoring goes, it was masterful. As defining moments go, it needs work.

In deconstructing the legacy of Emily Carr, I came to the conclusion that until land claims are honourably settled and Canada, as a nation and a community of newcomers, comes to terms with its legacy of appropriation, there will be no way to honourably claim Carr as a national icon. The same can be said for a great many other things in Canadian life. This is not a plea for outpourings of guilt, it is a plea for the work of reconciliation to include the wider public and address the mainstream need for connection with the past through the present ... which brings me back to Howard Adams.

Howard was a scholar, teacher, and activist. He was also a leader in the Métis community and a seasoned politico who lent his energy and acumen to many progressive causes, which is how I met him through the Writers' Union and the "Writing Thru Race" Conference of 1994. Our friendship led to conversations about his projects (he was writing *A Tortured People* then) as well as mine, and I often wondered what Great-Uncle would have thought ... a glib question worth taking seriously for a moment. What *would* young Captain Crean, then aged twenty-six, have known about the life and achievements of someone like Howard's remarkable grandfather Ambroise Lépine? Lépine was the adjutant general in Riel's provisional government who had been tried and sentenced to hang for the murder of Thomas Scott, though granted a last-minute pardon.[15] A tall, handsome, educated man, he and his brother were legends on the prairie, fiercely loyal to Riel and the dream of co-existence, collaboration even, with white society. How would Great-Uncle have conceived of that idea? For that matter, how would he have viewed the displacement of Indigenous people happening before his eyes? To me, the parallel with the displaced Irish, ravaged by famine and left to rot in the bogs, seems unavoidable. To Great-Uncle, such comparisons might have seemed a luxury.

Such questions are not answerable, of course, and are not meant to be. The personal contact with history does not need to be through benighted ancestors, but through personal connection in the here and now with the survivors of assimilation. Think of the success of Aboriginal artists, the accessibility of Indigenous culture, and the presence of urban Aboriginal communities right across Canada. It is, I believe, through reconciliation that dots grow, circles expand, and patterns change.

The author would like to thank the Aboriginal Healing Foundation for providing the resources below.

NOTES

[1] A sampling of historical insight from a First Nations or Native American perspective can be found in the following: Grinde, Donald A., Jr. and Bruce E. Johansen (1991). *Exemplar of Liberty: Native America and the Evolution of Democracy.* Los Angeles, CA: University of California, American Indian Studies Center (draft version retrieved 12 January 2009 from:http://www.ratical. org/many_worlds/6Nations/EoL/); Anderson, Kim (2000). *A Recognition of Being: Reconstructing Native Womanhood.* Toronto, ON: Second Story Press; Cherokee Nation official website (http://www.cherokee.org); Debo, Angie (1983). *A History of the Indians of the United States,* Seventh Printing. Norman, OK: University of Oklahoma Press; Allen, Paula Gunn (2004). *The Sacred Hoop: Recovering the Feminine in American Indian Traditions* (originally published 1986). Boston, MA: Beacon Press; Bruchac, Joseph (2000). *Trails of Tears, Paths of Beauty.* Washington, DC: National Geographic Society; Birchfield, D.L. (2004). *The Trail of Tears.* Milwaukee, WI: World Almanac Library: and Cherokee Nation (no date). *Trail of Tears Era.* Retrieved 22 January 22 2009 from: http://www.cherokee.org/Culture/History/TOT/ Cat/Default.aspx

[2] Crean, Susan (2001:178). *The Laughing One: A Journey to Emily Carr.* Toronto, ON: HarperCollins Publishers Publishers Ltd.

[3] Nurse, Andrew (2001). "But Now Things Have Changed": Marius Barbeau and the Politics of Amerindian Identity. *Ethnohistory* 48(3):432–472.

[4] Adams, Howard (1989). *Prison of Grass: Canada from a Native Point of View,* Revised Edition. Saskatoon, SK: Fifth House Publishers.

[5] Government of Canada (1920:63). *Report of the Special Committee of the House of Commons examining the Indian Act amendments of 1920* (Duncan Campbell Scott testimony on 30 March 1920). Library and Archives Canada, RG10, volume 6810, file 470-2-3, part 7.

[6] See Government of Canada (1920). *Report of the Special Committee of the House of Commons examining the Indian Act amendments of 1920.* Library and Archives Canada, RG10, volume 6810, file 470-2-3, part 7. See also the letter from D.C. Scott to Minister of Justice, Ottawa, 18th December 1916. LAC, RG10, volume 3629, file 6244-3. In 1884, the potlatch, along with other

ceremonies, was banned, and later amended in 1914 through the influence of D.C. Scott to ensure enforcement of this law by changing from criminal to summary conviction. The inclusion for the gradual enfranchisement of Indians in the *Indian Act* was first introduced in 1869 and later amended in 1920 to include the provision for *involuntary* enfranchisement. All *Indian Act* amendments can be found in the National Aboriginal Document Database retrieved 13 January 2008 from: http://epe.lac-bac.gc.ca/100/205/301/ic/cdc/aboriginaldocs/m-stat.htm

[7] Morse, Bradford W. (2007:237-238). Reconciliation Possible? Reparations Essential. In Marlene Brant Castellano, Mike Degagné, and Linda Archibald (eds.), *From Truth to Reconciliation: Transforming the Legacy of Residential Schools*. Ottawa, ON: Aboriginal Healing Foundation: 233–256.

[8] Trutch, Joseph W. (1871). Correspondence to the Secretary of State for the Provinces, 26 September 1871. In Government of British Columbia (1875:101). *Papers Connected with the Indian Land Question. 1850-1875*. Victoria, BC: Government Printing Office. Retrieved 14 January 2009 from: http://www.archive.org/details/papersconnectedw00britiala

[9] Kanakos, Jeannie L. (1982). *The Negotiations to Relocate the Songhees Indians, 1843-1911*. [Unpublished M.A. thesis.] Retrieved 26 January 2009 from: http://ir.lib.sfu.ca/bitstream/1892/7545/1/b16167624.pdf

[10] See: *Mathias v. The Queen*, 2001 FCT 480. Retrieved 5 March 2009 from: http://decisions.fct-cf.gc.ca/en/2001/2001fct480/2001fct480.html

[11] Haig-Brown, Mary (2006). Arthur Eugene O'Meara: Servant, Advocate, Seeker of Justice. In Celia Haig-Brown and David A. Nock (eds.), *With Good Intentions: Euro-Canadian and Aboriginal Relations in Colonial Canada*. Vancouver, BC: University of British Columbia Press: 258–296.

[12] See: *An Act to amend the Indian Act, 1927*, S.C. 1926-27, c. 32. Retrieved 13 January 2008 from: http://epe.lac-bac.gc.ca/100/205/301/ic/cdc/aboriginaldocs/m-stat.htm

[13] Government of British Columbia (1875), see note #5.

[14] Government of Canada (1927:ix). Appendix No. 2: Special Committees of the Senate and House of Commons. Meeting in joint session to inquire into the claims of the Allied Indian Tribes of British Columbia, as set forth in their petition submitted to Parliament in June 1926, Session 1926-27, *Proceedings, Reports and the Evidence*. Ottawa, ON: King's Printer.

[15] Siggins, Maggie (1994). *Riel: A Life of Revolution*. Toronto, ON: HarperCollins Publishers Ltd.

Photographer: Fred Cattroll

Rita Flamand

Liza Rita Flamand is a Métis Elder born 28 August 1931 in the community of Camperville, Manitoba. She attended Christ the King School, a day school taught by nuns and priests of Pine Creek Residential School and the Roman Catholic Church. Rita and her husband raised eight children, and she is known as *Kohkum* to her sixteen grandchildren and six great-grandchildren. Rita completed an LPN course at St. Boniface, Manitoba, in 1948 and later nursed in several hospitals throughout Manitoba, Ontario, and British Columbia.

Rita is currently President of Mine'igo Sipi Senior Inc. and of Camperville Métis Cemetery. She was President of Home & School and Councillor on the Community Council. She also coordinated and facilitated programs such as Community-Based University Entrance, Literacy, and Métis Education School Services programs and was employed with Community Education Development Association. Rita is a member of the Dauphin Legal Aid Advisory and Restitution committees, was certified as a Justice of the Peace Officer and Commissioner for Oaths, and worked as a Court Communicator. Rita was the first elected President of Manitoba Métis Women's Association and is a board member of both the Native Association of Community Councils and the Manitoba Métis Federation. She later became the first Coordinator of the Métis Child and Family Support program of the Manitoba Métis Federation. It was in this capacity that Rita was the first to be able to repatriate a Sixties Scoop Métis child back to her home community. Rita is endeavouring to preserve the Michif language she feels may disappear if there is no one who will take on this daunting task. Rita has put all her efforts into this since the 1980s and has since developed a Michif writing system with the assistance from two linguists: Peter Bakker, University of Aarhus, Denmark, and Robert Papen, Université du Québec à Montréal, Quebec. In 2000, she began teaching and tutoring both adults and children the Michif language from lessons she developed herself.

Since 1999, Rita has translated into Michif numerous books, guides, and newsletters on Métis language, history, recipes, and stories for both adults and children. In 2006, she contributed to the book *In the Words of Our Ancestors: Métis Health and Healing*. Rita continues to translate and teach the Michif language.

Truth about Residential Schools
and Reconciling this History:
A Michif View

Oppression by the Government of Canada and the Catholic Church has had a major negative influence on the Métis people. The natural evolution of a culture, a nation of people, and a society in all its aspects was thwarted by the government-sanctioned influence of the Church. Inadequate education, loss of language, and loss of culture were the results. *Culture* is defined as "the integrated pattern of human knowledge, belief, and behavior that depends upon the capacity for learning and transmitting knowledge to succeeding generations ... the customary beliefs, social forms, and material traits of a racial, religious, or social group."[1]

The effects of colonization and its mission are intergenerational and have resulted in the many social problems affecting today's generation. In addition, many Métis people suffered mental, physical, and emotional abuse caused by the intergenerational effects of residential school, and it still continues today through the loss of language and culture. In order for our children to know where they are going, they must know where they came from so that they can move forward in a healthy way. There is also a need for adequate and accessible healing programs and therapies that should be made available to Métis people.

My good friend and pupil, Darlene Kemash, sat down with me recently to assist in the telling of my story. You see, I speak and write in Michif, and Darlene helped to translate and organize my words. This is my story ...

Ni Maamaa Ste-Anne de Lima Fagnan

My mother, the storyteller of our family, related this story to us about the residential school she attended when she was a little girl:

> *Kétatawé iko ni'kushopayhin* (all of a sudden I came to), I was standing on top one of the corner beds in our dormitory. *Trwaa kémaa kaatr lii seur ota aanavañ kaa niipawichihk* (there were three or four nuns there standing around in front of me). As

I tried to take in what happened, I focused my eyes on Sister Frances who was standing directly in front of me. The headpiece of her habit was dangling on her shoulder all askew. Forgetting everything, my eyes popped open! SHE HAD HAIR!! Us girls used to wonder if the nuns had hair, and we sometimes wondered if they had feet the way they used to glide around in their long skirts. I was horrified when I learned that I had grabbed Sister Frances' headpiece off her head! As I looked around, the beds were all messed. I was apparently jumping from bed to bed as they tried to catch me.

Having some kind of breakdown, my mother had started fighting with the Sisters. My mother was Métis, and the reason she was in the residential school was to fill the quota while they were in the process of rounding up Treaty Indian children from the north to fill the school. In the meantime, Métis children would do. After six or seven years in the residential school, my mother could barely write her name. It always bothered her that she could not read or write. My dad would just hold that over her. After all, he went up to grade 4. She would ask him to teach her to read and write and, inevitably, their sessions would end in a fight with my mom accusing my dad of teasing and laughing at her. She wanted her children to have the education she never had. Little did she know that her children and grandchildren, second and third generation, would suffer some of the same fate with the priest and nuns, although we went to a Catholic day school.

My Parents

My mother, Ste-Anne de Lima Fagnan, was known by the name of Anne, although a lot of people still called her Ste-Anne, and she was called *"mii mii"* by her grandchildren. She did not want to be called Ste-Anne. She used to say that she was not a saint. She was born in Camperville, Manitoba, on 7 October 1905. Her parents lived on a little farm a couple of miles outside of Camperville. They used to come to town once in a while to get some supplies. My father, Peter Flamand, was born on 27 March 1886 in St. John's, North Dakota, a year after the Riel Resistance. It was not safe for my grandmother to have her baby in Canada, as the Métis people were always on the run from the RCMP. This was a very sad time for the Métis. But my dad's parents, my grandparents, still managed to run a farm in the Inglis, Manitoba area.

In the early nineteen hundreds, my grandparents, Joseph Flamand and Agathe Fleury, along with a lot of Métis people from the south, came to the Camperville area, drawn by the good fishing in Lake Winnipegosis. My Uncle Cyril was the first son to get here, as my mother recollects. She said the girls were talking about him as the "new guy in town." Not long after, she said the girls were saying "another one of Joe Flamand's sons got here and he's better-looking." My Mother said, "I saw him and I didn't think he was good-looking." With my mom this meant that she thought he *was* good-looking. She said she only saw him a few times, until one Sunday one of her sisters was shaking her awake early in the morning, "*wanishkaa, wanishkaa ki wii wiikitoon*" (get up, get up, you are getting married). She asked her sister, "What are you talking about?" Her sister told her, "Last night, Pete Flamand came to see Papa while you were sleeping and we heard them talking. He asked Papa for your hand in marriage and Papa said 'yes.'"

WHERE WE WERE BORN

My older brothers were born in Saskatchewan because my parents, after they were married, went where the jobs were. My mom used to tell us that two or three families would travel together by horse and wagon across the Prairies. They would meet different Métis and Indian families also travelling by wagon and would set up their tents and visit together for a few days while they rested their horses. Later on, my parents settled back in Camperville where the rest of us were born. There were five girls and five boys in my family. I often wonder how my dad fed us all. I only remember everything tasting so good, but maybe it was because I was always hungry.

Of course we lived off the land. We ate nothing but wild meat and fish, and my dad always had a big garden. We picked berries in the summer. There were so many berries in those days, and we lived in the blueberry patch for part of every summer. I was quite young, and all we did as kids was play! It was so nice and sandy where we pitched our tents; this place was called *kaa napaksakokaatek* (where it is flat). The tents were pitched all around and we, the kids, would play in the middle where it was safe. We always played outside, not like the kids today, playing video games and becoming dangerously overweight. When I was a kid, there were no overweight kids around.

We're mindful of one thing, and that is traditionally the Catholic Church does not apologize," said Mr. Fontaine, national chief of the Assembly of First Nations. "But we hope and pray that there will be an apology, one that will acknowledge the harms inflicted upon innocent children and an acceptance of responsibility for their role in the tragic experience.

Phil Fontaine
National Chief
Assembly of First Nations
Cited in "Residential school survivors granted audience with the Pope"
by Joe Friesen
Globe and Mail
14 April 2009

My mom would take us all to pick blueberries, and we, being the younger ones, would have a nap in the bush. My mom used to put cotton batting in our ears so the bugs would not crawl in. When we would get back to camp later, we would see fires starting outside the tents and women making supper. What I remember is my mom cooking fried blueberries in lard with sugar right away because it was quick to prepare and it would turn into a blueberry *rubaboo*. We would eat that with *la galet* to tide us over until the meat and veggies were cooked. Those are such good memories.

SCHOOL

We lived about a mile from the school. It was hard trudging to school through the high snow in the wintertime and in water in the spring. I was six when I started school. I could not speak English. I only spoke Michif. The schoolroom was overflowing with kids—there were kids standing all around the room. Our teacher was a young Ukrainian man. All I remember was us kids standing around him while he was doing a strange dance called the *Kolomeika*. His long legs were flying off the floor. We were used to jigging, but this was a new twist.

English, Saulteaux, and Michif were being spoken in the classroom. It was confusing. When the teacher said to someone, "Go to the cloakroom," they would come out crying. I learned that they got the strap when they went in there. One day he looked straight at me and said, "Go to the cloakroom." I was terrified and hung my head and started to cry. He must have forgotten about me in the chaos when he saw me crying, as he told my sister to ask me if I was sick. I understood the word "sick," so when she asked me, I said "yes." He sent me home and my mother kept me home for the rest of that year.

DAY SCHOOL

When I went back the following year, there was a change in our school. It was now called Christ the King School, and the nuns from the residential school were in charge. We were not allowed to speak our language. Everything was in English. I was learning two languages in school, English in the classroom and Saulteaux out in the schoolyard. A quarter of us kids spoke Michif and the rest spoke Saulteaux. I understood

> We were not allowed to speak our language. Everything was in English. I was learning two languages in school, English in the classroom and Saulteaux out in the schoolyard.

some Saulteaux words because my mom and my *kohkum* used to speak Saulteaux when they did not want us to understand something. English was totally alien, but coming from a day school, we did not lose our language completely because we spoke it at home in the evenings.

The nuns would arrive by horse and buggy every morning with their supplies and lunch for the day. They would start warming up their food at around 11:30 A.M. They would fry potatoes in butter. Oh, how that used to smell so good! By the time we went home for our lunch or ate it in the corner at school, it was hard to swallow bannock and lard or the morning's cold porridge with that smell lingering in your nose. The priests were always there having lunch with the nuns. After lunch, a priest would play with us and take us girls to the mission on the pretense of helping him in the Shomoo Hall. There, he would grab and touch us inappropriately. I did not feel right, but he was like God after all. That is how holy we thought they were.

Our family, parents, and grandparents were always in church. My grandma used to dress like a nun in long black dresses with a big cross around her neck. We would never tell them when the priests would rub us against them, especially Father "B..." I can still hear his high-pitched, excited laughter when he would be around us. We were so innocent we thought they loved us, and that is how they got away with it. They knew we would not say anything. We were about eight to ten years old. They controlled us right from when we started going to confession—that dark confessional in the back we seemed to be always attending—which was a form of control and abuse. We had to confess everything, our bad thoughts as well as all our sins. Did we have bad thoughts about a boy? What were they? If we kissed him it was a mortal sin, at least twenty Hail Marys.

Although we went to day school, the priests controlled all the Métis people in many different ways. I remember when the second-hand clothing would arrive. The women would come to get clothes for their kids and themselves. The priest would get the women to try on the tops and blouses, touching them on the breasts and saying, "Oh, it's too big" or "too small," while running his hands down the breasts pretending to straighten the blouse. The women would laugh embarrassingly. My girlfriend used to have big breasts, and we used to think the nuns were jealous because they were always making mention of her "big *tootoosh*" in a derogatory way. She used to make me tie a folded *koosh* (diaper) around her chest. I would pin it in the back with safety pins so she would have a flat chest.

PAGAN BABIES

We used to have a big drawing of a pyramid on the wall of our classroom. Our names were written on a coloured star at the bottom. Every time we brought a penny to school, our star would move up a notch. We worked our way up that pyramid with every cent we could muster up (there were not as many pennies to be had in them days). By the time we got to the top, it was five dollars and, *voila*!! We had bought a pagan baby! I used to wonder where these pagan babies were. I always thought they were some poor babies somewhere across the ocean. Imagine my surprise when I later learned the pagans were my Indian cousins and relatives.

PRAYING IN SCHOOL

We used to pray a lot in school. We would kneel down and pray when we arrived in the morning, when we went for recess, before lunch, after lunch, and again before we went home. I kid you not, my knees used to be red, flat, and sore. One day, when the nun was going to strap my sister (we had a big, black leather strap that was used in class), I got so angry that I told the nun, "We don't learn anything in here anyway, all we do is pray." I went home but my dad brought me back. The nun made me stand in front of the class and apologize for being mad at her.

RESIDENTIAL SCHOOL

The church and residential school were two or three miles from my home, and we used to walk to the "mission," as we called it. That is where the church, residential school, Fathers' and Sisters' residences, and barns were clustered. It used to be so cold to walk to church, especially when you would hit the field close to the church. The wind used to be so cold off the lake, but we were promised we would go straight through to heaven if we went to Holy Communion for nine consecutive first Fridays of each month. We would be there for early Mass, and we would make several of those first Fridays. So you see, I will be going straight to heaven when I die.

On Sundays, we would go to church in the big church. Each Sunday, we would watch these two doors open on each side of the altar, and the little girls would come out of one door and the boys out of the other. The girls would be all dressed in cotton dresses, all the same kind. Their hair was cut straight across the forehead and below the ears. I used to envy their nice dresses and shoes as I did not have nice dresses like that. The boys came out of the other door, all dressed in black suits and neckties and with short hair. They too had to march to the back of the church and up to the balcony where there was a big pipe organ. They had the sweetest voices you ever wanted to hear. I remember on Christmas Eve they used to sing *Christ the Messiah*. They were every bit as good as any choir. The choir sang in Latin, and the altar boys served the priests during Mass, answering the priests in Latin.

I do not remember seeing them smile. They always looked serious. I did not know where they came from. They just seemed to always be there. I would hear *"aasha mina kii tapaashiiwak aatit"* (some of them ran away again) and *"Maaka kii mishkawewak"* (but they caught them). Then, during Sunday Mass, they would be lined up in front of the church where the entire congregation would see them. Sometimes they would be a mixture of boys and girls, but most times they would either be all girls or all boys. Their heads would all be shaven. They would stand there with their heads down, very embarrassed. I used to wonder where they were from. I never heard anyone talk about them around the village, just in whispers, as if the people were scared the priests and nuns would hear them.

When my cousins from Tanner's Reserve[2] started attending the mission school, I became more aware that the kids who appeared in church actually lived at the mission. After that, we would go with my grandparents every Sunday after Mass. We were allowed to see them in the waiting room for just one hour. Even those kids that were from the reserve were only allowed to see their parents for one hour. Sometimes, the nuns would take the "mission kids," as we used to call them, for a walk on the highway. There would be nuns in front of them, on each side of them, and behind them, walking them like prisoners. We could not even wave at our cousins. We would run in the ditch, trying to get their attention, but the nuns would chase us away.

I'll say I'm Métis or other young people that I know that are Métis have been confronted with the same question: 'Oh, I didn't think you were Métis. You don't look it.' You know, it's not a biological issue. It's a cultural, historical issue and it's a way of life issue; and it's not what you look like on the outside, it's how you carry yourself around on the inside that is important, both in your mind and your soul and your heart.

Delbert Majer
Saskatchewan Metis
Addictions Council
Speaking at the public hearings of the Royal Commission on Aboriginal Peoples Regina, Saskatchewan 10 May 1993

Culture is conveyed through language. The government must recognize the importance of the Michif language as an integral part of health and wellness for Métis people.

The Catholic Church has so many rituals, and we seemed to be always going to church. We went for catechism, Benediction, and Lent and, during the month of May, honoured the Virgin Mary. The priests were always behind the holy altar. To us they seemed so mysterious and holy, almost Christ-like. That is how the people saw them. Our parents did not teach us the Bible or catechism, the nuns and priests did. I completed grade 8. For us, education ended at grade 8 as there was no further class for Métis children. Our school only went up to grade 8, there was no high school. After that we had to get out and find a job. We were cheated out of a high school education.

Truth and Reconciliation

The Canadian government must acknowledge the cultural genocide and abuse of the Métis people at the hands of the government and the Catholic Church. A public acknowledgement and apology by the Government of Canada and the Catholic Church is the first step towards reconciliation. With acknowledgement, the true history of Métis people must be made available in the school curriculum, not only for our Métis children, but for all Canadian children. Research, curriculum development, and implementation must happen. Human and financial resources must be allocated. Elders must be interviewed and their history documented. We were an integral part of the forming of this nation, and we remain so.

Also, the Michif language must be taught in schools where Métis children attend. Culture is conveyed through language. The government must recognize the importance of the Michif language as an integral part of health and wellness for Métis people. This should include curriculum development and implementation, with human and financial resources allocated for this. Also, Michif Elders and speakers must be consulted while they are still living. As my story shows, along with many other Métis people's stories, there were many Métis who were also victimized by residential schools (including day schools), so we too should be a part of the truth and reconciliation process.

Notes

[1] Merriam-Webster's Collegiate Dictionary, Tenth Edition, s.v. "culture."

[2] Also called Gambler's Reserve at Silver Creek in Manitoba. During my childhood, the people living there were almost all from the Tanner family and were all Michif speakers. *See* Barkwell, Lawrence J. with Dr. Peter Lorenz Neufeld (2007). *The Famous Tanner Family and Tanner's Crossing, now Minnedosa, Manitoba.* Winnipeg, MB: Louis Riel Institute. Retrieved 5 February 2009 from: http://www.metismuseum.ca/resource.php/07238

Métis family at Fort Chipewyan, Alberta, 1899
Photographer unknown
Glenbow Archives, NA-949-118

[Reprinted from the Legacy of Hope Foundation's *Where Are the Children?* exhibit catalogue (2003)]

IAN MACKENZIE

John A. (Ian) MacKenzie is a retired archdeacon who continues to live a full and enriched life by offering his knowledge and expertise through his continued work for the Anglican Church and other organizations. Ian received his Bachelor of Arts in Psychology and History from Dalhousie University (Halifax, Nova Scotia), a Bachelor of Divinity from the University of King's College (Halifax, Nova Scotia), and a Master of Sacred Theology from Union Theological Seminary (New York, New York). He also holds an honorary Doctor of Divinity from the Vancouver School of Theology (Vancouver, British Columbia).

Ian has spent the last 33 years in Caledonia as Rector of St. John's, Old Massett, a Haida parish (1974–1979), Rector of St. Andrew's Church, Laxgalts'ap (1979–1982), a Nisga'a parish, Archdeacon of Caledonia (1982–2000), Director of the Native Ministries Program, Vancouver School of Theology (1989–2000), and as an appointed member of the Nisga'a Tribal Council (1979–2001). Ian has been adopted by the Haida and Nisga'a nations, and he is a member of the Raven tribe. He is also a member of the Alaska Native Brotherhood. Since retirement, Ian is still active as the chair of TEENET, (a global network for theological education by extension) of which he was a founding member. He is an Emeritus member of the Native Ministries Consortium, which he helped start in 1984. Since 2005, he works as a volunteer Associate Rector for St. Philip's Church in Wrangell, Alaska and for the Diocese of Alaska, Episcopal Church, USA. Ian continues to tutor for the Vancouver School of Theology Native Ministries Program. He is a founding member of the David Lochhead Institute for Religion, Technology and Culture and of the Indian Ecumenical Conference. Ian continues to work on the interface of Christianity and First Nations traditional religion as one of the founding members of the Centre for Indian Scholars.

Ian has written several works, including *Native communities are not the same* (1995), *A Legend in His Own Time: Some Initial Reflections on the work of Robert K. Thomas* (1998), *Caledonia – Thirty Years of Change and Development* (1999), and *Canadian Native Activist Movements* (2001).

FOR EVERYTHING THERE IS A SEASON

There is a time to be born, and a time to die; a time to plant, and a time to reap; a time to kill, and a time to heal.[1]

NOW IS THE TIME TO HEAL

My most emotional memory of Indian residential schools is a visit I made in 1970 to the abandoned Anglican Shingwauk Indian Residential School[2] in Sault Saint Marie. At the time, I was a board member of the Nishnawbe Institute,[3] a First Nations-run post-secondary educational institution located in Toronto. A group of First Nations people from Sault Saint Marie, led by Carol and Rolland Nadjiwon, was interested in establishing a similar centre in the Sault. They had heard that this school was being sold by the federal government and that they might be able to acquire it for a nominal fee. Carol had asked Robert K. Thomas[4] and me to join her and Rolland in visiting the property so that we could decide if it was appropriate for our needs. I remember that as we prepared for this visit, we were very enthusiastic about the possibilities such a property might bring to our mutual vision for the institute we wanted to establish.

We arrived in Sault Saint Marie, connected with Carol and Rolland, and, with great anticipation, visited the building. I remember the four of us entering the building and looking at the various areas. Throughout the visit no one spoke, and when we left, we walked out of the building without saying a word. Finally, someone broke the silence with something like, "We should not acquire this building." Throughout this visit, I felt a deep sadness, depression, unhappiness, fear, and anxiety and the desire to get out of there as fast as possible. It was as if the walls of the place had absorbed the pain of the hundreds of Aboriginal young people who had lived there over the years. The experience has haunted me ever since.

Even though the Anglican Church of Canada had closed most of its residential schools by 1969,[5] the recognition of the devastating effects of these schools on most Aboriginal children was still a long time coming. The apology of the Anglican and United churches was still many years away, and the apology of the Government of Canada was to come thirty-

> It was as if the walls of the place had absorbed the pain of the hundreds of Aboriginal young people who had lived there over the years. The experience has haunted me ever since.

nine years later. As of 2009, the Roman Catholic Church has yet to issue an apology.[6] The federal government's apology, four decades later, may bring a measure of closure to some of those men and women who experienced the schools or to their children and grandchildren who have also suffered so much. Who can possibly comprehend the effects over generations of the loss of language, culture, identity, religion, and parenting skills caused by the desire of churches and governments to Christianize the "pagan Indians" and to solve the so-called "Indian problem" through education?[7] Compounding all of this was the scandal of sexual abuse, which was often passed on within the families of the abused victims.

The truth is unbearably painful, but accepting the truth can be the first step in setting us free. Both Aboriginal people and the successors of the colonizers can achieve reconciliation only if we are free of the domination of the past. We are now called upon to enter into a period of sharing with the hope that reconciliation and healing will take place. Many Aboriginal persons are prepared to enter into this discussion.[8] The challenge for the rest of Canadian society, particularly churches and governments, is to respond with actions as well as words in order to set the context for a permanent new relationship between all Canadians and Aboriginal people. While many Aboriginal persons are prepared to engage in the process of truth and reconciliation, are the leaders and members of churches, governments, and their institutions and the general public prepared to do the same? I suggest there are three areas of radical change that must take place if there is to be meaningful reconciliation.

THE CHURCHES

Some of the mainline churches have heard the critique of Aboriginal peoples since the late sixties and implemented policies and programs, which have changed some things for the better,[9] but such change has usually been slow and has not been sustained. Moreover, it has only been a partial change at best. For example, while the Anglican Church of Canada, supported by some mainline churches, fostered the Indian ecumenical movement[10] that brought together First Nations traditional religious leaders and doctors with First Nations Christians, churches across the country renewed their attacks on what they called "pagan" religious practices. Some denominations began to replace parish clergy in Aboriginal congregations with clergy from those communities, and this often resulted in replacing fully supported, salaried white clergy with non-stipendiary Aboriginal clergy. For reconciliation to take place, the churches, for one thing, need to support salaried, Aboriginal clergy.

Most urgently, churches need to consider opening a serious dialogue with Aboriginal theologians, doctors, and healers who represent part of the many diverse aspects of what the Royal Commission on Aboriginal Affairs has called the *North American intellectual tradition*. One of the common threads Aboriginal writers who have already shared their stories in the first volume of *From Truth to Reconciliation* is the call for recognition of the truth of past injustices and respect for their civilizations. Most of all, this is a call for respect for their traditional religious thoughts and practices. The only legitimate North American intellectual tradition comes from the diverse tribal societies in our midst!

Sustainable reconciliation will only take place when every Canadian seminary includes a course on Aboriginal religious traditions;[11] when every congregation includes ongoing discussion and reflection on the North American intellectual tradition by initiating and inviting Aboriginal religious leaders to lead such discussions; when every Sunday school includes in its materials the truth about our past relationships and respect for the religious traditions of Aboriginal people living in their area; when Aboriginal peoples achieve real self-government within their churches; and when Christian theology not only respects Aboriginal thought, but learns from it. If this happens, it would make a reality of Bishop Mark MacDonald's idea that, in this century, the gospel is finally coming to North America as Aboriginal theologians take their proper place within this society.[12]

GOVERNMENTS AND THEIR AGENCIES

In 2008, the Prime Minister of Canada issued an apology to Aboriginal people for their treatment over the years at residential schools. Many people have called for this apology for many years as a first step in moving towards reconciliation between the two civilizations. However, an apology without significant program development and massive funding directed at settling the many challenges of land claims, treaty issues, lifestyle issues, and village infrastructure and the rapidly growing

> However, an apology without significant program development and massive funding directed at settling the many challenges of land claims, treaty issues, lifestyle issues, and village infrastructure and the rapidly growing social challenge of Indians in the cities makes a mockery of the Prime Minister's words.

Fundamentally, we are human beings. We live together on this earth and, if we recognize what Native spirituality says, we are all children of this earth. I don't like it. We have to recognize that all of us live here together on this continent. Native people are not going to disappear, but European people are not all going to go back to England or France; it's impossible. Let us begin to live together in respect and work out our differences.

Jim Penton
Speaking at the public hearings of the Royal Commission on Aboriginal Peoples Lethbridge, Alberta 24 May 1993

social challenge of Indians in the cities makes a mockery of the Prime Minister's words. For over a hundred years, First Nations peoples have called for the federal government to honour their treaties. Now, governments are involved in modern-day treaty negotiation processes. Several First Nations have entered into these processes in good faith and have signed treaties only to find that the federal government is breaking these treaties within the first five years.[13] Provincial governments must also be required to reaffirm their commitment to a new beginning with funding and actions. For example, the Province of British Columbia's words of commitment are contradictory. Here is what Willard Martin, Chief Councillor of the Nisga'a village of Laxgalts'ap said recently in an email following a suicide in the Nisga'a Nation:

I inform you all, with a lot of sadness, the loss of another Nisga'a youthful member. Sometime between late Saturday and early Sunday, a male young adult committed suicide ... Not much detail is yet available. It is utterly disturbing that in the midst of all this, Health Canada continues to shun pleas for increased support to mental health and addictions. It is even more disturbing that, a week ago, the media informed British Columbians about the Liberal Government diverting considerable amounts of funds from mental health to something else. I think the senior governments will have to become more realistic in their approaches and we must confront them directly on the matter. It is clear that the underlying cause of despairs is the continuing poverty or lack of economic activity. My village government accepts that fact and is inclined towards initiatives that might service a better quality of life for all. The Church has to step up and do their part in assisting any change in the conditions that cause despair. I would urge those appointed to conduct activity with the Truth and Reconciliation processes to be sure that they address these kinds of occurrences as they surely stem from the lingering effects of the infamous residential schools. If the governments and churches want to create rewarding commemoration to the lives of thousands of aboriginal peoples victimized at those institutions, they had better ensure that infrastructure and programming to redirect the lives of future generations are well placed in strategic places for effective change. The situation cannot be continually minimized. We can no longer be acquiescent about these occurrences and the ongoing impoverished First Nations communities.[14]

Governments and their institutions often make decisions out of ignorance of the real situations facing Aboriginal peoples and with no sense of the history of their own continuing colonialism. In fact, many argue that present-day governments and their bureaucracies are still operating on the colonial model. In order for reconciliation between Aboriginal peoples and the Canadian nation to take place, every elected government official should be required to participate in an Aboriginal cultures and history orientation session. The same needs to happen with bureaucrats. It is usually at the interface between individual Aboriginal people and those in bureaucracies administering programs that systemic racism operates. Every civil servant should participate in an orientation on this issue. Those who work directly with Aboriginal peoples should be required to attend an in-depth cross-cultural workshop lead by Aboriginal people whose primary foundation is in the North American intellectual tradition.[15]

Duncan Campbell Scott directed the Indian residential school program from 1913 to 1932. His stated objective was clear:

> I want to get rid of the Indian problem. I do not think as a matter of fact, that this country ought to continuously protect a class of people who are able to stand alone … Our object is to continue until there is not a single Indian in Canada that has not been absorbed into the body politic, and there is no Indian question, and no Indian Department, that is the whole object of this Bill.[16]

Today, the leaders of our educational systems would like to think that the statement applied only to an earlier period of time. While there are now thousands of programs in educational institutions that are more orientated to Aboriginal cultures and history than ever before, the fact is that the underlying educational theory and practice continue to ignore the fundamentally different world views and methods of learning that characterize those following the North American intellectual tradition.

In simplified terms, the difference is that the Western mind thinks in linear terms, whereas Aboriginal people think in circular terms. In most of our educational systems, these two processes never meet.[17] When our educational systems recognize the validity of Aboriginal methods of thinking, we will be on the way to true reconciliation.

The challenge to Canadian academic institutions is well stated by Marie Battiste. She contends that academia must:

> support the agenda of Indigenous scholarship, which is to transform Eurocentric theory so that it will not only include and properly value Indigenous knowledge, thought, and heritage in all levels of education, curriculum, and professional practice but also develop a cooperative and dignified strategy that will invigorate and animate Indigenous languages, cultures, knowledge, and vision in academic structures.[18]

There is some movement in this direction; University of Northern British Columbia continues to dialogue with First Nations post-secondary centres they support, such as Wilp Wilxo'oskwhl Nisga'a Institute.[19] The Freda Diesing School of Northwest Coast Art[20] at Northwest Community College in Terrace, British Columbia, is working at teaching First Nations art, but also reflecting on the relationship between these art forms and Aboriginal land. The Native Ministries Consortium[21] has successfully sought accreditation for arts transferable courses from Open Learning that are taught by First Nations religious leaders who have no formal degrees. Many other Aboriginal-controlled post-secondary institutions and Aboriginal programs within mainstream institutions across the country are embarking on similar activities.

THE EARTH

Canadians could be the recipients of a huge gift. As people in churches, governments, and communities open to the offer of reconciliation and dialogue by First Nations peoples, we will be greatly enriched. The North American intellectual tradition could change all of us in its understanding of the relationships among humans, all sentient life, and Earth itself. It would mean that instead of thinking of Earth as something to exploit for humankind's benefit, we could begin to think of how we can live in harmony with Earth in all of its manifestations. I remember years ago when Bob Thomas and I were driving across the western United States and arrived at the Mississippi River. I had never seen or crossed that great river, so we found a place where we could park[22] next to it and walk by its shores. I picked up some pebbles and began to skip them across the water. After awhile, Bob asked me why I was hurting the river. For the first time in my life, I began to see rivers and lakes as having a being of their own. What a gift to me! And what a gift Aboriginal peoples might offer to the world if, through them, we began to understand what it means to live in harmony with Earth. It might be the catalyst that would save our planet from what looks more and more like its inevitable destruction.

Many Aboriginal people are offering Canadians an unimaginably generous hand of forgiveness and are prepared to enter into discussion with the colonizers. The time is now for churches, governments and their institutions, and for all Canadians to begin the process of exploration that will lead to change. If we can do this, in the words of the Royal Commission on Aboriginal Peoples, we will then

> resolve a fundamental contradiction at the heart of Canada: that while we assume the role of defender of human rights in the international community, we retain, in our conception of Canada's origins and make-up, the remnants of colonial attitudes of cultural superiority that do violence to the Aboriginal peoples to whom they are directed.[23]

There is a time to be born, and a time to die; a time to plant, and a time to reap; a time to kill, and a time to heal.

Now is the time to heal.

> *Our traditional spiritual beliefs are not a religion. Ours is a holistic spiritual way of life. This spiritual way of life is our traditions, beliefs and government.*
>
> **Dennis Thorne (Tungán Cikala) Speaking at the public hearings of the Royal Commission on Aboriginal Peoples Edmonton, Alberta 11 June 1992**

Notes

1 Adapted from Ecclesiastes 3:1–8 King James Version.

2 For more information on this school, visit The Shingwauk Project website. Retrieved 25 September 2008 from: http://www.shingwauk.auc.ca/welcome.html

3 The Nishnawbe Institute, formally called the Rochdale College Institute for Indian Studies, was founded by Wilfred Pelletier, Carol Nadjiwon, Jeannette Corbiere, Edna Manitowabi, and me in 1967. The Institute was the first Native-run post-secondary institution in Canada.

4 Thomas was a Cherokee anthropologist who was a major resource person and teacher for the Institute in delivering cross-cultural and Canadian Indian workshops. At the time, he was on the faculty of Wayne State University, Detroit, Michigan. See Pavlik, Steve (ed.) (1998). *A Good Cherokee, A Good Anthropologist: Papers in Honor of Robert K. Thomas*. Los Angeles, CA: University of Calfornia. See also many of Thomas' published papers and articles. Retrieved 25 September 2008 from: http://works.bepress.com/robert_thomas/

5 For a complete list and dates of all the residential schools run by the Anglican Church, please visit the Remembering the Children website. Retrieved 25 September 2008 from: http://www.rememberingthechildren.ca/history/school-list-acc.htm

6 See appendices 2 and 3.

7 This was the position of the Government of Canada as stated by Duncan Campbell Scott, deputy superintendent of the Department of Indian Affairs, 1913–1932. *See the transcript of the* Special Committee of the House of Commons, 30 March 1920. Library and Archives Canada, RG10, volume 6810, file 470-2-3, part 7. *See also:* Titley, E. Brian (1986). *A Narrow Vision: Duncan Campbell Scott and the Administration of Indian Affairs in Canada*. Vancouver, BC: University of British Columbia Press.

8 Many resist participating in this process for a variety of reasons ranging from personal pain to the conviction that society and its institutions of church and state continue to implement the goal of total assimilation through programs like self-government.

9 The Anglican Church implementation of the *Hendry Report*, formation of Project North, the support of Native opposition to the Trudeau *White Paper*, the first MacKenzie River pipeline proposal, the initial funding of the Indian Ecumenical Conference, the gradual placing of First Nations clergy in First Nations congregations to name a few of the many positive activities over the past 40 years. *See also*: MacDonald, David (2008). A Call to the Churches: "You shall be called repairer of the breach." In Marlene Brant Castellano, Linda Archibald, and Mike De Gagne (eds.), *From Truth to Reconciliation:*

Transforming the Legacy of Residential Schools. Ottawa, ON: Aboriginal Healing Foundation: 341–358.

[10] For a description of the Indian Ecumenical Conference, *see:* Treat, James (2003). *Around the Sacred Fire: Native Religious Activism in the Red Power Era.* New York, NY: Palgrave MacMillan; see also: http://www.centreindianscholars.com/history.htm

[11] Vancouver School of Theology now offers several courses by Dr. Martin Brokenleg on this subject.

[12] MacDonald, Mark (2006). *The Gospel Comes to North America.* Ministry Matters, Anglican Church of Canada online journal. Retrieved 26 September 2008 from: http://ministrymatters.ca/2006/fall/mm04.html

[13] Terrace Standard (2008). Budget Issue upsets Nisga'a. Quoting Kevin McKay, Chairman, Nisga'a Lisims Government, July 2, 2008, "'What the most frustrating thing for us is that we signed the treaty and so did Canada and there's the mandate in there to renegotiate the fiscal agreement and they are not doing it,' said McKay. 'It's as if they regard the treaty as something that was over when they signed it, but it's not.' 'When our negotiators sit across from their negotiators what they say to us is they don't have the mandate to sign a new [fiscal] agreement.' McKay said the Nisga'a leadership is perplexed by the federal stance because it holds up the Nisga'a treaty as an example of what modern day treaties can accomplish."

[14] Willard Martin sent this email on 18 August 2008.

[15] Between 1967 and 1971, the Nishnawbe Institute conducted seven cross-cultural workshops attended by clergy and a large number of civil servants. We found that we needed 10 days in order to cause significant change in attitudes. It is important to remember the impact of government bureaucracies on both the creation and implementation of government philosophy.

[16] Scott, Duncan Campbell (1920:54–55, 63), see note #6.

[17] Fixico, Donald Lee (2003). *The American Indian Mind in a Linear World: American Indian Studies and Traditional Knowledge.* New York, NY: Taylor & Francis Books, Inc.

[18] Battiste, Marie (ed.) (2000). *Reclaiming Indigenous Voice and Vision.* Vancouver, BC: University of British Columbia Press.

[19] As the former president of WWNI, I was part of the team negotiating a relationship with University of Northern British Columbia (UNBC). At one point, we suggested to the director of Graduate Studies that their future Ph.D. program might need to consider the possibility of an oral thesis rather than a written one. He was not enthusiastic. However, I understand that in the last few years, UNBC First Nations graduate students have begun to challenge the existing academic process as inappropriate for their way of thinking.

[20] For more information, see: http://www.nwcc.bc.ca/FredaDiesing/Index.cfm

[21] For more information, see: http://www.vst.edu/nativemin/nmc.php

[22] When one drove with Bob Thomas, stopping to park was an unusual event. With the exception of stopping to eat or gas up, he drove until we arrived at our destination, be it 10 or 3,000 miles.

[23] Royal Commission on Aboriginal Peoples (1996:5). *Report of the Royal Commission on Aboriginal Peoples, Volume 1: Looking Forward, Looking Back.* Ottawa, ON: Minister of Supply and Services Canada.

Inuit children who lived too far away and had to stay at school during the summer
Anglican Mission School
Aklavik, NWT, 1941
Photographer: M. Meilke
National Archives of Canada, PA-101771

[Reprinted from the Legacy of Hope Foundation's *Where Are the Children?* exhibit catalogue (2003)]

Drew Hayden Taylor is an award-winning playwright, author, columnist, filmmaker, and lecturer. Originally from Curve Lake First Nation (Ojibway) in central Ontario, he has spent the last two decades travelling the world spreading the gospel of First Nations literature. Drew writes about his travels from an Aboriginal perspective and manages to bridge the gap between cultures by tickling the funny bone.

During the last 25 years, Drew has done many things during his literary career, from performing stand-up comedy at the Kennedy Center in Washington D.C. to lecturing at the British Museum on the films of Sherman Alexie. Over the last two decades, he has written award-winning plays (resulting in 70-plus productions of his work), writes a column in five newspapers across the country, short stories, novels, and scripts for *The Beachcombers*, *StreetLegal*, *North of Sixty*, and currently, he is the head writer for the APTN comedy series *Mixed Blessings*. He has also worked on 17 documentaries exploring the First Nations experience; most notably, he wrote and directed *Redskins, Tricksters, and Puppy Stew!* a documentary on First Nations humour for the National Film Board of Canada. In addition, he is also former Artistic Director of Canada's premiere Native theatre company, Native Earth Performing Arts.

Drew was the artist/writer-in-residence at the University of Michigan (2006) and the University of Western Ontario (2007). He has written and edited over 20 fiction and non-fiction books, including recently published *The Night Wanderer: A Native Gothic Novel* and *Me Sexy*, a follow-up to his highly successful non-fiction book on First Nations humour, *Me Funny*.

CRY ME A RIVER, WHITE BOY

Aabwehyehnmigziwin is the Anishnawbe word for apology. That is what Prime Minister Stephen Harper delivered in the House of Commons on the eleventh of June 2008 to the Survivors of Canada's residential school system.[1] Quoting the immortal words of singer Brenda Lee, who put it so eloquently,

> I'm sorry, so sorry ...
> Please accept my apology ...
> You tell me mistakes
> Are part of being young
> But that don't right
> The wrong that's been done

Harper said, "We are Sorry." Sorry. Surprising words from a surprising source. Brenda had put it much more eloquently. But the First Nations people of Canada listened. There were thousands of Aboriginal people on the front lawn of the Parliament buildings, eager to hear this historic admission of responsibility. Televisions were set up in community centres, band offices, halls, and schools in Aboriginal communities all across the country. And then the people cried. They cried at the memory of what had been done, and what was being said. This event made a lot of people cry, and for many, it was a good cry—a cathartic one. Psychiatrists and Elders will tell you that.

Since the late 1800s, over 150,000 Aboriginal children were forcibly taken away from their families and shipped off to one of 130-plus schools scattered across seven provinces and two territories. There, they were robbed of their language, their beliefs, their self-respect, their culture, and, in some cases, their very existence in a vain attempt to make them more Canadian. The key phrase I kept hearing during the apology and in the opposition responses was the misguided belief that *in order to save the child, you must destroy the Indian.* How on earth did those two thoughts become entwined? Another fine example of an un-researched and unintelligent government policy like the Chinese head tax[2] or sending a small Inuit community five hundred kilometres further north in an

The official *Aabwehyehnmigziwin* was a long time in coming, and hopefully it will close the chapter on this unfortunate part of First Nations history so that an entirely new book can begin, hopefully, this time with Aboriginal people as co-authors.

attempt to establish Arctic sovereignty. The thought processes of many a politician can truly be baffling when it comes to people of another race.

The official *Aabwehyehnmigziwin* was a long time in coming, and hopefully it will close the chapter on this unfortunate part of First Nations history so that an entirely new book can begin, hopefully, this time with Aboriginal people as co-authors. All of the churches who ran residential schools—Roman Catholic, United, Anglican, and Presbyterian—have issued their own version of *aabwehyehnmigziwin* over the years. In 1998, the Liberals offered a kind of watered down, wimpy, anemic version. Essentially, it was something about having "profound regrets."[3] I have a lot of regrets too. Most people do. For instance, I have had sincere regrets about some of my past relationships, but that does not mean I apologize for them. Big difference.

Perhaps it is my working-class origins and artsy nature, but I do find it odd that it was the Conservative government who found the balls to issue the *aabwehyehnmigziwin*. It makes one wonder why the Conservative lawyers saw this as possible when ten years earlier, an army of government lawyers under the Liberals likely advised against it. You would think the residential school system would be something the Conservatives would admire. On the surface, it fits into their political and economic agenda. The government promised, in a number of treaties, to educate the youth from over 600 reserves across the world's second biggest country. They managed to download the cost of educating these youth by transferring it to the four main religious groups and their churches. Sounds like a sound economic decision, does it not?

In 2005, the Liberal government was all set to adopt the Kelowna Accord and address many of the serious issues plaguing First Nations communities. Then prime minister Paul Martin had long been concerned with Aboriginal issues. Yet no apology. Fast forward to 2006 when the Conservatives took power and offered Canada a new way of doing business, which basically involved shelving the Kelowna Accord and hiring Tom Flanagan, author of the controversial book *First Nations? Second Thoughts*, as a top Conservative advisor. Things did not look good for First Nations communities in this new century. Then came Harper's 180-degree turn. One could almost hear the snow falling in hell. Perhaps the official bean counters had taken into account the fact that an official apology would be in their best interest, as it would shift responsibility to the Aboriginal communities. The government could then wash a lot of it off their hands.

How could the federal government know the whole issue of accountability for residential schools would later be classified as—and I love this term frequently used to describe screwed up governmental policies—a boondoggle? It has literally come back to bite them in their fish-belly white asses. On average, over 1.9 billion dollars[4] has already been paid out to many of the approximately 80,000 Survivors of Manifest Destiny High. That is a hell of an expensive education. And the price tag is still rising. Canadian taxpayers will be buying bandages for the physical and psychological wounds their ancestors inflicted for generations.[5]

It had been obvious for a long time that apologizing was not high on the Liberals to-do list. Pierre Trudeau did not want to bother with an *aabwehyehnmigziwin*. I think he felt it would just open the floodgates to more apologies that would quickly become unfortunate road bumps on the highway of proud Canadian history. I think he would have been right. Jean Chretien did not believe current social beliefs should be applied to past issues, yet it was Brian Mulroney's Conservatives who issued an apology to Japanese Canadians for the country's misdoings during World War II.[6] And now, Harper is regretting the Aboriginal people's historical treatment. Who would have thunk it? In all fairness, it should be mentioned that it was the Conservatives that gave Aboriginal people the right to vote in 1960. Way to go Progressive Conservatives! … a phrase I thought I would never say. Though many would argue old-school Conservatives are substantially different from the New World Conservatives. Personally, I think Diefenbaker could whip Harper's ass. Still, Harper is the current boss and I guess that is why the Ojibways call him the *Kichi Toodooshaabowimiijim*, which translates to "the Big Cheese" or, perhaps even more literally, to "Much Sour Milk."

Of course, there is always one spoilsport at every party, a pisser in the pool, known as the Conservative *brain trust* a.k.a. Pierre Poilievre and his amazingly insensitive comments about Survivors just needing a stronger work ethic and his opinion that giving these people reparation money was a waste of time. Otherwise, things might have been just fine and dandy. Evidently, Harper took the boy out to the proverbial woodshed, and a new and different apology by a contrite Poilievre soon followed. It should have been expected, just like there is one drunk at every party, one ex-girlfriend at every powwow, and one veggie burger at every barbecue. It was bound to happen in the volatile world of Canadian politics, somebody was going to pee in the pool. Conservative politicians are seldom known for their subtlety.

Was the *aabwehyehnmigziwin* sincere and do I buy it? Yes, I suppose it was sincere enough for me to buy it, however naïve that may sound. I suppose something is better then nothing. I also know that, by very definition, politicians should not be trusted nor believed any more than a Jerry Springer guest, especially when it comes to commitments to Aboriginal people. But Harper looked sincere, as did Dion, Duceppe, and Layton—all privileged white men apologizing for the actions of other privileged white men and also eager to curry First Nation favour. It is amazing how good education can make you the empathetic leader of a federal party and a bad education can get you an *aabwehyehnmigziwin*. They probably listened to Brenda Lee and her apologetic song. They are of that generation. Brenda probably knew little or nothing about Canadian politics or Aboriginal issues, though nobody could apologize like her.

I know a lot of people who were a little cynical about the sincerity of the apology. That is their right. If an abusive husband apologizes to his abused wife and kids, however sincere it might sound, some may doubt the authenticity of that apology. Same as in this situation, an admission of responsibility is as good a place as any to start. Ask any lawyer. But the healing must start somewhere.

I am very fortunate. Neither I nor any of my immediate relatives attended a residential school. Instead, we were schooled at the Mud Lake Indian Day School located directly on the Curve Lake Reserve in eastern Ontario. Still, many of the residential school policies extended to the communities. My mother tells of not being allowed to speak Anishnawbe on school grounds, which were located just a few hundred metres from where she lived. Just the other night, I heard her reminiscing with one of her sisters about how they made sure they never played under the windows of the school so the teacher would not hear them speaking in Anishnawbe. One usually does not think of one's seventy-seven-year old shy mother as a rebel. Maybe that is why Anishnawbe is still her first language and English a distant second.

There is a lot of collateral damage from that era as well. Hot on the heels of residential school Survivors are those who went through the Sixties Scoop, where Aboriginal kids were taken away by various social services and farmed out for adoption, usually to white families, sometimes to Europe and to the United States. They were part of the same larger, overall policy of eliminating Aboriginal culture by wiping away the memories and heritage of Aboriginal children and Canadianizing them. If you cannot get them through the front door, try the back, or even the window.

Interestingly, many Aboriginal people watching the historic *aabwehyehnmigziwin* were not actual students of residential schools. But I think it is safe to say that they were all affected by the practice in some way. Most Aboriginal people who watched knew somebody or several somebodies who attended residential school or were descended from, or a relative of, a Survivor. As a result, they were forced to deal with the repercussions of that experience. It now permeates our culture. Harper and Canada's apology was for all of us—those who attended the schools and those who are living with the fallout. Just as all Jewish people were affected by the Holocaust in some way (if I may be allowed to say this), all Aboriginal people were victims of what happened in those institutions. It is collateral damage in sort of an intergenerational way.

What happens now? I do not know. Maybe Phil Fontaine and the gang should contact Maher Arar. He might have some suggestions. If memory serves me correctly, Mr. Arar was kidnapped suddenly for no logical reason, taken far away from his family for a long period of time, beaten, starved, and terrified for the greater good. He finally returned to his family a changed man and is now seeking justice. Geez, you would think he was an Aboriginal kid or something.

As the similarly sympathetic Connie Francis who, like Brenda Lee, was neither Aboriginal nor a residential school Survivor, also sang many years ago, "I'm sorry I made you cry." Did Harper get his words right (that were chosen for him by lawyers)? Harper had said, "We are sorry … We apologize for having done this." He must not forget that there is

Our first thoughts today are for our elders. Many of them have suffered lifelong physical and emotional pain because of their residential school experiences. We are so proud that many Anishinabek lived long enough to hear Canada's apology to them. But the true test of Mr. Harper's words will be his government's actions to help our children have a better future than their parents and grandparents.

John Beaucage
Grand Council Chief
Anishinabek Nation
of Ontario
In response to Stephen
Harper's apology
11 June 2008

still a Canadian issue here that all Canadians need to address as part of an ongoing relationship. Closing the book on residential schools does not mean that the "Aboriginal problem" has been solved—at least not in the eyes of the government. Thus, I will let Connie Francis finish with her poignant lyrics:

I'm sorry I made you cry
Won't you forget, won't you forgive
Don't let us say goodbye

I'm just glad Harper did not try to sing the *aabwehyehnmigziwin*.

NOTES

[1] *See* Appendix 2.

[2] For a brief review on the history of the Chinese head tax, please see pages 238–239 of Bradford W. Morse's article "Reconciliation Possible? Reparations Essential" in Castellano, Marlene Brant, Linda Archibald, and Mike DeGagné (2008). *From Truth to Reconciliation: Transforming the Legacy of Residential Schools*. Ottawa, ON: Aboriginal Healing Foundation: 233–256.

[3] Government of Canada (1998). *Statement of Reconciliation*. Ottawa, ON: Indian and Northern Affairs Canada. Presented on 7 January 1998 by The Honourable Jane Stewart, Minister of Indian and Northern Affairs Canada. Retrieved 15 September 2008 from: http://www.ainc-inac.gc.ca/gs/rec_e.html

[4] Indian and Northern Affairs Canada (no date). Indian Residential Schools Resolution Canada 2007-2008 Departmental Performance Report. Retrieved 31 March 2009 from: http://www.tbs-sct.gc.ca/dpr-rmr/2007-2008/inst/ira/ira-eng.pdf

[5] *See*: Bowlus, Audra, Katherine McKenna, Tanis Day and David Wright (2003). *The Economic Costs and Consequences of Child Abuse in Canada*. Ottawa, ON: The Law Commission of Canada; *and* Native Counselling Services of Alberta (2001). *A Cost-Benefit Analysis of Hollow Water's Community Holistic Circle Healing Process*. Ottawa, ON: Solicitor General Canada and Aboriginal Healing Foundation.

[6] For a brief review on the apology and redress to Japanese Canadians, please see pages 237–238 of Bradford W. Morse's article "Reconciliation Possible? Reparations Essential" in Castellano, Marlene Brant, Linda Archibald, and Mike DeGagné (2008). *From Truth to Reconciliation: Transforming the Legacy of Residential Schools*. Ottawa, ON: Aboriginal Healing Foundation: 233–256.

Boys from the Spanish Indian Residential School

Courtesy of Father William Maurice, S.J. Collection – The Shingwauk Project

MICK DODSON

Mick Dodson, born in Katherine, Northern Territory, is a member of the Yawuru peoples, the traditional Aboriginal owners of land and waters in the Broome area of the southern Kimberley region of Western Australia. Mick completed a Bachelor of Jurisprudence and a Bachelor of Laws at Monash University in Victoria. He was awarded an honorary Doctor of Letters from the University of Technology in Sydney and an honorary Doctor of Laws from the University of New South Wales, also in Sydney.

Mick has been a prominent advocate on land rights and other issues affecting Aboriginal and Torres Strait Islander peoples, including Indigenous peoples around the world. He was Australia's first Aboriginal and Torres Strait Islander Social Justice Commissioner with the Human Rights and Equal Opportunity Commission, serving from 1993 to 1998. Previously, he has worked extensively on matters mostly relating to Aboriginal legal issues, notably as counsel assisting the Royal Commission into Aboriginal Deaths in Custody. Mick has sat on many boards, commissions, and advisory panels on Indigenous matters; of note, he is a board member and co-chair of Reconciliation Australia, and he was a founding member and chairman of the Australian Indigenous Leadership Centre. He is now the current director for the National Centre for Indigenous Studies and a professor of law, both at the Australian National University. He also has his own legal and anthropological consulting firm. In 2005, Mick accepted a three-year appointment as a member of the United Nations Permanent Forum on Indigenous Issues. He was recently reappointed for a further three years. Mick had participated in the crafting of the text of the *Declaration on the Rights of Indigenous Peoples*, which was adopted overwhelmingly in 2007 by the United Nations General Assembly.

WHEN THE PRIME MINISTER SAID SORRY

It's strange isn't it? We apologize for taking away the children of the Stolen Generations but we didn't apologise for anything else ... And it made us feel good. You know, we had finally acknowledged we were at fault. We are only on the edge of what we have done to these people. We have ripped away everything, language, culture, land, self-esteem, you name any of the things that make you a human being and they have all been stripped away from Aboriginal people. It's not that they're powerless to overcome that, it's just that it's unhuman of us to expect them to do it without assistance.[1]

Official apologies are very important. They are about the need for Indigenous peoples as nation-states to be allowed to have their stories told and let their history be known. Official apologies can change the terms and meaning of the membership of a political community in which they are given. Apologies no doubt help bring history into the conversation, but they also bring other topics into that conversation like racism and bigotry. Any casual glance at a newspaper or televised talk-back show during the lead up to the apology in the Australian Parliament clearly demonstrates this. Apologies can serve to justify political and policy changes and reforms, and this seems to have been the impetus here in Australia, although we must be vigilant in ensuring that those changes and reforms are positive and do not slip back into old bad practices.

The apology here in Australia will accomplish nothing if all it is about is the validation of the experience of the Stolen Generations. For example, where do those Indigenous Australians not part of the Stolen Generations and, therefore, not a subject of the apology now stand? What of their dispossession, marginalization, and exclusion? Can the apology advance societal reconciliation and strengthen democratic consolidation for Australia? There are many bridges to cross to get there, although signs are encouraging. Talk of constitutional recognition of Indigenous Australians is certainly about fundamental reform, although we need to be clear about what this means and particularly what Indigenous Australians think it means.

Rights and self-determination were not at the heart of the Australian apology. If the current Australian government is to achieve its stated ambition of "closing the gaps," rights and particularly the right to self-determination for Indigenous Australians must be up front and centre.

Apologies may focus our attention on the past but have implications for the future. We have to be focused on the future post-apology and escape from apology politics to accomplish anything. To get to that point, we must deal with the past here in Australia, and the past is not just about the Stolen Generations. We have to deal with the trans-generational effects as well as with all the other horrible things done to Indigenous Australians for over two centuries; otherwise, the memory and resentment will stay alive for centuries. Dealing with this other stuff was not a feature of the Australian apology, because it was confined to the Stolen Generations and their experiences. Rights and self-determination were not at the heart of the Australian apology. If the current Australian government is to achieve its stated ambition of "closing the gaps," rights and particularly the right to self-determination for Indigenous Australians must be up front and centre. With the apology there is now a platform for new, just, and fair arrangements that can be established to "make peace with the Aborigines to get the place right."[2]

The apology can also be a source of pride for the nation giving it, and I believe that for many Australians this is the case. Feeling pride about what has been done is important in order for us to move forward. Pride is another foundation to help our nation attempt to repair the past. What Australia now needs to decide is whether we intend to continue to have successive generations of Australians, black and white, negotiate the terms of association. Or, do we want to point to the apology and say here is the opportunity where we can now put our relationship on a proper philosophical footing that understands and underpins respect for Aboriginal difference and our status as Original Peoples?

An apology in itself will not deliver appropriate public policy frameworks that will result in self-determination and, in turn, deliver self-government for Indigenous Australians. The point is that the apology ought to allow the government to use it as a platform for the achievement of Indigenous aspirations in this regard and to use this goodwill to generate the policy framework that will allow it to happen. The public must be taken on this policy path.

The apology does make a start in overcoming the public's general lack of knowledge of Indigenous peoples and its alarming ignorance of national history and the history of the laws and policies that have shaped the landscape that is now present-day Indigenous Australia. This historical experience grounds the grievances and demands for actions, like an apology, in the first place. The problem with trying to manipulate history with so-called "wars"[3] is that, in such circumstances, your historical policy base is going to be false. False historical assumptions do not make for good policy.

History is important because the need for apologies arises from history. If you can manipulate history then you can wash out the need for an apology, as Australia's former prime minister, John Howard, attempted to do with his utterances and encouragement of the so-called history wars.

The Australian government has linked the apology to closing the gaps while dismissing the call to compensate the members of the Stolen Generations. The desire of government and just about every other Australian, including Indigenous Australians, to close the gaps is a given, but the grievance for compensation will not go away. The government needs to have an understanding of the trans-generational carriage of grievances and the fact that they do not just go away if ignored by those most able to accommodate them. In fact, in Australia, we cannot expect to fully close the gaps unless all the gaps are included in the policy and the practical push, which means the unfinished business, like compensation, must be in the mix. What the Rudd government is now doing is using the apology as a justification for its policy approach to Indigenous affairs.

Prime Minister Rudd's apology will allow us to validly reinterpret our history into what is now Australia's "new public," one that is more accepting of including Aboriginal history. The trick is to now make Aboriginal history in this country more accessible to a wider public Australia. The apology goes part of the way in correcting the historical record, as you cannot expect to deal with the present disadvantage of closing the gaps if you try to disconnect it from the historical record. The apology does not change the legal status of Aboriginal and Torres Strait Islander peoples, but it does serve to emphasize "the moral burden of Aboriginal mistreatment"[4] as something we now have to deal with as a nation. The apology does not alter the terms of national membership, but it does provide the emotional dimensions to that membership. What the apology has done is provide a cathartic and positive psychological

Reconciliatory justice requires an ongoing commitment to future peace-building, sustained in deeds and not just words.

Robert Andrew Joseph
Māori
Excerpt from the first volume, From Truth to Reconciliation: Transforming the Legacy of Residential Schools

effect for the peoples who are the subject of the apology and, indeed, for the nation as a whole.

Whatever happens now in Australia, there is one thing we cannot say, and that is: Now that the nation has apologized, the mistakes of the past do not matter. They matter even more now, and, as a nation, we have an obligation to address and to correct those mistakes. The national apology has been a key piece in the jigsaw puzzle that is reconciliation in Australia. It is like the corner piece of the puzzle, the piece that is essential if we wish to complete the picture. I think the apology has been seen as a major change in the reconciliation environment in our country. The change of government at the national level has offered a new sense of possibility. We now believe we can do things differently. We have surmounted a central object blocking the road to reconciliation.

In his speech to Parliament on 13 February 2008, the Prime Minister said, "The mood of the nation is for reconciliation now." He said the nation was calling on politicians "to move beyond our infantile bickering, our point-scoring and our mindlessly partisan politics and elevate at least this one core area of national responsibility to a rare position beyond the partisan divide ... Surely, at least from this day forward, we should give it a go."[5]

The apology was a marginally transformative experience for Australia and a fundamental step in building a respectful relationship between Indigenous and non-Indigenous citizens. It is now fair to say that the majority of Australians feel better knowing that the apology has been made and that they are keen to build on this corner piece of the reconciliation puzzle. They are open to doing things differently to get the results we all want. While the rhetoric around Indigenous affairs has changed for the better, it is not yet clear if this will translate into sound policy, bipartisanship, and cross-jurisdictional cooperation. No single government can carry the task on its own. True bipartisanship would allow us to learn from past mistakes, use the evidence at hand, and make success in Indigenous affairs policy a determined national priority. This is the formula needed for success, and success is the key to securing Australians' support and engagement.

Today, Australia changes its position. We do this in the spirit of rethinking the relationship between indigenous and non-indigenous Australians.

Jenny Macklin
Indigenous Affairs Minister
Parliament House
Canberra, Australia
3 April 2009

I think that the parliamentary apology made to members of the Stolen Generations will forever change the relationship between Aboriginal and Torres Strait Islanders and the rest of the population of Australia. The apology has the potential to transform Australia and, once and for all, to put black and white relationships in this country on a proper footing. As stated by Reconciliation Australia in its submission to the Inquiry into the Stolen Generations Compensation Bill:

> It was a fundamental step in building a respectful relationship between Indigenous and non-Indigenous citizens and has generated widespread support for doing things differently - to ensure our actions are the right ones to deliver meaningful, measurable results.[6]

The apology was about dealing with one aspect of unfinished business in our country: the Stolen Generations. We have now accepted this as a historical truth at the highest political level. It is only us, as Australians, who can heal the wounds of the past, and the first step is to recognize and acknowledge the truths of the past. The apology validates the life experience of those who were taken away; it is their vindication.

While the apology is hugely symbolic for our country, it does and should not end there; we still have to tackle all the unfinished business if we are to obtain a true and lasting reconciliation. We have to deal with the health, housing, education, and life expectancy gaps and a host of other problems of disadvantage, exclusion, and racism if we want lasting reconciliation. But this apology is the start. What is real and important to Aboriginal people is how we feel about ourselves. It is immensely important to us that we can feel that our history and our culture are respected by the rest of the country. This is central in our capacity to face our problems and those that are shared with the rest of the nation. It is also about who we are and where we stand in this country and about our culture, our land, our heritage, and all our peoples. Our spiritual and psychological health is just as important as our physical health.

What is reconciliation? Reconciliation means two groups settling their differences and coming to terms with the past so that they can move forward into the future together. Reconciliation is about Indigenous and non-Indigenous Australians learning from each other and dealing with some of the hurt endured by Indigenous peoples in the colonization process. When Europeans came to our country they did not respect our land rights. We were dispossessed of our lands without treaty or agreement. Many of our people were killed, others were treated very harshly, and our kids were taken away. Reconciliation is important because, as Australians, we all now share this history and this land. Reconciliation is not about guilt or blame, it is about learning, understanding, and working together. We have yet to come to terms with how we are to share this land in a just and fair way that acknowledges the past and seeks to repair the damage of that past. This is the heart of reconciliation, and it can come closer to being achieved on the back of the apology.

For too long some Australians have denied the past as having an impact on the present. This is a denial of what makes this country what it is. Governments inherit from previous governments, sins and all. The laws and practices of the past get handed on to the next generations, so too does the responsibility for past actions. The pain and hurt endured by Indigenous peoples are also part of that history and what has been inherited. The apology demonstrates our preparedness to face up to and accept the mistakes of the past. This is about healing and reconciliation for the benefit of all. We have to look at the past. You do not have to be Sigmund Freud to know that past experiences shape the present life of an individual person. The same principle can be applied to the collective experience of a people. You cannot even begin to understand, let alone address or change the present, and address the future unless you understand the past.

We Aboriginal peoples want honest recognition of the truths about Australia's past, because the scars from the past are inscribed in the lives of the present. Prime Minister Rudd has embraced that honesty by getting Parliament to apologize to the Stolen Generations. At least we now have acceptance at the highest official level that it happened, even though there are some in Australian society who are still denying that it did. It is the history of the Stolen Generations that bears directly on the lives of Indigenous children and families today. These are the policies and practices of assimilation and, in particular, of the separation of Aboriginal and Torres Strait Islander children from their families.

I spent two years of my life as a commissioner sitting at hearings of the National Inquiry into the Separation of Aboriginal and Torres Strait Islander Children from Their Families.[7] I spent hundreds of hours pouring over reams of files that documented in clinical detail the lives of children transported from one abusive institution to the next. I have read official documents outlining the repugnant scientific motivations and justifications for removal. I have sat with Indigenous women and men as they have spoken about their lives, about being taken away from their own families, or about having their own children or relatives removed. I cannot begin to describe the inhuman treatment that was inflicted on thousands of Indigenous families.

These children were denied the right to grow up knowing and being cared for by their mothers, fathers, brothers, sisters, aunties, uncles, and grandparents. Those families were, in turn, denied the right to grow up and experience the joy of their own children. Children who were removed were denied the right to learn about their culture or to learn and speak their own language. They were denied the right to live in and be a part of their indigenous environment—their lands, their totems, their inherited memories, and their communities. They were denied the most basic right of a child: to grow up and to belong to a loving environment. The repercussions are immeasurable. The taking of Aboriginal children, to this day, has produced the background for many years of horrific memories, distress, and mental health problems.

The devastating experiences of Aboriginal parents and their families brought on by the removal of their children—the loss of control of their lives, powerlessness, prejudice, and hopelessness—have left many problems for us to deal with today. These problems are not limited to the people who were themselves removed. There are trans-generational effects of removal. This means that separation not only affects the many adults and their families and communities who experienced separation themselves, but also affects the children of those who were separated. This, in turn, affects the children of the children, which result in a continuous cycle of effects.

The evidence presented during the inquiry was not just the narrative of individual abuse, it was the story of the endeavour to destroy a people. The result was not simply thousands of fractured lives, but of sustained

> The devastating experiences of Aboriginal parents and their families brought on by the removal of their children—the loss of control of their lives, powerlessness, prejudice, and hopelessness—have left many problems for us to deal with today. These problems are not limited to the people who were themselves removed. There are transgenerational effects of removal.

policies of removal that have fractured the skeleton of Indigenous families and people. It is into this type of fractured family and cultural system that the Aboriginal children of today are born. It is dangerous to speak about Aboriginal families or cultures as dysfunctional, but the fact cannot be denied that many of yesterday's damaged children do not have the resources today to provide their own children with a healthy or nurturing family environment. Much of the instability of Indigenous families today can be directly attributed to the past practices of separating Indigenous children from their families. The official apology will begin the process of healing these people.

Given this history, it is hardly surprising that Indigenous families are loathe to trust any person identified as part of the welfare system or, sadly, for that matter, any person who wishes to help. When you begin to think about advocating for Aboriginal children you must understand that your intentions and attempts will automatically provoke suspicion and fear, unless you make it very clear that your interventions will empower Indigenous people and not take over for them, which is what Indigenous Australians know and experienced in the past. You will only make the problem worse if this past is the starting point for learning about the problems faced by our children.

In 2007, the United Nations General Assembly overwhelmingly adopted the *Declaration on the Rights of Indigenous Peoples*, which recognizes that Indigenous families and their communities retain the right to the upbringing, training, education, and well-being of their children consistent with the rights of the child. The past Howard government had, at that time, voted against the resolution to endorse the *Declaration*. The present Rudd government promised to reverse this position and endorse the resolution supporting it, which they did on 3 April 2009.[8] We now look forward to the implementation of a plan, developed in conjunction with Aboriginal and Torres Strait Islander Australians, within the context of the provisions of the *Declaration* at a domestic level.

NOTES

[1] Australian Broadcasting Corporation (2008). Transcript of "Germaine Greer joins Lateline." Broadcast: 13/08/2008. Reporter: Leigh Sales. Retrieved 2 October 2008 from: http://www.abc.net.au/lateline/content/2008/s2334393.htm

[2] *Cited in* Independent Monthly (1993:14). Tales of the True Believers: Exclusive Authentic Keating. Transcript of address to staff by the Prime Minister, The Hon. P.J. Keating MP. Imperial Peking Restaurant, Sydney, March 12, 1993.

[3] This is a reference to the so-called "culture wars" in Australia encouraged by the previous conservative prime minister and largely conducted publically by non-Aboriginal historians. The "war" is of competing narratives; on the one hand, there are those who say Australia was peacefully settled and, on the other hand, there are those who say it was invaded and Aboriginal resistance brutally put down. The war is pretty much over now and it is impossible to declare a winner.

[4] Nobles, Melissa (2008:146). *The Politics of Official Apologies*. New York, NY: Cambridge University Press.

[5] Rudd, The Honourable Kevin (2008). *Prime Minister of Australia Speech - Apology to Australia's Indigenous Peoples*. House of Representatives, Parliament House, 13 February 2008. Canberra, AU: Prime Minister of Australia (*see* Appendix 6). Retrieved 2 October 2008 from: http://www.pm.gov.au/media/Speech/2008/speech_0073.cfm

[6] Reconciliation Australia (2008). Submission to the Inquiry into the Stolen Generations Compensation Bill, 11 April 2008. Retrieved 1 October 2008 from: http://www.aph.gov.au/Senate/committee/legcon_ctte/stolen_generation_compenation/submissions/sub76.pdf

[7] Human Rights and Equal Opportunity Commission (1997). *Bringing Them Home: National Inquiry into the Separation of Aboriginal and Torres Strait Islander Children from Their Families*. Sydney, AU: Commonwealth of Australia.

[8] *See* United Nations (2008). *United Nations Declaration on the Rights of Indigenous Peoples* (retrieved 2 March 2009 from: http://www.un.org/esa/socdev/unpfii/documents/DRIPS_en.pdf); *and* Macklin, Jenny (2009). *Statement on the United Nations Declaration on the Rights of Indigenous Peoples*. Statement made by the Minister for Families, Housing, Community Services and Indgenous Affairs to Parliament House Canberra, 3 April 2009 (retrieved 16 April 2009 from: http://www.fahcsia.gov.au/internet/jennymacklin.nsf/content/un_declaration_03apr09.htm

RECONCILIATION, RESTITUTION, RHETORIC

Aboriginal children in class at the
Roman Catholic-run Fort George Catholic Indian Residential School
Fort George, Quebec, 1939
Archives Deschâtelets

[Reprinted from the Legacy of Hope Foundation's *Where Are the Children?* exhibit catalogue (2003)]

Heather Igloliorte is an Inuk artist, writer, and curator from Labrador. After graduating from the Nova Scotia College of Art and Design University with a Bachelor of Fine Arts in painting and a minor in art history, she moved to Ottawa to pursue her Master's in Canadian Art History, specializing in Inuit art. While in the master's program, Heather completed a year-long internship as a curatorial assistant at the Canadian Museum of Civilization, became involved with the Aboriginal Curatorial Collective (ACC), and was hired by the Carleton University Art Gallery to be the Curator of Inuit Art for the 2005–2006 academic year. Her artwork has been shown and sold all over the east coast and can be found in several public and private collections.

Heather is now pursuing a doctorate in Inuit and other global Indigenous art histories at Carleton University with the Institute for Comparative Studies in Language, Arts, and Culture. Her dissertation research centres on the historic and contemporary visual arts of the Labradorimiut.

She is also currently working on several upcoming exhibitions, including the nationally touring exhibit *We Were So Far Away - The Inuit Experience of Residential Schools*, which features the stories of eight Inuit former students of residential schools.

INUIT ARTISTIC EXPRESSION
AS CULTURAL RESILIENCE

Inuit artists have maintained cultural resilience through their artwork since the beginning of the contemporary Inuit art period, despite the many changes that threatened Inuit knowledge, languages, and lifeways. I have discovered that despite the small number of artworks that specifically address the Inuit residential school experience, there is a sizeable and growing body of Inuit art that deals with and critiques the entangled impacts of nearly a century of colonialism and Christianity in the Arctic, which includes residential schools. This flourishing sub-genre of contemporary Inuit art can provide us with valuable insights concerning the impact of the onslaught of European culture in the Arctic during the mid-twentieth century. These works also show us how Inuit artists have challenged that colonial legacy with tremendous grace, humour, and resilience.

Inuit have overcome many obstacles on the path to healing and reconciliation, and some examples will show how Inuit have utilized the visual arts to resist the forces of the European colonial legacy. Despite the numerous affronts deployed to protect Inuit society from the early to mid-twentieth century to the present, artmaking, as a consistent and positive presence in many Arctic Inuit communities over the past sixty years, has been an important factor in supporting Inuit cultural resilience.[1]

PROCESSES OF COLONIZATION
AND CHRISTIANITY IN THE NORTH

While Western discourse often separates, classifies, or compartmentalizes its objects of study, it would be imprudent to engage in a discussion of the impact of residential schooling on Inuit culture in isolation from the other nearly simultaneous and traumatic events experienced by Inuit communities during the mid-twentieth century. Following centuries of a relatively uninterrupted and fundamentally semi-nomadic lifestyle, even the prolonged contact with European whalers and explorers throughout the nineteenth century could not have prepared the Inuit for the rapid onslaught of European colonization in the Arctic over the span of the first half of the twentieth century. Residential schooling was only one facet of the numerous threats to Inuit sovereignty from the hegemonic colonial society that imposed a multitude of changes in the North. In many ways, Inuit culture is still reeling from the combined impacts of a number of detrimental changes. As such, it is not surprising that many Inuit artists have not often dealt directly or solely with residential schooling as artistic subject matter, but instead addressed the issues and impacts that have emerged from the elaborate convolution of these outside forces. For example, intergenerational trauma is one of the legacies of residential schools. Its effects occur when victims of trauma develop unhealthy ways of coping, such as self-medicating with drugs or alcohol and then unwittingly pass these dysfunctional behaviours on to their children.

Alcoholism is one impact that arose out of residential schools and is represented through Inuit art. More famous for his drawings of birds and Arctic animals, Kananginak Pootoogook has created a significant

This is the beginning of Alcoholism
1996, Kananginak Pootoogook, Cape Dorset
Pencil crayon and ink on paper
Collection of Edward J. Guarino, New York

series of narrative drawings that provide cogent examples of the ills of alcoholism in his community, despite only hinting at the origin of the problem. One of these drawings, which appeared in the Spring 2007 edition of *Inuit Art Quarterly*, is captioned by the artist: "*This is the Inuk man's first drink ever. Even though it's only wine he is very intoxicated. This is the beginning of Alcoholism.*"[2] In the image, a white man attired like a trapper looks on with detached amusement while a clearly intoxicated Inuk sloshes a glass of red wine around.

Sculptor Ovilu Tunnillie and graphic artist Annie Pootoogook, two women artists of the Inuit avant-garde, have also provided variations on the theme of impacts of alcohol. They too intertwine a variety of complex issues in their art by examining the relationship of alcohol with spousal abuse, negative self-image, and community impacts—all legacies of the colonial incursion in the North and, in some circumstances, the direct result of residential schools.

DRAMATIC CHANGES TO INUIT LIFESTYLE

In the few short decades preceding the introduction of the residential school system to the North, the traditional way of life in the Arctic was already under threat of erosion due to the impact of Euro-Canadian culture throughout the North. Unlike the South, where the changes to Aboriginal communities were spread out over a century of increased Western European colonization and evangelization, Inuit culture had remained relatively intact and unscathed until the 1950s, largely because the Inuit had been ignored by the Canadian government and was isolated from prolonged contact with southerners. Beginning in the late nineteenth century (and much earlier in Labrador), Christian missionaries were dispatched to the Arctic and Subarctic, but it was not until the 1910s and 1920s that massive numbers of Inuit were rapidly and almost wholly converted primarily to the Catholic and Anglican faiths. The churches banned the Inuit converts from practicing numerous spiritual customs and cultural traditions, believing that the Inuit way of life to be fundamentally heathen and savage. At the same time, Hudson's Bay Company trading posts had been established throughout the North, encouraging Inuit to abandon their semi-nomadic lifestyle and to settle in the communities established around the posts.[3] This often led to the over-hunting of wildlife in the areas of settlement and further dependency on canned goods and packaged foods from the South. Diseases such as smallpox and tuberculosis spread quickly throughout these new settlements as well.[4]

Seemingly overnight, Inuit populations had been converted to Christianity, were concentrated in settlements and threatened by disease, and had become dependant on trade goods. Sled dogs are alleged to have been slaughtered by RCMP officers throughout the eastern Arctic and elsewhere, further grounding the already partially immobilized Inuit.[5] In northern Quebec and Labrador, Inuit communities were wholly relocated under the pretence of benefiting the community, but in reality serving government interests only.[6] This had devastating consequences on the relocatees as well as on the settlements they overcrowded. Amidst this cultural turmoil, residential schools were introduced across the North under the pretext that the residential school system would be "the most effective way of giving children from primitive environments, experience in education along the lines of civilization leading to vocational training to fit them for occupations in the white man's economy."[7] Inuit children were taken from their homes in large numbers and forced to learn the *Qallunaat* (Inuktitut for Europeans and Euro-Canadians) way of life at the expense of their own. Prior to 1955, less than 15 per cent of school-aged Inuit children were enrolled in residential schools; within a decade, this number would climb to over 75 per cent.[8]

The Survivors, while grateful for the education they received, had suffered greatly as children, and many grew up to be traumatized adults. Inuit children were forbidden to speak their own language or practice any aspect of their culture in the schools, dormitories, hostels, and other residences. The crux of assimilation lies in the adoption of the English language, so the prohibition on traditional languages was often strictly enforced with harsh punishments. Many students were physically, mentally, and sexually abused by those responsible for their care. Furthermore, Inuit children were made to feel ashamed of their traditional way of life, and many had developed disdain toward their parents, their culture, their centuries-old practices and beliefs, and even for the country foods their parents provided. The deleterious effects that the residential school system had on the health and well-being of these Survivors and their families were evident everywhere in their communities and were compounded by the other converging impacts of colonialism and evangelization.

THE CONTEMPORARY INUIT ARTS INDUSTRY IN THE ARCTIC

The aforementioned changes ushered in a new era of impoverishment to Inuit culture that took hold in the span of mere decades, and this had continued unabated throughout the 1950s and on into the next four decades. In the beginning of this era, the newly settled Inuit were presented with few opportunities for wage employment, and the fur trade was in sharp decline. Following the conclusion of World War II and the beginning of the Cold War, Inuit were becoming increasingly dependent on the support of the federal government, and the federal government was becoming increasingly concerned with maintaining

Arctic sovereignty, which dealt with it by way of taking responsibility for its Arctic citizens.[9] During this period of increased and reluctant paternalism, the arts industry was one of the first experimental developments introduced to replace the fur trade. As an industry that required little machinery or overhead, it seemed to be work well-suited to remote northern areas, and the government sentiment seemed to be that the development of Inuit handicrafts was an avenue "for which nature has fitted them."[10] Most significantly, it was also one of the first opportunities for subjugated Inuit to regain a necessary measure of self-reliance.

Instrumental in the success of this fledgling venture was teacher and artist James Houston, who travelled throughout the North during the 1950s and 1960s instructing Inuit on what things would sell in the South and liaised with the Hudson's Bay Company, the Canadian Handicrafts Guild, and the federal government to purchase works, hold exhibitions, and market Inuit art to southerners. Under Houston's guidance, the industry quickly grew into a viable economic substitute for the rapidly declining fur trade.

Because Inuit had always carved and produced beautiful handmade clothing and personal adornments, they were already skilled for this arts industry. Furthermore, Inuit were quite accustomed to the process of manufacturing carvings for trade and sale; there are reports from as early as 1821 of Inuit bartering ivory figurines and models with seamen from whalers and other ships that visited Arctic waters.[11] Moreover, there were many positive effects from the early carvings and handicrafts trade. Welfare administrator and teacher Margery Hinds reported on the improvement in morale in the encampments around Port Harrison;[12] and RCMP officers reported similar accounts for other locales where welfare payments had decreased.[13] Government administrators, and even many teachers, encouraged the production of handicrafts in the manner that Houston had laid out, and sales of arts and crafts went up in the communities where Houston was involved. Port Harrison, for example, experienced an increase in purchases from $76 in 1948 to $11,700 in 1952. In Povungnituk, the increase was from $90 to $1,900 for the same time span.[14]

The Inuit were once a proud and independent people who provided all their economic and spiritual needs, successfully educated their children, and cared for their elderly, the weak and the unfortunate. But thanks to the paternalism of government policy and money, only a minority can now claim to be truly proud and independent.

Saali Peter
Speaking at the public hearings of the Royal Commission on Aboriginal Peoples Iqaluit, NWT 26 May 1992

> While all around them their culture was being debased, devalued, and actively oppressed by the dual forces of colonialism and Christianity, these same values were revered, celebrated, and voraciously collected in their arts.

Perhaps it was more significant that Inuit were being asked to depict their traditional and, in many cases, forbidden cultural practices in stone and, later, on paper and in textiles. Artists could illustrate the stories they had told for millennia as well as the Indigenous knowledge bestowed on them by their ancestors, the animals they had studied since childhood, and the traditional lifestyle they had so recently lived. While all around them their culture was being debased, devalued, and actively oppressed by the dual forces of colonialism and Christianity, these same values were revered, celebrated, and voraciously collected in their arts.

For artists, there is no doubt that there was an economic motivation behind the creation of artworks that featured traditional themes, as their main audience in the beginning were the primitive art enthusiasts of the international art market; those who had romanticized notions about the daily lives of Inuit.[15] The traditional subject matter of the artwork held a different meaning for this audience than it did for the makers. Inuit art buyers were able to imagine the Inuit as an untouched society, of which representations of this traditional lifestyle sold well, and Inuit were no doubt aware of this fact. It is undeniable that Inuit artists have been highly successful in creating traditional art that suits Western tastes, as the global market for Inuit art attests.[16] However, as long as Inuit knowledge, stories, or practices portrayed in the artwork are not distorted or falsified to make them more saleable, the artwork can both appeal to a Western audience as well as act as an expression of cultural knowledge and cultural resilience. In fact, these motivate many Inuit artists today to continue making art about what life was like before colonization.

Despite being his primary source of income, stone sculptor Uriash Puqiqnak stated, "When I carve, I try to convey what it was like for Inuit in the early 1940s."[17] Graphic artist Mayureak Ashoona has said of her artwork that "These are all about history – what has been going on. They are memories; the whole truth about all of life for those who forget about their history; to make sure that the young people know what really happened; to work both sides, from the past to the future; to communicate with people in the South because I can't speak English. I am proud of that lifestyle – my Inuit life."[18]

IMPACTS OF COLONIZATION AND CHRISTIANITY AND UTILIZING ART IN THE HEALING PROCESS

In recent years, some artists have daringly stepped outside this framework to provide us with a number of divergent perspectives on the transformation of the North. These new artworks, uncommon and introspective, are a significant departure from the traditional imagery usually found in past decades, but I would argue that they serve similar ends: to strengthen from within a culture threatened by dominant outside forces and to examine the way of life as Inuit know it. As the second and third generation of Inuit artists emerge, the possibility of remembering a traditional and unmediated lifestyle becomes less likely, and the artwork is shifting to reflect this reality. The movement towards depicting the intercultural encounter between Inuit and Western worlds most prominently began with Pudlo Pudlat, the artist who first combined traditional Inuit transformation iconography with modern transportation technologies, such as depicting planes, ships, and helicopters in his art from the 1960s onward.[19] This new approach to Inuit art seems to be accelerating of late and includes more social commentary and critique.

This emergent socially conscious art is indicative of the increased ability of Inuit to reflect upon and respond to the multiple stressors of contemporary life. There has been a noticeable shift over the last two decades to a focus on daring, new intercultural or transcultural subject matter (as demonstrated in the work of Napatchie Pootoogook, Mike Massie, Toonoo Sharky, Floyd Kuptana, and many others) and what is hopefully a growing body of work that directly calls into question the legacy of trauma and colonization of the Arctic (as in the work of, Manasie Akpaliapik, Annie Pootoogook, and Oviloo Tunnilee).

The aforementioned graphic artist, Annie Pootoogook, for example, presents an impressive self-reflexive and autobiographical account of her personal challenges. In one work, entitled *Memory of My Life: Breaking Bottles* (2001-02), Pootoogook expresses her frustration with family alcoholism by depicting the time she gathered all the liquor bottles up and smashed them.[20] Such bold statements are novel to Inuit art, but indicate a willingness of Inuit artists to begin the difficult process of self-examination and a desire to rebound from adversity to become fortified and more resourceful—the essence of resilience.

Yet to date, nowhere has this resilience and self-reflexivity been more evident than in the work of brothers Abraham Anghik Ruben[21] and David Ruben Piqtoukun. Piqtoukun and Ruben are pioneers in the field who have drawn directly from their experiences as students of the residential school system to inspire their artwork. For the majority of students who attended residential school, the wounds inflicted by the system have left deep scars that continue to affect many aspects of their daily lives; so, from these two artists who have poured their memories and emotions into their artwork, we may be able to learn much about the power of self-expression to heal and fortify.

For Ruben, becoming an artist was the catalyst for self-healing. In a 1991 interview, Ruben recounted the eleven years he spent suffering from the legacy of residential schooling until he met Alaskan Inupiaq artist Ron Senungetuk, a professor at the Native Arts Centre at the University of Alaska in Fairbanks, and began professional art training: "For the first time in years, I felt at home."[22] Since then, Abraham has gone on to create several bold works of social critique that bring awareness to the issues he holds dear: *Kittigazuit* (1999–2000), for example, narrates in the abstract a community decimated by foreign disease; and *The Last Goodbye* (2001) depicts with vivid clarity the pain he remembers his mother had experienced as she sent her two older children to residential school.

For Piqtoukun, the solo exhibition *Between Two Worlds: Sculpture by David Ruben Piqtoukun* was a revelation for artist and audiences alike. The artist created 62 works with such titles as *Bearing Wounds* (1995), *Angst* (1995), and *Tradition Lost* (1996). Taken together, these works expose the complexities and difficulties of cross-cultural translation and provide the viewer unmitigated access into Piqtoukun's traumatic past and his continuing effort to strike

Tradition Lost
1996, David Ruben Piqtoukun
Brazilian soapstone, slate
Private collection

a balance between two worlds. One of his most powerful messages of Inuit cultural resilience is present in *The Ever-Present Nuns* (1995), of which Piqtoukun wrote, "The four faces pointing in four directions represent the all-seeing nuns. They attempted to watch over and control the Inuit children in their school, even to control their inner lives. But the nuns could not see everything. They were blind to the owl spirit hovering directly above them."[23]

From the tremendous efforts of these two siblings we have been given a remarkable insight into the potential of artmaking as a tool for both resisting colonization and strengthening Inuit voice. In fact, all of the artists featured in this essay have shown us that art can be creatively utilized as a vehicle to preserve and fortify our cultural heritage and as an instrument of both personal and collective healing. However, as we enter this period of unprecedented nationwide awareness around residential schools, the artwork of Inuit, First Nations, and Métis people can play another important role. The power of visual art to speak across linguistic, cultural, and generational divides presents an opportunity for artists to tell these stories to a broad audience and to support the continued strengthening and revitalization of the national reconciliation process.

NOTES

[1] The Aboriginal Healing Foundation explains that resilience "is most often defined as the capacity to spring back from adversity and have a good life outcome despite emotional, mental or physical distress.... the adoption of "mature defenses" (i.e., humour and altruism) can help individuals overcome a lifetime of adversity; whereas anti-social or self-injurious coping strategies can aggravate existing risk factors and conditions. Breaking with the past and disrupting negative chain reactions are, therefore, critical steps in desisting from such negative strategies.... Culture and resilience intersect and help shape traditions, beliefs and human relationships. Traditional Aboriginal societies have placed great emphasis on fostering resilience for children and youth, but an oppressive colonial experience has often cut off Aboriginal parents from such cultural moorings. Notwithstanding, the resurgence of Aboriginal beliefs and practices, accompanied by traditional resilience promotion strategies, has given rise to promising interventions." Stout, Madeleine Dion and Gregory Kipling (2003:iii - iv). *Aboriginal People, Resilience and the Residential School Legacy.* Ottawa, ON: Aboriginal Healing Foundation. It is my contention that artmaking is one of these promising interventions that may strengthen the resilience of Inuit culture against past and continued oppressions.

[2] *Cited in* Kardosh, Robert (2007:14). The Other Kananginak Pootoogook. *Inuit Art Quarterly* 22(1):10–18.

[3] Unfortunately, these government-created communities "were usually constructed at the site of the trading posts, inspite of the fact that these locations had been chosen to satisfy the demands of the fur trade (access to ports, for instance) and were not necessarily suited to supporting large colonies of people." Mitchell, Marybelle (1993:336). Social, Economic, and Political Transformation among Canadian Inuit from 1950 to 1988. In *In the Shadow of the Sun: Perspectives on Contemporary Native Art*. Gatineau, QC: Canadian Museum of Civilization: 333–356.

[4] Norget, Kristen (2008:222). The Hunt for Inuit Souls: Religion, Colonization, and the Politics of Memory. In Gillian Robinson (ed.), *The Journals of Knud Rasmussen: A Sense of Memory and High-Definition Storytelling*. Montreal, QC: Isuma Productions: 217–236.

[5] These allegations are currently under investigation by the Qikiqtani Inuit Association.

[6] In 1959, the Hebronimiut of Labrador, for example, had their community forcibly relocated to more southern Labrador communities because the non-Inuit administrators in Hebron felt that it was too expensive to continue to fly supplies to the coast; Inuit were promised new homes and jobs, yet those promises were never fulfilled. Brice-Bennett, Carol (2000). *Reconciling with Memories: A Record of the Reunion at Hebron 40 Years after Relocation*. Nain, NL: Labrador Inuit Association.

[7] NAC RG85 volume 1507, file # 600-1-1, part 7. Report on Education in Canada's Northland, 12 December 1954.

[8] King, David (2006). *A Brief Report of the Federal Government of Canada's Residential School System for Inuit*. Ottawa, ON: Aboriginal Healing Foundation.

[9] Diubaldo, Richard (1985). *The Government of Canada and the Inuit: 1900-1967*. Ottawa, ON: Research Branch, Corporate Policy, Indian and Northern Affairs Canada.

[10] Canada. Department of the Interior (1928:10). Annual Report of the Department of the Interior for the Fiscal Year Ended March 31, 1928. Ottawa, ON: Department of the Interior.

[11] In order to obtain early trade goods from European whalers and other Arctic travellers, Inuit began producing quantities of figurines and miniatures specifically for the purpose of bartering. As early as 1821, William Parry recounted that Inuit who met his ships along the shores of Baffin Island were eager to trade their ivory models for "any trifle we chose to give them." In Parry, William E. (1824:24). *Journal of the Second Voyage for the Discovery of a North-West Passage from the Atlantic to the Pacific*. New York, NY: Greenwood Press.

Certain types of carvings and models of traditional tools, toys, and amulets were in high demand. In response, Inuit carvers produced these carvings in quantity for trade with Europeans. As George Swinton has pointed out in *Sculpture of the Inuit*, it was in this period that Inuit commercial art production truly first began. In Swinton, George (1999). *Sculpture of the Inuit*, 3rd revised edition. Toronto, ON: McClelland and Stewart.

[12] Goetz, Helga (1985). *The Role of the Department of Indian and Northern Affairs in the Development of Inuit Art*. Ottawa, ON: Inuit Art Section, Indian and Northern Affairs, Research and Documentation Centre [unpublished manuscript].

[13] Graburn, Nelson H.H (2004). Authentic Inuit Art: Creation and Exclusion in the Canadian North. *Journal of Material Culture* 9(2):141–159.

[14] These figures were estimates by Goetz, and include prices paid by the Guild, the HBC, the Catholic and Anglican missions, and military personnel.

[15] It should be noted that several scholars have examined the motivations behind the avid collection of early contemporary Inuit art and, particularly, its acceptance into the international art market intrinsically linked as it was to the perception of Inuit as "primitive" peoples. This monetary motivation has been critiqued repeatedly by non-Inuit art historians over the short history of contemporary Inuit art, particularly because the promoters of Inuit art seem to have actively tried to conceal or minimize the importance of economic incentives to Inuit artists. This idea was capitalized upon by Inuit art's most passionate promoter, James Houston, who keenly understood the mid-century modernist fascination with primitive peoples and used it to market Inuit art as the products of an untouched, exotic, and primitive society. This is in sharp contrast to the realities of Inuit life previously mentioned in this essay. For more information see, for example, Igloliorte, Heather (2007). Sanajatsarq: Reactions, Productions, and the Transformation of Promotional Practice. *Inuit Art Quarterly* 22(4):14–25.

[16] Furthermore, Inuit artists have been often criticized for focusing on traditional themes and for representing themselves in a way that is different from the realities of daily life. These critics, while acknowledging that, as Robert Kardosh has said, "the expression of traditional subjects serves an important purpose by helping to preserve and sustain Inuit identity in an era of globalization," still denounce this traditional art form as primarily motivated by the international art market's nostalgic desire for the products of an authentic and primitive society. Kardosh, Robert (2007:16). The Other Kananginak Pootoogook. *Inuit Art Quarterly* 22(1):10–18.

[17] *Cited in* Mitchell, Marybelle (1991:12). Seven Artists in Ottawa. *Inuit Art Quarterly* 6(3):6–17.

[18] *Cited in* Feheley, Patricia (2001:14). Focus on Mayureak Ashoona. *Inuit Art Quarterly* 17(1):14–19 [italics removed].

[19] Hessel, Ingo (1998). *Inuit Art: An Introduction.* New York, NY. Harry N. Abrams, Inc.

[20] *See page 13 for this image printed in* Feheley, Patricia (2004). Modern Language: The Art of Annie Pootoogook. *Inuit Art Quarterly* 19(2):10–15.

[21] Ruben's 2001 Brazilian soapstone carving, *Wrestling With My Demons*, was featured on the cover of the 2008 AHF publication, *From Truth to Reconciliation: Transforming the Legacy of Residential Schools.*

[22] *Cited in* Gunderson, Sonia (2005:20). Abraham Apakark Anghik Ruben: A View from the Top of the World. *Inuit Art Quarterly* 20(4):18–25.

[23] *Cited in* Gillmor, Alison (1996:32). Between Two Worlds: Sculpture by David Ruben Piqtoukun. *Inuit Art Quarterly* 11(4):30–34.

Inuit boy in front of Oblate Mission hospital
Chesterfield Inlet, Nunavut, 1958
Photographer: Charles Gimpel
Hudson's Bay Company Archives, Archives of Manitoba, HBCA-N13340

(Photo: Courtesy of Legacy of Hope Foundation's
"We were so far away...": The Inuit Experience of Residential Schools exhibit)

RICHARD WAGAMESE

Richard Wagamese is an Ojibway from the Wabasseemoong First Nation in northwestern Ontario. He has been a lecturer in creative writing with the University of Regina's Saskatchewan Indian Federated College, a writer for the Royal Commission on Aboriginal Peoples, a faculty advisor on journalism for Grant MacEwen Community College and the Southern Alberta Institute of Technology (SAIT), and a scriptwriter for the CBC-Alliance production *North of 60*. Recognized for his free-flowing style, Richard has been a book, film, and music reviewer, general reporter, and feature writer for numerous newspapers and journals across Canada. He has also worked extensively in both radio and television news and documentary.

Following a distinguished journalism career in which he became the first Aboriginal in Canada to win a National Newspaper Award for column writing, he moved into the realm of fiction writing. The result was the award-winning bestseller *Keeper'n Me* (1994), followed by an anthology of his newspaper columns, *The Terrible Summer* (1996), his second novel, *A Quality of Light* (1997), a memoir entitled *For Joshua: an Ojibway Father Teaches His Son* (2002), his third novel *Dream Wheels* (2006), his fourth, *Ragged Company* (2007), and finally his latest book, his second memoir, *One Native Life* (2008). Richard has been listed in *Canadian Who's Who*.

RETURNING TO HARMONY

I am a victim of Canada's residential school system. When I say victim, I mean something substantially different than "survivor." I never attended a residential school, so I cannot say that I survived one. However, my parents and my extended family members did. The pain they endured became my pain, and I became a victim.

When I was born, my family still lived the seasonal nomadic life of traditional Ojibwa people. In the great rolling territories surrounding the Winnipeg River in Northwestern Ontario, they fished, hunted, and trapped. Their years were marked by the peregrinations of a people guided by the motions and turns of the land. I came into the world and lived in a canvas army tent hung from a spruce bough frame as my first home. The first sounds I heard were the calls of loon, the snap and crackle of a fire, and the low, rolling undulation of Ojibwa talk.

We lived communally. Along with my mother and siblings, there were my matriarchal grandparents, aunts, uncles, and cousins. Surrounded by the rough and tangle of the Canadian Shield, we, moved through the seasons. Time was irrelevant in the face of ancient cultural ways that we followed.

But there was a spectre in our midst.

All the members of my family attended residential school. They returned to the land bearing psychological, emotional, spiritual, and physical burdens that haunted them. Even my mother, despite staunch declarations that she had learned good things there (finding Jesus, learning to keep a house, the gospel), carried wounds she could not voice. Each of them had experienced an institution that tried to scrape the Indian off of their insides, and they came back to the bush and river raw, sore, and aching. The pain they bore was invisible and unspoken. It seeped into their spirit, oozing its poison and blinding them from the incredible healing properties within their Indian ways.

For a time, the proximity to family and the land acted as a balm. Then, slowly and irrevocably, the spectre that followed them back from the

Each of them had experienced an institution that tried to scrape the Indian off of their insides, and they came back to the bush and river raw, sore, and aching.

schools began to assert its presence and shunt for space around our communal fire. When the vitriolic stew of unspoken words, feelings, and memories of their great dislocation, hurt, and isolation began to bubble and churn within them, they discovered that alcohol could numb them from it. And we ceased to be a family.

Instead, the adults of my Ojibwa family became frightened children. The trauma that had been visited upon them reduced them to that. They huddled against a darkness from where vague shapes whispered threats and from where invasions of their minds, spirits, and bodies roared through the blackness to envelope and smother them again. They forgot who they were. They struck back vengefully, bitterly, and blindly as only hurt and frightened children could do.

When I was a toddler, my left arm and shoulder were smashed. Left untreated, my arm hung backwards in its joint and, over time, it atrophied and withered. My siblings and I endured great tides of violence and abuse from the drunken adults. We were beaten, nearly drowned, and terrorized. We took to hiding in the bush and waited until the shouting, cursing, and drinking died away. Those nights were cold and terrifying. In the dim light of dawn, the eldest of us would sneak back into camp to get food and blankets.

In the mid-winter of 1958 when I was almost three, the adults left my two brothers, sister, and me alone in the bush camp across the bay from the tiny railroad town of Minaki. It was February. The wind was blowing bitterly and the firewood ran out at the same time as the food. They were gone for days, drinking in Kenora sixty miles away. When it became apparent that we would freeze to death without wood, my eldest sister and brother hauled my brother, Charles, and me across the bay on a sled piled with furs.

They pulled us across that ice in a raging snowstorm. We huddled in the furs on the leeward side of the railroad depot cold, hungry, and crying. A passing Ontario provincial policeman found us and took us to the Children's Aid Society. I would not see my mother or my extended family again for twenty-one years.

I lived in two foster homes until I was adopted at age nine. I left that home at age sixteen; I ran for my safety, my security, and my sanity. The seven years I spent in that adopted home were filled with beatings, mental and emotional abuse, and a complete dislocation and disassociation from anything Indian or Ojibwa. I was permitted only the strict Presbyterian ethic of that household. It was as much an institutional kidnapping as a residential school.

For years after, I lived on the street or in prison. I became a drug user and an alcoholic. I drifted through unfulfilled relationships. I was haunted by fears and memories. I carried the residual trauma of my toddler years and the seven years in my adopted home. This caused me to experience post-traumatic stress disorder, which severely affected the way I lived my life and the choices I would make.

The truth of my life is that I am an intergenerational victim of residential schools. Everything I endured until I found healing was a result of the effects of those schools. I did not hug my mother until I was twenty-five. I did not speak my first Ojibwa word or set foot on my traditional territory until I was twenty-six. I did not know that I had a family, a history, a culture, a source for spirituality, a cosmology, or a traditional way of living. I had no awareness that I belonged somewhere. I grew up ashamed of my Native identity and the fact that I knew nothing about it. I was angry that there was no one to tell me who I was or where I had come from.

My brother Charles tracked me down with the help of a social worker friend when I was twenty-five. From there, I returned to the land of my people as a stranger knowing nothing of their experience or their pain. When I rejoined my people and learned about Canada's residential school policy, I was enraged. Their political and social history impelled me to find work as a reporter with a Native newspaper. As a writer and a journalist, I spoke to hundreds of residential school Survivors. The stories they told, coupled with my family's complete and utter reticence, told me a great deal about how my family had suffered. I knew that those schools were responsible for my displacement, my angst, and my cultural *lostness*.

> The truth of my life is that I am an intergenerational victim of residential schools. Everything I endured until I found healing was a result of the effects of those schools.

It was very difficult growing up with family who have gone to residential schools, we have been very, and must say, are very dysfunctional (speaking for me certainly), we have been through a fair share, alcoholism, drug abuse, violence, among many other situations.

The common characteristics most families like mine all share are that there has been a lack of love and affection, there were no 'I love you' words, no hugs and no kisses.

**Norman Achneepineskum
Kanehsatake
CBC News online posting
11 June 2008**

For years I carried simmering anger and resentment. The more I learned about the implementation of that policy and how it affected Aboriginal people across the country, the more anger I felt. I ascribed all my pain to residential schools and to those responsible. I blamed churches for my alcoholism, loneliness, shame, fear, inadequacy, and failures. In my mind I envisaged a world where I had grown up as a fully functioning Ojibwa, and it glittered in comparison to the pain-wracked life I had lived.

But when I was in my late forties, I had enough of the anger. I was tired of being drunk and blaming the residential schools and those responsible. I was tired of fighting against something that could not be touched, addressed, or confronted. My life was slipping away on me and I did not want to become an older person still clinging to a disempowering emotion like the anger I carried.

So one day I decided that I would visit a church. Churches had been the seed of my anger. I had religion forced on me in my adopted home and it was the churches that had run the residential schools that shredded the spirit of my family. If I were to lose my anger, I needed to face the root of it squarely. I was determined that I would take myself there and sit and listen to the service. As much as I knew that I would want to walk out and as much as my anger would direct me to reject it all, I would force myself to sit and listen and try to find something that I could relate to. I chose a United Church because they had been the first to issue an apology for their role in the residential school debacle. They had been the first to publicly state their responsibility for the hurt that crippled generations. They were the first to show the courage to address wrongdoing, abuse, forced removal, and shaming. They had been the first to make tangible motions toward reconciliation. It put them in a more favourable light with me.

I was uncomfortable at first. No one spoke to me as I took my seat in a pew near the back. There were no other Native people there and I used that fact as a denunciation. When the service began, I heard everything through the tough screen of my rage. Then I noticed the old woman beside me sitting with her eyes closed as the minister spoke. She looked calm and peaceful, and there was a glow on her features that I coveted. So I closed my eyes too and tilted my head back and listened.

I ceased to hear the liturgy that day. I could not hear doctrine, semantics, proselytizations, or judgment. Instead, with my eyes closed, all I could hear was the small voice of the minister telling a story about helping a poor, drug-addicted woman on the street despite his fear and doubt. All I heard was the voice of compassion. All I heard was a spiritual, very human person talking about life and confronting its mysteries.

So I went back the next week. I went back and took my seat, and I listened with my eyes closed. After the scriptural text was read, the minister analyzed it by placing it in the context of his impatience and the lessons he had learned in the grocery line and in the freeway traffic. Here was a man responsible for directing the lives of a congregation talking about facing his own spiritual shortcomings. There was no self-aggrandization, no inferred superiority. There was only a man telling us how hard it was to behave like a spiritual being.

I went back to that church for many weeks. The messages I heard were all about humanity and about the search for innocence, comfort, and belonging. I do not know just exactly when my anger and resentment disappeared. I only know that there came a time when I could see that there was nothing in the message that was not about healing. I heard about compassion, love, kindness, trust, courage, truth, and loyalty and an abiding faith that there is a God, a Creator. There was nothing to be angry about in any of that; in fact, there was nothing different from what Native spirituality talks about. After I came home to my people I sought out teachers and healers and ceremonies. I had committed myself to learning the spiritual principles that allowed our peoples to sustain, define, and perpetuate themselves through incredible changes. I had adopted many of those teachings into my daily life, and every ceremony I attended taught me more and more about the essence of our spiritual lives. What I heard from that minister those Sunday mornings was not any different from the root message of humanity in our teachings. With my eyes closed there was no white, no Indian, no difference at all; the absence of anger happened quietly without fanfare.

It has been a few years now since I sat in that church. I have not receded back into the dark seas of resentment, rage, or old hurt. Instead, I have found a peace with churches and, in turn, with residential schools, with Canada. See, that church changed my personal politics. Sure, there are genuine reasons to be angry. The hurt caused by the residential school experience, both of the Survivors and of those like me who were victimized a generation or more later, are huge, real, and overwhelming. But healing happens if you want it bad enough, and that is the trick of it, really. Every spiritually enhancing experience asks a sacrifice of us and, in this, the price of admission is a keen desire to be rid of the block of anger.

When the Truth and Reconciliation Commission makes its tour of the country and hears the stories of people who endured the pain of residential schools, I hope it hears more stories like mine—of people who fought against the resentment, hatred, and anger and found a sense of peace. Both the Commission and Canada need to hear stories of healing instead of a relentless retelling and re-experiencing of pain. They need to hear that, despite everything, every horror, it is possible to move forward and to learn how to leave hurt behind. Our neighbours in this country need to hear stories about our capacity for forgiveness, for self-examination, for compassion, and for our yearning for peace because they speak to our resiliency as a people. That is how reconciliation happens.

It is a big word, *reconciliation*. Quite simply, it means to create harmony. You create harmony with truth and you build truth out of humility. That is spiritual. That is truth. That is Indian. Within us, as nations of Aboriginal people and as individual members of those nations, we have an incredible capacity for survival, endurance, and forgiveness. In the reconciliation with ourselves first, we find the ability to create harmony with others, and that is where it has to start—in the fertile soil of our own hearts, minds, and spirits.

That, too, is Indian.

New arrivals at Moose Fort Indian Residential School
Moose Factory, Ontario

Courtesy of Janice Longboat

PETER HARRISON

Peter Harrison is a professional geographer and holds a Bachelor of Arts (First Class Honours) from the London School of Economics and Political Science (United Kingdom), a Masters of Arts from the University of Victoria (British Columbia), and a doctorate from the University of Washington (Seattle, Washington).

Peter has been the Skelton-Clark Fellow at Queen's University since June 2008. Prior to this, he has held a number of deputy minister and senior government positions; most notably, he was Senior Associate Deputy Minister of Indian and Northern Affairs Canada where he was responsible for the Northern Affairs Program and the Inuit Relations Secretariat. Concurrently, Peter was the Executive Director and Deputy Head (Deputy Minister) of Indian Residential Schools Resolution Canada where he was responsible for implementing the largest court-ordered out-of-court settlement (Indian Residential Schools Settlement Agreement) in Canadian history. He was also responsible for the common experience payment, the creation of an independent adjudication process (to deal with specific cases of abuse), and the creation of the Truth and Reconciliation Commission. He also shepherded the development of the Government of Canada's apology in the House of Commons to First Nations, Inuit, and Métis Survivors of residential schools.

Peter is a Fellow of the Royal Geographical Society; a Fellow, Governor, and Vice-President of the Royal Canadian Geographical Society; and Adjunct Professor at the World Maritime University (Malmö, Sweden). He is a recipient of Her Majesty Queen Elizabeth II's Golden Jubilee Gold Medal for Public Service, and the J.B. Nicholls award for his lifetime contribution to ocean and coastal management in Canada.

DISPELLING IGNORANCE OF RESIDENTIAL SCHOOLS

In the late summer of 2007, the conversation among a group of senior federal officials turned to the question of immigration. The discussion was wide-ranging and covered both the challenges and the opportunities that Canada, as a country dependent on immigration, continues to face. At one point, a comparison was made between Canada's experience and that of European countries such as France, Germany, the United Kingdom, and other members of the European Union. The question was raised as to why the integration of immigrant populations into Canadian society has seemingly been more successful than elsewhere. One hypothesis raised was that, unlike many European nations, Canada has never been a colonial power. The argument was that since Canada has never had overseas dependencies—such as the Belgians in the Congo, the French in Algeria, or the British in Hong Kong or India—entitlements to residence in the colonizing jurisdiction had not been created. Furthermore, it was also argued that some of the current tensions in European societies may well be an ongoing result of previous colonial policies and attitudes.

As a participant in this conversation, I must admit to taking great exception to the statement that Canada has never been a colonial power, whatever the comparison with experience elsewhere. While Canada has not extended its hegemony to other lands and continents, national objectives have historically been heavy with domestic colonial policies and attitudes regarding First Nations, Inuit, and Métis peoples. And, as I noted at the time, this is nowhere more evident than in the legacy of the residential school system and the impact these schools have had on individuals, families, and communities and will have on future generations. Taking children away from their families and communities, often forcibly, and attempting to eradicate all vestiges of their language, culture, and spirituality in order to assimilate them into mainstream society can only be described as a colonial objective. Add to this the psychological, physical, and sexual abuse that many of these children were subjected to in institutions that should have had the duty to protect them, and the only conclusion to be reached is that Canada, despite its virtues, has been as much a colonizer of its own people as other countries have been in their overseas dependencies.

What this and other conversations have convinced me of is the enormous challenge of educating the Canadian public about this dark chapter of our history so that informed debate can take place and reconciliation can begin. This is the challenge of coping with ignorance, which the Truth and Reconciliation Commission will face at the beginning of and throughout its mandate. At the time of the conversation noted above, the *Indian Residential Schools Settlement Agreement*,[1] which had been negotiated and accepted by the national Aboriginal organizations, the churches that ran the schools, and the Government of Canada, had also received approval from the courts in the nine jurisdictions where the schools had been located. The future fate of the *Settlement Agreement*, which is the largest out-of-court settlement of a class action in Canadian history, was at that point still in the hands of the residential school Survivors. As members of the class action, they could accept the *Settlement Agreement* as a whole or opt out and pursue their own legal remedies. If more than 5,000 of the estimated 86,000 Survivors had opted out, then the *Settlement Agreement* would have become void. In any event, fewer than 400 Survivors opted out, and the court-monitored *Settlement Agreement* came into effect on 19 September 2007, at which time began its five-year life.

Much has happened in the intervening year. The common experience payment has been paid out to over 61,473 claimants as at 31 March 2008 (for a total of over $1.19 billion), and the process of reconsideration of disputed claims is under way.[2] The independent assessment process for assessing and compensating individual cases of abuse has been put in place, and adjudication hearings have begun. An additional endowment ($125 million) has been provided to the Aboriginal Healing Foundation, and the Truth and Reconciliation Commission (TRC) has been created. In addition, the business of the House of Commons was suspended for the day on 11 June 2008, and the Right Honourable Stephen Harper, the Prime Minister of Canada, on behalf of the Government of Canada and all Canadians, apologized to the Survivors of residential schools and asked for their forgiveness.[3] Many Survivors were present in the chamber while national Aboriginal leaders addressed Members of Parliament and the whole country from the floor of the House of Commons, and countless others watched the proceedings in communities and at gatherings across Canada and around the world.

While much has happened, much more remains to be done. As many Aboriginal leaders and residential school Survivors have pointed out, the payments under the *Settlement Agreement* are important in the process of healing and reconciliation, but they are by no means sufficient by themselves. The increased public awareness occasioned by the Apology was welcomed and timely, but it needs to be nurtured and built upon. And so there are great expectations that the TRC—the jewel in the crown of the *Settlement Agreement*—will be able to achieve its objectives in a lasting way.

Toward Reconciliation

There are many layers to the goal of reconciliation with many different players involved: individual Survivors struggle to reconcile their residential school experience with its ongoing impact on their lives; spouses and family members are on journeys of understanding and healing; whole communities are trying to cope with social issues resulting from the abuse suffered in the residential schools; and reconciliation with the institutions responsible for the schools—the churches and the government—is an ongoing challenge with its own set of dynamics. But what of the Canadian public—civil society—as a whole? How can they be informed about the legacy of residential schools? Is reconciliation possible without a clear understanding of the role and impact of these institutions? Judging by the conversation outlined above (and I have had many others like it), even informed professionals are unaware of the enormity of the residential school phenomenon. So how much more difficult will it be to engage a public that has even less knowledge and, in some cases, less interest? The education of the Canadian public is thus one of the key objectives of the TRC, and this will be a mammoth task.

When first faced with the facts of residential schools many people are incredulous, and their disbelief leads to a plethora of questions, such as: How could this have happened in a society that sees itself as caring and tolerant? This quickly evolves into a deeper understanding of the situations still faced by many Aboriginal people in Canada, their families, and their communities. This often turns to outrage and the desire for further action. This empathy can be a wellspring of support for the TRC and its work and could strengthen the relationship between Aboriginal and non-Aboriginal people in Canada if tapped into effectively. It would

> The increased public awareness occasioned by the Apology was welcomed and timely, but it needs to be nurtured and built upon. And so there are great expectations that the TRC—the jewel in the crown of the *Settlement Agreement*—will be able to achieve its objectives in a lasting way.

153

be a great gift to Canada if the story of suffering and despair endured in residential schools gives rise to greater understanding and leads to positive partnerships with Aboriginal peoples.

FACING THE SCEPTICS

There are sceptics and those who simply dismiss the residential schools issue as being of little consequence. The TRC will undoubtedly hear from such individuals. Indeed, if the TRC is to rewrite this dark chapter in Canadian history, it *should* hear such views; there would be merit in seeking these individuals out so that myth can be replaced with fact and ignorance thereby dispelled. I have heard many sceptical comments in the conversations referred to above. What are some of these? How can these be countered? The remainder of this article will deal with some of the more egregious ones. It is only to be hoped that these comments arise because of a lack of knowledge, information, and understanding by the commentator. If so, then the TRC is well placed to face them head-on and to correct the record in a definitive way.

DISPELLING THE IGNORANCE OF TYPICAL COMMENTS

This happened long ago, so why bring it up now?

Those few who are aware that residential schools had existed at all often have the perception that they were a phenomenon only of the late nineteenth and early twentieth centuries. It comes as a complete surprise to them that even though many schools closed in the 1960s and 1970s, the last school (Gordon Indian Residential School in Saskatchewan) did not close until 1996. (In fact, the youngest recipient of the common experience payment was only 17 years old and present on the floor of the House of Commons for the Prime Minister's apology.) This misperception is an impediment to fruitful dialogue because it is easier to dismiss something that happened in the past than to face the fact that over 80,000 former students are still alive, even though their number is continually declining as older Survivors die. Perhaps as individual stories begin to emerge from the activities of the TRC, and as the tremendously powerful work of organizations such as the Legacy of Hope Foundation become known, civil society will realize that Indian residential schools are as much a part of recent history as they are of the distant past.

There are sceptics and those who simply dismiss the residential schools issue as being of little consequence. The TRC will undoubtedly hear from such individuals. Indeed, if the TRC is to rewrite this dark chapter in Canadian history, it should hear such views; there would be merit in seeking these individuals out so that myth can be replaced with fact and ignorance thereby dispelled.

The churches were only doing what the government asked them to do …

The residential schools were sponsored and funded by the Government of Canada and were operated by the mainline churches (Catholic, Anglican, Presbyterian, and United). A total of 132 of these schools[4] are recognized pursuant to the *Settlement Agreement* (this number could increase as appeals of the schools listed are considered). As the TRC grapples with the legacy of the schools, it will be important to clarify who was responsible for what. While the government policy was clearly one of assimilation of Aboriginal children into the dominant society, how this was undertaken was largely a matter for those who administered the schools. Strict discipline and acceptance of abusive practices in individual institutions and lack of protection from abusers are issues that will need to be aired if reconciliation is to take place. The TRC will need to hear directly from government and administrators of the institutions, or their representatives, in order to probe these matters.

The policies were well-meaning and in tune with their times …

It is easy to look back in history and to justify certain actions because that was the way things were done then and because policy-makers were well-meaning. This approach is too simplistic and requires much further analysis. Providing children with an education is undoubtedly a laudable objective of any society, but doing it in a way that demolishes cultures and demeans the children is surely unacceptable at any time. Add to this the physical and sexual abuse suffered by many students at the residential schools, then it has to be asked: Was this ever acceptable as the way things were done? Certainly not! A role of the TRC should be to have this question answered in a fulsome way.

They got an education, did they not?

This is perhaps the most common reaction to the question of residential schools. It is usually mixed with the sentiment: complaining about the experience in the schools is somehow a lack of gratitude. This reaction is probably the most insidious because it continues to be based on the perceived superiority of the dominant society.

Many former students did get an education, and some of the schools have been recognized as having played a major role in supporting the development of Aboriginal leadership throughout the decades. But, even where success was evident and in cases where former students are of the view that their education at a residential school was a key to this success, the question is not about the *what* of the education process, but about the *how*.

Sadly, many students at the schools got little or no education of a lasting nature, and the quality of the education many received was inferior to that of non-Aboriginal people. Even worse, being forced to live for many years in an institution and in an environment where abuse of all kinds was rampant often led to learned behaviour of a negative kind. The prevalence of sexual predators, and what they did to little children, is perhaps the most terrible of the impacts. This education continues to have an impact on later generations—the children, grandchildren, and great-grandchildren of Survivors. The TRC will be instrumental in shedding light on how such learned behaviour has led to challenges within Aboriginal communities and how it has affected the condition of Aboriginal peoples generally.

But everyone got the strap in those days...

It seems that everyone has a tale to tell about how they were punished at school for various infractions. Somehow, this is seen as a justification for the abuse that occurred within residential schools. While corporal punishment may have been more prevalent in past years than it is today, the scale of such punishment at residential schools was beyond any level of acceptability. The lawyers and adjudicators refer to the standards of the time in determining levels of abuse. The TRC will hear many stories from Survivors that will dispel the myth of the strap because the abuse meted out often far exceeded any of the standards of the time, or of any time: to be hunted down for running away from school; to be put in a cage for several days for all to see; to be humiliated before the entire student body; and to be deprived of nourishment and access to sanitary facilities during this time. This was not just the strap.

Non-Aboriginal people in Canada had similar experiences, so what is so different about this?

Unfortunately, there were similar experiences: the Duplessis orphans,[5] the Barnardo children,[6] and Mount Cashel.[7] Even more cases are coming to light at seemingly respectable educational and religious institutions in Canada and elsewhere.

The fact that there were similar experiences does not simply justify any of them. Each has to be dealt with in a way that promotes healing and reconciliation based on the circumstances involved. However, residential schools and their impact were, and are, different. They were created as a matter of national policy and had the express objective of *taking the Indian out of the child*. This is why a national process of reconciliation and the role that the TRC will have in this process are so important.

Why can people not just get over it?

This opinion is closely related to the perception that residential schools are part of ancient history and not of the present, and this is usually based on ignorance of the gravity of the abuse suffered by former students. How does someone come to terms with having been raped on multiple occasions as a child? How can current infirmities and dependencies resulting from previous abuse be overcome, if at all? Where is the hope that has been systematically destroyed? While many former students are on a healing journey that involves coping with the past and building for the future, many are not. This will be a major challenge for the TRC as it tries to dispel the myth in civil society that somehow this whole matter was an aberration while at the same time promotes reconciliation through healing.

This whole thing is not fair to the many good people involved …

The *Settlement Agreement* came into being because of the number of class action suits for alleged abuse being brought against the defendants—Canada and the churches that ran the schools. It came into being to right many wrongs, not to laud the contribution of dedicated people of whom there were undoubtedly many. So it is not surprising that the dialogue to date has focused on the many terrible things that happened in the

The tragic legacy of residential education began in the late nineteenth century with a three-part vision of education in the service of assimilation. It included, first, a justification for removing children from their communities and disrupting Aboriginal families; second, a precise pedagogy for re-socializing children in the schools; and third, schemes for integrating graduates into the non-Aboriginal world.

Report of the Royal Commission on Aboriginal Peoples Volume 1: Looking Forward, Looking Back

schools. This will continue as the TRC begins its work. The challenge will be to hear all sides of the residential school story—the good, the bad, and (equally important) the indifferent—while not diminishing in any way the suffering of former students and the negative impact the schools have had on Aboriginal societies.

The location and operation of many of the residential schools was such that these were isolated entities, often with little outside contact or input. This undoubtedly contributed to the flourishing abusive practices. However, surely little can remain hidden for long in such closed environments. So, particular interest will be of any observations and conclusions the TRC will reach as to why many of those good people were oblivious to the abuse that was happening around them. Or, if they were not oblivious, then why did not more of them step forward and take action to protect the children in their care?

Is it not time to just move on and let bygones be bygones?

This opinion is dismissive of the trauma experienced by many Survivors of residential schooling and underestimates the difficulty of coping with the ongoing impact of such trauma. It is the naive view that somehow a page can be turned and all will be well—a matter of pulling oneself together and getting on with things. Anyone who has ever grieved or suffered trauma knows how enormously wrong such statements are and how they reflect a fundamental misunderstanding of the human condition.

There may well be a time to move on, but only when individual Survivors, families, and communities have the strength and support to cope with their past experiences and to deal with the trauma that has been inflicted on them. Each healing journey is different; some are more difficult than others, others have never begun. The nature and the pace of each journey can only be determined by each traveller, but the TRC can be instrumental in helping so many travellers reach their destination.

In October of 2007, I had the privilege of addressing a group of professionals who were to become adjudicators in the independent assessment process mandated by the Settlement Agreement. I urged them to remember that those who were abused in a residential school were defenceless little children and that what happened to each of the Survivors they help, whatever their age, happened when they were a child. My message to them was that, as they adjudicate individual cases of abuse, they have an enormous gift to impart above and beyond a financial settlement, and that is the gift of hope. With institutions such as the Aboriginal Healing Foundation continuing their critically important and acclaimed work, and now with the Truth and Reconciliation Commission beginning its activities, maybe the gift of hope will be granted to all Aboriginal children—past, present, and future.

NOTES

[1] Indian Residential Schools Resolution Canada [IRSRC] (2006). *Indian Residential Schools Settlement Agreement*. Retrieved 7 October 2008 from: http://www.ainc-inac.gc.ca/rqpi/content/pdf/english/IRSSA%20Settlement%20Agreement/IRSSA-Settlement.pdf

[2] Indian and Northern Affairs Canada (no date). Indian Residential Schools Resolution Canada 2007-2008 Departmental Performance Report. Retrieved 31 March 2009 from: http://www.tbs-sct.gc.ca/dpr-rmr/2007-2008/inst/ira/ira-eng.pdf

[3] *See* Appendix 2.

[4] Government of Canada (2007). Application for Common Experience Payment for Former Students Who Resided at Indian Residential School(s). Retrieved 7 October 2008 from: http://www.ainc-inac.gc.ca/rqpi/content/pdf/english/Service%20Can%20Former%20Students%20Eng.pdf

[5] During the 1940s to 1960s, under the leadership of Maurice Duplessis, the Quebec government was responsible for having healthy, orphaned children diagnosed as mentally challenged and having them sent to psychiatric institutions. Many had suffered from physical and sexual abuse while at these institutions. For more information on the Duplessis orphans, see: Roy, Bruno (1994). *Memoire d'asile: La Tragedie des enfants de Duplessis*. Les Éditions du Boréal; and Perry, J. Christopher, John J. Sigal, Sophie Boucher, and Nikolas Paré (2006). Seven Institutionalized Children and Their Adaptation in Late Adulthood: The Children of Duplessis (Les Enfants de Duplessis). *Psychiatry* 69(4):283–301.

[6] The "Barnardo children" were young British children sent to live and work in Canada and Australia between 1870 and 1939. Approximately 30,000 children, considered orphaned but many were from foster homes, had been shipped to Canada and, once there, were neglected, abused, and treated as servants. For more information, see: Bagnell, Kenneth (2001). *The Little Immigrants: The Orphans who came to Canada*. Toronto, ON: Dundurn Press Ltd.; and

Corbett, Gail H. (2002). *Nation Builders: Barnardo Children in Canada.* Toronto, ON: Dundurn Press Ltd.

[7] Between 1898 and 1990, the Christian Brothers of Ireland in Canada operated the Mount Cashel Orphanage, a facility for boys in St. John's, Newfoundland. In the late 1980s, allegations of sexual abuse began to surface. An investigation by a royal commission found that there was evidence of abuse, and eventually nine Christian brothers were convicted and sentenced. The institution was subsequently closed in 1990, and the Government of Newfoundland has since paid compensation to the victims. For more information, see: Royal Commission of Inquiry into the Response of the Newfoundland Criminal Justice System to Complaints (1991). *Volume One: Report.* St. John's, NL: Office of the Queen's Printer; Harris, Michael (1990). *Unholy Orders: Tragedy at Mount Cashel.* Markham, ON: Penguin Books; and Berry, Jason and Andrew M. Greely (2000). *Lead Us Not Into Temptation: Catholic Priests and the Sexual Abuse of Children.* Champaign, IL: University of Illinois Press.

"How would you feel if your children were forced to go to a school surrounded by barbed wire fence?"

Photographer: Peter Harrison

SCOTT SERSON

Scott Serson was born in Ottawa, Ontario, but grew up in nearby Arnprior. He received his Bachelor of Arts in Sociology from Carleton University in 1970.

Scott began his career in the public service as a counsellor for Manpower Canada in 1973. For his first ten years in the public service, he held various positions in social policy during which time he also graduated from the Career Assignment Program. From 1985 to 1987, he was Assistant Secretary to the Cabinet, Office of Aboriginal Constitutional Affairs in the Federal-Provincial Relations Office. In 1987, Scott moved to the Department of Finance initially as General Director, Social Policy and Federal-Provincial Relations, and later as General Director, Fiscal Policy and Economic Analysis. Returning to the Federal-Provincial Relations Office as Deputy Secretary to the Cabinet, Intergovernmental and Aboriginal Affairs in 1989, he provided strategic advice on federal-provincial relations and Aboriginal constitutional issues and co-chaired the Indigenous Peoples working group during the Charlottetown Accord. Scott then became Associate Deputy Minister at Health Canada in 1993 and, in 1994, assumed the position of Associate Deputy Minister of Human Resources Development Canada. In 1995, he was appointed Deputy Minister of Indian Affairs and Northern Development where he was instrumental in the successful development of the Government's response to the Royal Commission on Aboriginal Peoples. Scott was appointed President of the Public Service Commission of Canada in 1999 where he worked until his retirement in 2003 from the public service. During this time, he was also one of the Champions for Values and Ethics in the Public Service. Since his retirement, Scott had worked as a policy advisor to the National Chief of the Assembly of First Nations. He now works as a private consultant.

Scott received the Outstanding Achievement Award in 1999 for his efforts in the field of social justice and his interest in public service leadership. He is a member of the Auditor General's Advisory Committee on Aboriginal Issues and the Advisory Committee of the Carleton Centre on Values and Ethics. He is also Chair of the Board of the Institute on Governance and a member of the Audit Committee of the Canadian Food Inspection Agency.

RECONCILIATION:
FOR FIRST NATIONS THIS MUST INCLUDE
FISCAL FAIRNESS

The 1996 *Report of the Royal Commission on Aboriginal Peoples* (*RCAP Report* or *Report*) was by far the broadest and most comprehensive effort to define a plan of reconciliation between the Aboriginal peoples of this land and the rest of Canadian society. But did the *RCAP Report* ever get the kind of attention from the government of Canada it warranted? It can be argued that it was not given the warranted long-term, detailed attention and that a decision was taken around the time of its release that continues to seriously undermine the progress of First Nations of which RCAP and the initial government response to it had envisioned.

When thinking about reconciliation in the current context, there are many reasons to turn back to the *RCAP Report*. One reason is the following reference in the Prime Minister's recent apology to former residents of Indian residential schools: "Two primary objectives of the residential schools system were to remove and isolate children from the influence of their homes, families, traditions and cultures, and to assimilate them into the dominant culture. These objectives were **based on the assumption** aboriginal cultures and spiritual beliefs were inferior and unequal."[1] If the Government of Canada has finally admitted that this assumption was false, surely we need to ask whether there are other false assumptions motivating government policy on Aboriginal peoples. And if there are, will they not continue to confound efforts to achieve reconciliation at the societal level until they too are repudiated?

RCAP identified three other false assumptions in addition to what motivated and sustained the Indian residential schools:

1. The first held Aboriginal people to be inherently inferior and incapable of governing themselves.

2. The second was that treaties and other agreements were, by and large, not covenants of trust and obligation but devices of statecraft, less expensive and more acceptable than armed conflict ...

3. The third false assumption was that wardship was appropriate for Aboriginal people, so that actions deemed to be for their benefit could be taken without their consent or their involvement in design or implementation.[2]

The *RCAP Report* goes on to point out "The fact that many of these notions are no longer formally acknowledged does not lessen their contemporary influence ... they still significantly underpin the institutions that drive and constrain the federal Aboriginal policy process."[3] Indeed, it goes further to point out that even though "The four false assumptions may well be officially disavowed now ... this does not end the capacity of political institutions to devise new ones ... One such modern variant ... is that Aboriginal peoples constitute an interest group, one among many in a pluralistic society."[4]

Since the *RCAP Report* was released twelve years ago, it is fair to ask whether these assumptions continue to "drive and constrain the federal Aboriginal policy process."[5] First Nations leaders might argue that recent history indicates that they do. Efforts of First Nations to move toward self-government are given minimal support (unless they are combined with a land claim negotiation). There are no serious treaty implementation negotiations, although the current government has talked of starting some. Finally, the federal government continues to make significant unilateral policy moves. One recent example is *Bill C-44: an Act to Amend the Canadian Human Rights Act* to remove the exemption for band governments (Section 67). One reason for First Nations' early opposition to the application of the *Act* was the absence of studies and analysis of what costs the *Act*'s application would impose on them.[6] In the end, this legislation was introduced without any credible studies of the cost to First Nations, without consultation, and certainly without any effort to obtain First Nation consent.

The RCAP discussion of assumptions is fundamental, but it is just one small part of this comprehensive report. If only one assumption has been seriously addressed by government over a twelve-year period, it does raise questions about how seriously it treated the rest of the *Report*. One could argue that the initial government response to RCAP was a reasonable one, given the need to balance the challenge of analyzing a report of that length and substance with the political necessity of having a federal response shortly after the release of the *Report*. The federal response to RCAP was *Gathering Strength – Canada's Aboriginal Action Plan*.[7] It had four objectives:

1. to *renew the partnerships* that RCAP argued characterized the relations between Aboriginal Peoples and the newcomers in earlier times;

2. to *strengthen Aboriginal governance*, which built not only on RCAP but on the view of the Department of Indian Affairs and Northern Development (DIAND)'s senior management. When the federal government devolved the management of federal programs to Aboriginal people in the late 1980s, too little attention was paid to building and sustaining the governance capacity to successfully deal with those responsibilities;

3. to *develop a new fiscal relationship*, which again sought to marry RCAP's broad direction with DIAND senior management's view that Aboriginal governments and organizations could not move forward in a sustainable fashion without a more secure and modern legislated financial regime (somewhat similar to the Equalization Program) on which to base their governments; and

4. to *support strong communities, people, and economies* that, building on the elements above, sought to make a marked improvement in the quality of life enjoyed by Aboriginal peoples.

Of course, the Government of Canada also produced the *Statement of Reconciliation*: "As Aboriginal and non-Aboriginal Canadians seek to move forward together in a process of renewal, it is essential that we deal with the legacies of the past affecting the Aboriginal peoples of Canada, including the First Nations, Inuit and Métis."[8] In addition, as a sign of commitment to deal with the legacies of the past, the government invested $350 million "to support the development of community-based healing as a means of dealing with the legacy of physical and sexual abuse in the Residential School system."[9]

It is worth underscoring that the Minister of Indian Affairs of the day, Jane Stewart, fundamentally believed that partnership should characterize the day-to-day relations of her officials in their relations with Aboriginal peoples. In fact, she agreed that government officials

We are firmly convinced, however, that the Department of Indian Affairs, with its archaic structure and misguided philosophy, is incapable of participating in a sincere and intelligent process of consultation. We feel it is imperative that your Government create a new structure with which we, through the National Indian Brotherhood, can negotiate.

Harold Cardinal
President
Indian Association of Alberta
Speaking at the presentation by the Indian Chiefs of Alberta to the Prime Minister and Government of Canada
4 June 1970

So, we come
back to the basic
question: if RCAP
was a roadmap for
reconciliation and if
Gathering Strength
took a few steps,
however tentative,
to follow that
roadmap, why has the
RCAP promise to
Aboriginal people not
been fulfilled?

should work with the Assembly of First Nations to determine how the *Gathering Strength* framework could best be implemented with First Nations. The result was *An Agenda for Action with First Nations*, an initial work plan that First Nations and the government would jointly pursue. As stated earlier, the government response tried to address the challenge of dealing with a voluminous and substantive report in a timely manner. Certainly, the senior management of DIAND at the time recognized that as *Gathering Strength* was being implemented, they would also have to continue assessing the detail of the *RCAP Report*. DIAND senior management gave such assurances to the national Aboriginal leaders and, indeed, to the commissioners of RCAP.

So, we come back to the basic question: if RCAP was a roadmap for reconciliation and if *Gathering Strength* took a few steps, however tentative, to follow that roadmap, why has the RCAP promise to Aboriginal people not been fulfilled? The business of government is complex, but there are two obvious contributing factors examined here.

The first is that the minister of Indian Affairs changed. Having delivered the commitments of *Gathering Strength* on behalf of the federal government, Jane Stewart was moved shortly after and replaced by Bob Nault. The new minister's primary priority seemed to be a new *First Nations Governance Act*, which First Nations charged was not developed in partnership as the government seemed to have promised in *Gathering Strength*. Yes, the resources that were attached to *Gathering Strength* were invested, but the promise of reconciliation was lost. And, in fact, some First Nations leaders would argue that this is a pattern they have seen with the federal government over the past thirty years. One minister who works cooperatively and makes progress on First Nations issues is often replaced by a minister who prefers to work unilaterally. It seems fair to ask not only how reconciliation can be built in such circumstances, but also how First Nations can be expected to develop in the context of ever-changing directions in government policies and priorities.

The second contributing factor is one that seems to best exemplify the reality that the historic patterns of this relationship between the federal government and First Nations have not really changed. In the mid-nineties, as RCAP was preparing its report, the federal government was fighting to eliminate the deficit, in part, through a review of government expenditures referred to as *program review*. In the course of pursuing that objective, the minister and the senior management of DIAND were approached by central agencies to make a contribution. The idea was that there would be no absolute cuts to programs for First Nations, partly in recognition of the rapidly growing First Nation population. But, DIAND could contribute by reducing the year-to-year growth in those programs and then capping that growth at two per cent per year for the next couple of years.

Throughout the late 1980s, those programs had been experiencing double-digit growth based on a number of factors. Inflation and population growth were two basic factors, but there were two other unique aspects. The first was that the additional status Indian population created by the passage of Bill C-31 had to be accommodated. The second was that federal policy had always referred to certain First Nations' programs as quasi-statutory; these are programs that provincial governments make available to all citizens. The federal government's policy commitment had been to fund these programs at levels equivalent to the provinces so that First Nations people would not become second-class citizens. These programs include elementary and secondary education, social welfare, and child and family services. As the Bill C-31 population was accommodated and provinces began to cut back their programs to fight their own deficits, growth in First Nations programs had begun to decline throughout the early 1990s.

The specific program review proposal put to DIAND by central agencies was that the overall growth in First Nations' program funding would be six per cent in 1995–96, three per cent in 1996–97, and two per cent for the two years thereafter (that is, until the end of that particular fiscal framework).[10] Earlier efforts to move to this type of expenditure *cap* had been resisted by senior management at DIAND, and this proposal engendered much debate. At least one member of senior management believed that it would be naïve to expect the cap to be easily removed once in place. Others felt strongly that eliminating the deficit was an important objective and that, at the end of the fiscal framework and certainly once the deficit was eliminated, there would have to be a fair and open assessment of whether that cap on First Nations programs could be fairly sustained. It was in this belief that the DIAND minister and senior management had agreed to the cap, and it was those oral assurances given to First Nations leadership that tempered their protests against the decision.

Astoundingly, the overall growth in the DIAND envelope for basic services for First Nations remains capped at two per cent, eleven years after it was first capped at this same level. This raises the following questions:

- What kind of an impact is this arbitrary cap having?

- Is this the way other levels of government are being treated? Perhaps, deficit-fighting measures that applied to the provinces are still in place as well.

- What explains the length of time this measure has been in place for First Nations?

One way of beginning to understand the impact of the cap is to note that over this same timeframe, inflation had been growing at a rate of two per cent per year, the same as the First Nations population growth. As the auditor general already pointed out in 2006: "Funding for First Nations programs has increased in recent years, but not at a rate equal to population growth. Indian and Northern Affairs Canada's funding increased by only 1.6 percent, excluding inflation, in the five years from 1999 to 2004, while Canada's Status Indian population, according to the Department, increased by 11.2 percent."[11] The impact of the two per cent cap is complicated by the fact that, as noted earlier, some of the programs for First Nations are deemed to be quasi-statutory and therefore should keep track of provincial expenditures. What this has forced the Department to do is reallocate from First Nations programs such as capital, housing, and operations and management to programs such as elementary and secondary education and child and family services. In 2006, an internal study by the Department calculated that by 2004–5, they had already been forced to transfer $500 million in the two per cent cap era.[12] At this point, it should be noted that the government is not publishing any information about the impact of these reallocations on First Nations communities. For example, one might ask what kind of infrastructure deficit is being created in First Nations communities and whether this is creating a health and safety risk, but the answers to such questions are not publicly available. As an aside, it is worth noting that this lack of public data represents a poor example for a government that is often probing First Nations about accountability and transparency.

It is important to note here that successive governments have made additional investments in some of DIAND's First Nations programs, but those investments do not compensate for this cap and, without reasonable base funding, the impact of additional investments is reduced. As DIAND has noted: "Most of the adjustments are for targeted programs, many of which are to remedy backlogs and historical socio-economic gaps. Although valuable, these adjustments do not significantly help First Nations deal with most services' year-over-year volume and price pressures because the impact of these pressures has been greater than the funding growth provided by Parliament."[13]

The treatment of First Nations stands in sharp contrast to the treatment of provinces in the post-federal deficit world. There are two primary federal programs to support the provinces in their delivery of basic programs and services to their citizens, the Canada Health and Social Transfers to all provinces and the Equalization that provides support to the so-called have-not provinces. By 2009–10, the Canada Health and Social Transfers will have increased by 33 per cent over the previous five years. Equalization received increases of 9.9 per cent in 2004–05 and 8.4 per cent in 2005–06 and a growth rate of 3.5 per cent for the subsequent 10 years.

For those that think of Canada as a caring, compassionate country, the question becomes: What justifies leaving this two per cent cap on First Nations programming when it clearly does not allow their funding to keep pace with inflation and population growth?

+ Is it because the quality of life gap between First Nations and non-Aboriginal Canadians has closed significantly? No, in fact, by all reports, the narrowing of this gap has slowed since funding was capped.

+ Is it because our political leaders are unaware of the situation? This is unlikely since, as noted above, DIAND mounted a major review of the situation in 2006 and a draft report entitled *First Nations Basic Services Cost Drivers Project* was available in November of that year.

By the mid-1980s, it was widely and publicly recognized that the residential school experience, in the north and in the south, like smallpox and tuberculosis in earlier decades, had devastated and continued to devastate communities. The schools were, with the agents and instruments of economic and political marginalization, part of the contagion of colonization. In their direct attack on language, beliefs and spirituality, the schools had been a particularly virulent strain of that epidemic of empire, sapping the children's bodies and beings.

Report of the Royal Commission on Aboriginal Peoples Volume 1: Looking Forward, Looking Back

+ Is it motivated by a government desire to encourage First Nations to agree to *transform* these programs? Again, this would seem strange since this was one of the avowed purposes of the Kelowna Accord, which the current federal government has rejected.

+ Is it an effort by government to force First Nations to rely more heavily on their own-source revenues to finance basic services? This too would be strange because, as noted previously, the Assembly of First Nations had already agreed in the context of the federal response to RCAP, and that was to undertake a joint process with the federal government to examine the circumstances under which the principles of the Equalization Program, which takes into account of own-source revenues, could be adapted to a block transfer to First Nations. In fact, a joint First Nation-Federal Task Force had started working on this until the federal government withdrew.

+ Is it motivated by an ongoing concern with accountability in First Nation communities? Once again, if this was the case, why would the federal government not take the direct approach and pursue the initiatives the current National Chief of the Assembly of First Nations has repeatedly said he is prepared to champion, including the very extensive process that was part of the Kelowna Accord (including a national committee of Chiefs) and that actually began work after the agreement on Kelowna was first reached.

+ Is it because Canadian citizens generally are unaware of the quality of life in many First Nations communities? This is a plausible explanation and a helpful one for anyone who wishes to continue to believe that Canadians are a caring people. Most First Nations are in rural or remote locations. For whatever reasons, DIAND does not make an effort to focus its annual public documents on comparisons of quality of life statistics between First Nations and non-Aboriginal Canadians and it does not make an effort to explore comparisons between per capita funding for provincial schools and what it provides to First Nations schools. There are encouraging signs that if Canadians knew more of the poverty in First Nations communities, they would demand action. The polling around the Kelowna Accord seems to illustrate that, as does the public reaction when a member of International Save the Children Alliance drew attention to third world poverty in Northern Ontario First Nations communities in 2007.[14]

Of course, the dangerous thing about exploring these possible rationales is that they lead to the unfortunate conclusion that the federal government is practicing a subtle form of discrimination in the funding of First Nations. This is likely to continue to be the conclusion of more First Nations leaders as they understand the situation more clearly.

The rationale for the federal government's continued maintenance of a two per cent cap on the funding of First Nations core programs is not clear, but one is led to the belief that it has more to do with those false assumptions about Aboriginal people that RCAP discussed than any rational purpose. Returning to the Prime Minister's apology in the House of Commons, it is clear that for First Nations, "forging a new relationship between aboriginal peoples and other Canadians, a relationship based on knowledge of our shared history, a respect for each other and a desire to move forward together with a renewed understanding that strong families, strong communities, and vibrant cultures and traditions [that] will contribute to a stronger Canada for all of us"[15] requires that this issue be addressed in a straightforward and mutually acceptable manner.

Notes

[1] Prime Minister Stephen Harper's statement of apology [emphasis added] (see Appendix 1). Retrieved 24 November 2008 from: http://pm.gc.ca/eng/media.asp?id=2149

[2] Royal Commission on Aboriginal Peoples [RCAP] (1996:248). *Report of the Royal Commission on Aboriginal Peoples, Volume 1: Looking Forward, Looking Back*. Ottawa, ON: Minister of Supply and Services Canada.

[3] RCAP (1996:249).

[4] RCAP (1996:252).

[5] RCAP (1996:249).

[6] Hurley, Mary C. (2007). *Legislative Summary: Bill C-44: An Act to Amend the Canadian Human Rights Act*. Ottawa, ON: Library of Parliament.

[7] Government of Canada (1997). *Gathering Strength: Canada's Aboriginal Action Plan*. Ottawa, ON: Minister of Public Works and Government Services Canada.

8 Government of Canada (1998). *Statement of Reconciliation: Learning from the Past*, January 7, 1998 (see Appendix 1). Retrieved 30 September 2008 from: http://www.ainc-inac.gc.ca/gs/rec_e.html

9 Government of Canada (1998:1). Canada's Aboriginal Action Plan Focused on Communities, Founded on Reconciliation and Renewal. *News Release* 1-9801, Ottawa, January 7, 1998.

10 Based on author's personal knowledge.

11 Office of the Auditor General of Canada (2006:para. 5.4). Chapter 5: Management of Programs for First Nations. *A Status Report of the Auditor General of Canada to the House of Commons—May 2006*. Ottawa, ON: Minister of Public Works and Government Services Canada. Retrieved 30 September 2008 from: http://www.oag-bvg.gc.ca/internet/English/parl_oag_200605_e_1118.html

12 Indian and Northern Affairs Canada (2006). First Nations Basic Services, Cost Driver Project: Draft Final Report [internal unpublished document].

13 Indian and Northern Affairs Canada (2006:6). First Nations Basic Services, Cost Driver Project: Draft Final Report [internal unpublished document].

14 *See*: Silversides, Anne (2007). Poverty and human development: The North "like Darfur." *Canadian Medical Association Journal* 177(9):1013–1014. Retrieved 30 March 2009 from: http://www.pubmedcentral.nih.gov/picrender.fcgi?artid=2025628&blobtype=pdf

15 Prime Minister Harper offers full apology on behalf of Canadians for the Indian Residential Schools system. June 11, 2008. Ottawa, ON: Office of the Prime Minister. Retrieved 4 September 2008 from: http://www.pm.gc.ca/eng/media.asp?id=2149

PROGRAMME OF STU[DIES]

THE Programme of studies herein prescribed shall be followed by the

DIES FOR INDIAN SCHOOLS.

teacher as far as the circumstances of his school permit, &c.—*Continued.*

SUBJECT.	STANDARD I.	STANDARD II.	STANDARD III.	STANDARD IV.	STANDARD V.	STANDARD VI.
Geography			Development of geographical notions by reference to geographical features of neighbourhood. Elementary lessons on direction, distance, extent.	(d) General study from globe and maps. The hemisphere, continent, oceans and large islands, their relative positions and size. The continents: position, climate, form, outline, surroundings, principal mountains, rivers, lakes; the most important countries, productions, people, interesting facts and associations.	Simple study of the important countries in each continent, &c., &c.	(e) Observation to accompany the study of geography: apparent movements of the sun, moon and stars, and varying time of their rising and setting; difference in heat of the sun's rays at different hours of the day; change in the direction of the sun's rays coming through a school-room window at the same hour during the year; varying length of noon-day shadows; changes of the weather, wind and seasons.
Ethics	The practice of cleanliness, obedience, respect, order, neatness.	Right and wrong. Truth. Continuance of proper appearance and behaviour.	Independence. Self-respect. Develop the reason for proper appearance and behaviour.	Industry. Honesty. Thrift.	Citizenship of Indians. Patriotism. Industry. Thrift. Self-maintenance. Charity. Pauperism.	Indian and white life. Patriotism. Evils of Indian isolation. Enfranchisement. Labour the law of life. Relations of the sexes as to labour. Home and public duties.
Reading	First Primer	Second Primer	Second Reader	Third Reader	Fourth Reader	Fifth Reader.
Recitation	To begin in Standard II, are to be in line with what is taught in English, and developed into			pieces of verse and prose which contain the highest moral and patriotic maxims and thoughts.		
History			Stories of Indians of Canada and their civilization.	History of province in which school is situated.	Canadian History (commenced).	Canadian history (continued.)
Vocal Music	Simple Songs and Hymns. The subjects of the former to be interesting and patriotic.			The tones bright and cheerful.		
Calisthenics	Exercises, frequently accompanied by singing, to afford variation during work and to			improve physique.		
Religious Instruction	Scripture Reading. The Ten Commandments. Lord's Prayer. Life of Christ, &c., &c.					

NOTE.—ENGLISH.—Every effort must be made to induce pupils to speak English, and to teach them to
READING.—Pupils must be taught to read loudly and distinctly. Every word and sentence must
sentence, in their own words, in English, and also in their own language if the
GENERAL.—Instruction is to be direct, the voice and blackboard being the principal agents. The
N.B.—It will be considered a proof of the incompetency of a teacher, if pupils are found to read in
mark applies to all teaching, viz.:—Everything must be thoroughly understood, before a pupil

understand it; unless they do, the whole work of the teacher is likely to be wasted.
be fully explained to them, and from time to time they should be required to state the sense of a lesson or
teacher understands it.
unnecessary use of text books to be avoided.
"parrot fashion" only, i.e., without in the least understanding what they read. And the following re-
is advanced to further studies.

Photo: Courtesy of Legacy of Hope Foundation

(This photo can also be found, along with many other resources, at www.wherearethechildren.ca)

Apology and Reconciliation
A Timeline of Events

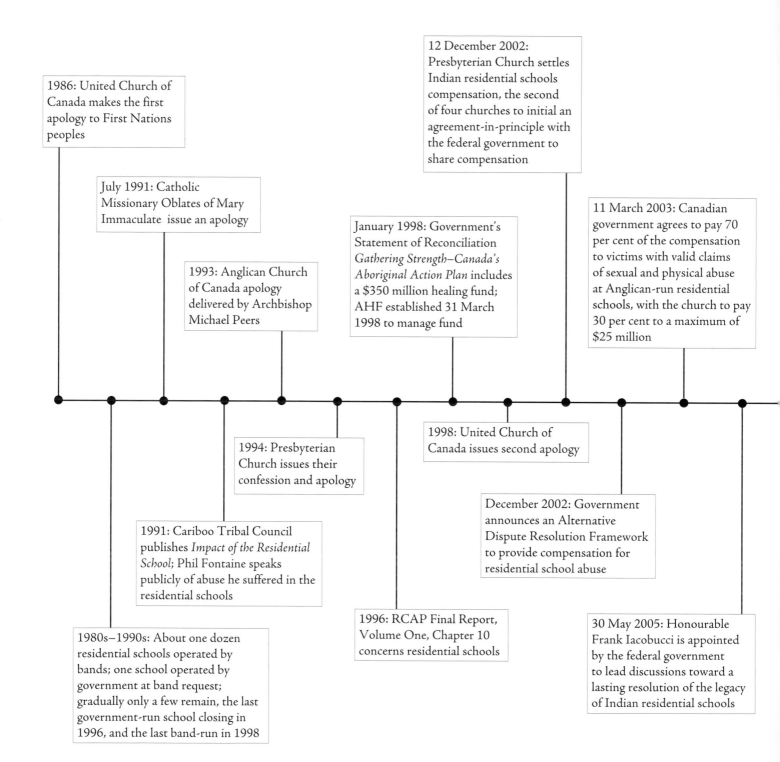

1986: United Church of Canada makes the first apology to First Nations peoples

July 1991: Catholic Missionary Oblates of Mary Immaculate issue an apology

1993: Anglican Church of Canada apology delivered by Archbishop Michael Peers

January 1998: Government's Statement of Reconciliation *Gathering Strength–Canada's Aboriginal Action Plan* includes a $350 million healing fund; AHF established 31 March 1998 to manage fund

12 December 2002: Presbyterian Church settles Indian residential schools compensation, the second of four churches to initial an agreement-in-principle with the federal government to share compensation

11 March 2003: Canadian government agrees to pay 70 per cent of the compensation to victims with valid claims of sexual and physical abuse at Anglican-run residential schools, with the church to pay 30 per cent to a maximum of $25 million

1994: Presbyterian Church issues their confession and apology

1998: United Church of Canada issues second apology

1991: Cariboo Tribal Council publishes *Impact of the Residential School*; Phil Fontaine speaks publicly of abuse he suffered in the residential schools

December 2002: Government announces an Alternative Dispute Resolution Framework to provide compensation for residential school abuse

1980s–1990s: About one dozen residential schools operated by bands; one school operated by government at band request; gradually only a few remain, the last government-run school closing in 1996, and the last band-run in 1998

1996: RCAP Final Report, Volume One, Chapter 10 concerns residential schools

30 May 2005: Honourable Frank Iacobucci is appointed by the federal government to lead discussions toward a lasting resolution of the legacy of Indian residential schools

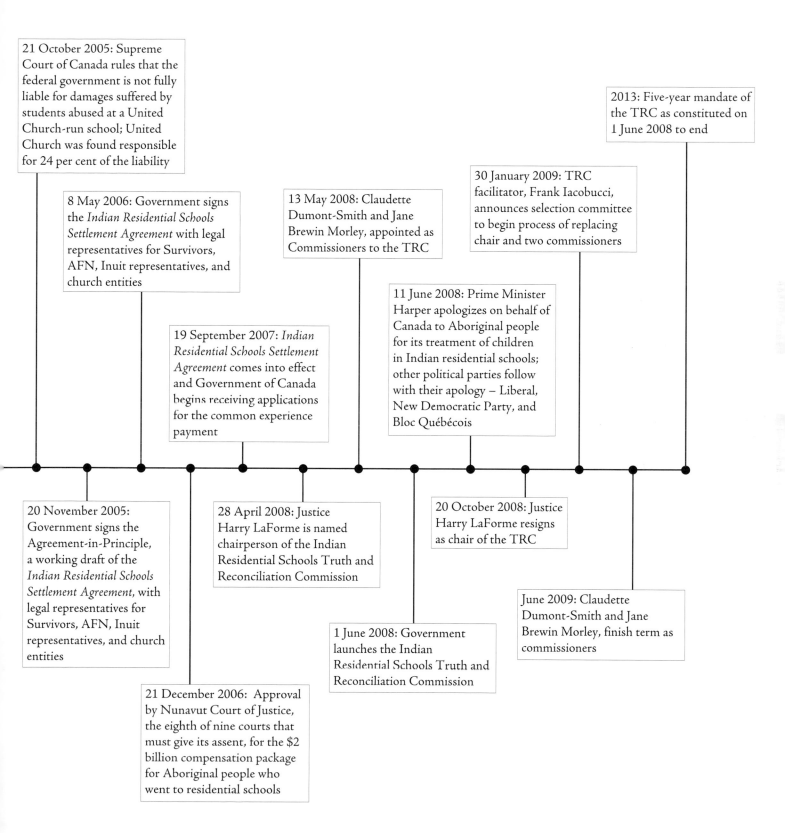

21 October 2005: Supreme Court of Canada rules that the federal government is not fully liable for damages suffered by students abused at a United Church-run school; United Church was found responsible for 24 per cent of the liability

2013: Five-year mandate of the TRC as constituted on 1 June 2008 to end

8 May 2006: Government signs the *Indian Residential Schools Settlement Agreement* with legal representatives for Survivors, AFN, Inuit representatives, and church entities

13 May 2008: Claudette Dumont-Smith and Jane Brewin Morley, appointed as Commissioners to the TRC

30 January 2009: TRC facilitator, Frank Iacobucci, announces selection committee to begin process of replacing chair and two commissioners

11 June 2008: Prime Minister Harper apologizes on behalf of Canada to Aboriginal people for its treatment of children in Indian residential schools; other political parties follow with their apology – Liberal, New Democratic Party, and Bloc Québécois

19 September 2007: *Indian Residential Schools Settlement Agreement* comes into effect and Government of Canada begins receiving applications for the common experience payment

20 November 2005: Government signs the Agreement-in-Principle, a working draft of the *Indian Residential Schools Settlement Agreement*, with legal representatives for Survivors, AFN, Inuit representatives, and church entities

28 April 2008: Justice Harry LaForme is named chairperson of the Indian Residential Schools Truth and Reconciliation Commission

20 October 2008: Justice Harry LaForme resigns as chair of the TRC

June 2009: Claudette Dumont-Smith and Jane Brewin Morley, finish term as commissioners

1 June 2008: Government launches the Indian Residential Schools Truth and Reconciliation Commission

21 December 2006: Approval by Nunavut Court of Justice, the eighth of nine courts that must give its assent, for the $2 billion compensation package for Aboriginal people who went to residential schools

177

Gerald Taiaiake Alfred

Gerald Taiaiake Alfred is a Kanien'kehaka (Mohawk) philosopher, writer, and teacher. Taiaiake was born in Montreal in 1964 and raised on the Kahnawake Mohawk Territory where he lived until 1996, except for his service in the US Marine Corps during the 1980s. He presently lives on Snaka Mountain in Wsanec Nation Territory in British Columbia with his wife and sons. He studied history at Concordia University in Montreal and holds a doctorate in Government from Cornell University. Taiaiake began his teaching career at Concordia University and is now Director and Professor of Indigenous Governance, a program he founded, at the University of Victoria.

Taiaiake has lectured at many universities and colleges in Canada, the United States, England, and Australia and has served as an advisor to the Royal Commission on Aboriginal Peoples, to the Mohawk Council of Kahnawake, and to many other Indigenous governments and organizations.

Taiaiake has been awarded a Canada Research Chair, a National Aboriginal Achievement Award in the field of education, and the Native American Journalists Association award for best column writing. His writing includes numerous scholarly articles and contributed essays in newspapers, journals, and magazines as well as three books, Wasáse (Broadview, 2005), a runner-up for the McNally Robinson Aboriginal Book of the Year in 2005; the influential and best-selling Peace, Power, Righteousness (Oxford University Press, 1999); and Heeding the Voices of Our Ancestors (Oxford University Press, 1995).

Restitution is the Real Pathway to Justice for Indigenous Peoples

It is my contention that reconciliation must be intellectually and politically deconstructed as the orienting goal of Indigenous peoples' political and social struggles. I see reconciliation as an emasculating concept, weak-kneed and easily accepting of half-hearted measures of a notion of justice that does nothing to help Indigenous peoples regain their dignity and strength. One of my concerns in any discussion of reconciliation is finding ways to break its hold upon our consciousness so that we can move towards a true and lasting foundation for justice that will result in meaningful changes in the lives of Indigenous peoples and in the return of their lands.

Without massive restitution made to Indigenous peoples, collectively and as individuals, including land, transfers of federal and provincial funds, and other forms of compensation for past harms and continuing injustices committed against the land and Indigenous peoples, reconciliation will permanently absolve colonial injustices and is itself a further injustice. This much is clear in our Indigenous frame of understanding of the past and present of our shared histories, even if Indigenous leaders are too afraid of the political repercussions and unwilling to make the necessary sacrifices to advance such an agenda.

Other people's understandings of the nature of the problem we are facing are a more complex issue. The complete ignorance of Canadian society about the facts of their relationship with Indigenous peoples and the wilful denial of historical reality by Canadians detracts from the possibility of any meaningful discussion on true reconciliation. Limited to a discussion of history that includes only the last five or ten years, the corporate media and general public focus on the inefficiently spent billions of dollars per year handed out through the Department of Indian and Northern Affairs system. The complex story of what went on in the past and the tangled complexities of the past's impact on the present and future of our relationships are reduced to questions of entitlements, rights, and good governance within the already established institutions of the state. Consider the effect of lengthening our view and extending society's view. When considering 100 or 300 years of interactions, it would become clear even to white people that the real problem facing their country is that nations are fighting over questions of conquest and survival, of empire or genocide, and of moral claims to be a just society. Considering the long view and true facts, the Indian problem becomes a question of right and wrong for justice at its most basic form.

Something was stolen, lies were told, and they have never been made right. That is the crux of the problem. If we do not shift away from the pacifying discourse of reconciliation and begin to reframe people's perceptions of the problem so that it is not a question of how to reconcile with colonialism that faces us but instead how to use restitution as the first step towards creating justice and a moral society, we will be advancing colonialism, not decolonization. What was stolen must be given back, and amends must be made for the crimes that were committed from which all non-Indigenous Canadians, old families and recent immigrants alike, have gained their existence as people on this land and citizens of this country.

Restitution is purification.

When I say to a settler, "Give it back," am I talking about them giving up the country and moving away? No. Irredentism has never been in the vision of our peoples. When I say, "Give it back," I am talking about settlers demonstrating respect for what we share—the land and its resources—and making things right by offering us the dignity and freedom we are due and returning enough of our power and land for us to be self-sufficient.

Restitution is not a play on white guilt; that is what reconciliation processes have become. Guilt is a monotheistic concept foreign to Indigenous cultures; it does not brood under the threat of punishment over past misdeeds to the point of moral and political paralysis. Restitution is purification. It is a ritual of disclosure and confession in which there is an acknowledgement and acceptance of one's harmful actions and a genuine demonstration of sorrow and regret, constituted in reality by putting forward a promise to never again do harm and by redirecting one's actions to benefit the one who has been wronged. Even the act of proposing a shift to this kind of discussion is a radical challenge to the reconciling negotiations that try to fit us into the colonial legacy rather than to confront and defeat it. When I speak of restitution, I am speaking of restoring ourselves as peoples, our spiritual power, dignity, and the economic bases for our autonomy. Canadians understand implicitly that reconciliation will not force them to question what they have done, but it will allow them to congratulate themselves for their forbearance and understanding once Indigenous peoples—or, to be precise, using the language of the conciliatory paradigm, *Aboriginal peoples*—are reconciled with imperialism. Reconciliation may be capable of moving us beyond the unpalatable stench of overt racism in public and social interactions. This would be an easy solution to the problem of colonialism for white people, and no doubt most would be satisfied with this obfuscation of colonial realities. But logically and morally, there is no escaping that the real and deeper problems of colonialism are a direct result of the theft of our lands, which cannot be addressed in any way other than through the return of those lands to us.

There are at least two aspects of this large problem. The first is comprehension of the economic dimension; the continuing effect upon our communities of being illegally dispossessed of their lands. The second is the social dimension; the political and legal denials of collective Indigenous existences. Recasting the *Onkwehonwe* (original people) struggle as one of seeking restitution as the precondition to reconciliation is not extremist or irrational, as most Indigenous intellectual and political leaders and certainly all white people will no doubt respond. Restitution, as a broad goal, involves demanding the return of what was stolen, accepting reparations (either land, material, or monetary recompense) for what cannot be returned, and forging a new socio-political relationship based on Canadians' admission of wrongdoing and acceptance of the responsibility and obligation to engage Indigenous peoples in a restitution-reconciliation peace-building process.

The other side of the problem is methodological; the lessons of Indigenous people's struggles for self-determination since the mid-twentieth century are that restitution and reconciliation can only be achieved through contention and the generation of constructive conflict with the state and with the Canadian society through the resurgence and demonstration of Indigenous power in the social and political spheres. From the Red Power Movement through to the Oka Crisis and the new generation of warrior societies, history has demonstrated that it is impossible either to transform the colonial society from within colonial institutions or to achieve justice and peaceful coexistence without fundamentally

Put simply, the imperial enterprise called "Canada" that is operating in the guise of a liberal democratic state is, by design and culture, incapable of just and peaceful relations with Indigenous peoples.

transforming the institutions of the colonial society themselves. Put simply, the imperial enterprise called "Canada" that is operating in the guise of a liberal democratic state is, by design and culture, incapable of just and peaceful relations with Indigenous peoples. The consistent failure of negotiated solutions to achieve any meaningful change in the lives of Indigenous peoples or to return control of the land over to them proves this fact (agreeing to govern and use the land as would a white man in return for recognition of your governing authority does not count as liberation from colonialism). Real change will happen only when settlers are forced into a reckoning of who they are, what they have done, and what they have inherited; then they will be unable to function as colonials and begin instead to engage other peoples as respectful human beings.

There are serious constraints to the recognition of Indigenous rights in this country because the imperative to assimilate all difference is, in fact, an inherent feature of liberal democracy. Attempts to move away from the racist paternalism so typical of all colonial countries are handicapped by the framing of the entire decolonization project in the legal and political context of a liberal democratic state. Detached from the colonial mythology of the settler society through the application of a disciplined logic of just principles, Indigenous-settler relations cannot be obviously reconciled without deconstructing the institutions that were built on racism and colonial exploitation. For justice to be achieved out of a colonial situation, a radical rehabilitation of the state is required. Without radical changes to the state itself, all proposed changes are ultimately assimilative.

There are fundamental differences between Indigenous and Canadian models of societal organization and governance. Indigenous cultures and the governing structures that emerged from within them are founded on relationships and obligations of kinship relations, on the economic view that sustainability of relationships and perpetual reproduction of material life are prime objectives, on the belief that organizations should bind family units together with their land, and on a conception of political freedom that balances a person's autonomy with accountability to one's family. Contrast this to the liberal democratic state in which the primary relationship is among rights-bearing citizens and the core function of government is to integrate pre-existing social and political diversities into the singularity of a state, assimilating all cultures into a single patriotic identity, and in which political freedom is mediated by distant, supposedly representative structures in an inaccessible system of public accountability that has long been corrupted by the influence of corporations.

How can anyone expect that these two totally different political cultures are reconcilable? They are not. Colonial institutions and the dysfunctional subcultures they have spawned within Indigenous communities are the result of failed attempts to force Indigenous peoples into a liberal democratic mould. Given the essential conflict of form and objectives between Indigenous and liberal governance, one or the other must be transformed in order for a reconciliation to occur. As majoritarian tyrannies within colonial situations, liberal democratic societies always operate on the assumption that Indigenous peoples will succumb and submit to the overwhelming cultural and numerical force of the settler society. Huge costs are involved, monetarily and socially, in the effort to make Indigenous individuals assimilate to liberal democracy and Judeo-Christian cultural values, with no justification other than those weak arguments formed on ideological and cultural prejudices toward the supposed superiority of Europe's cultural and intellectual heritage. This is why reconciliation, as it is commonly understood, is unjust; any accommodation to liberal democracy is a surrender of the very essence of any kind of an Indigenous existence.

Unprejudiced logics of decolonization point instead to the need to create coexistence among autonomous political communities. Eventual peaceful coexistence demands a decolonization process in which *Onkwehonwe* will be extricated from, not further entrenched within, the values, cultures, and practices of liberal democracy. If the goals of decolonization are justice and peace, then the process to achieve these goals must reflect a basic covenant on the part of both Indigenous peoples and settlers to honour each other's existence. This honouring cannot happen when one partner in the relationship is asked to sacrifice their heritage and identity in exchange for peace. This is why the only possibility of a just relationship between Indigenous peoples and the settler society is the conception of a nation-to-nation partnership between peoples, the kind of relationship reflected in the original treaties of peace and friendship consecrated between Indigenous peoples and the newcomers who started

But aboriginal rights, this really means saying "We were here before you. You came and took the land from us and perhaps you cheated us by giving us some worthless things in return for vast expanses of land and we want to re-open this question. We want you to preserve our aboriginal rights and to restore them to us." And our answer- it may not be the right one and may not be the one that is accepted but it will be up to all of you people to make your minds up and to choose for or against it and to discuss it with the Indians- our answer is "no."

Prime Minister Trudeau From a speech on Indian, Aboriginal, and treaty rights Vancouver, British Columbia 8 August 1969

arriving in our territories. The only way to remove ourselves from the injustice of the present relationship is to begin implementing a process of resurgence-apology-restitution and seeking to restore the pre-colonial relationship of sharing and cooperation among diverse peoples.

Canada rebukes attempts to reason logically through the problem in this way. Mainstream arguments about restitution and reconciliation always end up becoming conservative defences of obvious injustices against even the most principled and fair arguments for restitution. It should no doubt be commonly accepted that legitimizing injustices promotes further injustices. Tolerating crimes encourages criminality. But the present Canadian argument presumes that since the injustices are historical and the passage of time has certainly led to changed circumstances for both the alleged perpetrators and for the victims, the crime has been erased and there is no obligation to pay for it. This is the sophisticated version of the common settler sentiment: "The Indians may have had a rough go of it, but it's not my fault because I wasn't around one hundred years ago," or, "I bought my ranch from the government, fair and square!" In the wake of the Indian residential schools apology and the compensation of the *Settlement Agreement*, it must be said that half-hearted and legally constrained government apologies and small monetary payoffs of those remaining individuals who endured abuse in residential schools do not come close to true acknowledgement, much less moral, legal, or political absolution for the much larger crime of dispossession of an entire land mass.

The first argument—pro-restitution—is powerful in itself. It is precisely the reluctance of the settler to investigate and indict his own actions and those of his ancestors that allows the injustice to compound continuously and to entrench itself within the dominant culture. Given the facts and the reality that define Indigenous-settler relations, the counter-argument of historicity points to the necessity of restitution. Placing the counter-argument in an actual social and political context negates any power that it may otherwise have in a theoretical or mythical context. The key to this is in the assertion that the passage of time leads to changes in circumstance. This is fundamentally untrue, especially when made in relation to Indigenous peoples, Canadian society, and the injustice of a colonial relationship. Between the beginning of this century and the beginning of the last, people's clothes may have changed and their names may be different, but the games they play are the same. Without a substantial change in the circumstances of colonization, there is no basis for considering the historical injustice. The crime of colonialism is present today, as are its perpetrators, and there is yet no moral or logical basis for Indigenous peoples to seek reconciliation with Canada.

This essay is adapted from the author's discussion of reconciliation in *Wasáse: Indigenous Pathways of Action and Freedom* (Peterborough, ON: UTP/ Broadview Press, 2005).

Photographer: Jane Hubbard

Waziyatawin is a Wahpetunwan Dakota from the *Pezihutazizi Otunwe* (Yellow Medicine Village) in southwestern Minnesota. She received her doctorate in American history from Cornell University in 2000 and earned tenure and an associate professorship in the history department at Arizona State University where she taught for seven years. Waziyatawin currently holds the Indigenous Peoples Research Chair in the Indigenous Governance Program at University of Victoria. Her interests include projects centering on Indigenous decolonization strategies such as truth-telling and reparative justice, Indigenous women and resistance, the recovery of Indigenous knowledge, and the development of liberation ideology in Indigenous communities.

She is the author or editor of five volumes, including: *Indigenizing the Academy: Transforming Scholarship and Empowering Communities* (2004); *Remember This!: Dakota Decolonization and the Eli Taylor Narratives* (2005); *For Indigenous Eyes Only: A Decolonization Handbook* (2005); *In the Footsteps of Our Ancestors: The Dakota Commemorative Marches of the 21st Century* (2006); and, her most recent volume, *What Does Justice Look Like? The Struggle for Liberation in Dakota Homeland* (2008).

YOU CAN'T UN-RING A BELL:
DEMONSTRATING CONTRITION THROUGH ACTION

My grandfather, Eli Taylor, from the Sioux Valley Reserve in Manitoba, used to say, "There is no word for 'sorry' in the Dakota language. Just like you can't un-ring a bell, bad actions or words cannot be taken back." Thus, within this cultural world view, we must all act mindfully in order to maintain good relations with all of creation. In the event that we do not act respectfully and actually cause harm to others, our words cannot rectify the harm. Instead, we need to demonstrate contrition through our actions. In the context of a peoples-to-peoples relationship, it is also appropriate to think about the significance of action, rather than apology, as a means of addressing the harms perpetrated against Indigenous Peoples both in Canada and in the United States. Given the magnitude of these historical and ongoing harms, repairing the damage requires action on a colossal scale.

While the current initiatives in Canada are focusing on residential schools, settler society eludes responsibility for the broader harms perpetrated against Indigenous Peoples by narrowing the focus of the harms to be repaired. Because of the extensive violence of the residential school experience, we have been trained to forget that the schools were used as a tool to disconnect us from one another, from our spirituality and cultures, and from our lands. They were designed to compel our complete subjugation to the colonial state. Thus, the schools had served a larger colonial project. In stripping them from that context, settler society is attempting to maintain the colonial structure while throwing mere scraps to residential school Survivors for the terror and devastation wrought within colonial institutions. We need bigger solutions.

Similar experiences with colonial powers have meant similar legacies for Indigenous Peoples on both sides of the 49th parallel. In the Dakota homeland of *Minisota Makoce* (land Where the Waters Reflect the Skies), we are currently calling attention to the need for Minnesotans and the United States government to address these long-standing historical and contemporary harms. I have recently published a book entitled *What Does Justice Look Like? The Struggle for Liberation in Dakota Homeland*[1] to initiate what I hope will be a public discussion. In this book, I highlight a

When claims come to the table for our people we don't want society as a whole to be scared of what might come down because we are not looking at making changes that are going to be severely adverse to non-Aboriginal people. We are not looking at chasing them out of this land. We're prepared to sit and talk to them and negotiate and point out and work with them as to how we can both co-operate together.

Gerald Wesley
Hereditary Chief
Kitsumkalum Band
Speaking at the public hearings of the
Royal Commission on Aboriginal Peoples
Terrace, British Columbia
25 May 1993

four-step process for addressing the crimes of land theft, genocide, ethnic cleansing, and colonization. This process includes a need for a broad-scale truth-telling forum, a campaign to *TAKE DOWN THE FORT*, a program of land restoration and reparations, and, finally, the end of American colonization of Indigenous Peoples and homeland. While all Indigenous histories are not identical, they are similar enough to offer some relevancy to Indigenous Peoples in Canada.

Though the crimes of land theft, genocide, and colonization are well-documented on both sides of the Canadian-US border, most settlers still remain resistant to acknowledging the violent and morally reprehensible crimes perpetrated so that they could not only obtain Indigenous lands, but also so they could continue to inhabit them without fear of violent retribution. Thus, colonial governments were intent on eradicating the existence of Indigenous Peoples, either physically, culturally, or both. The genocidal practices range from outright attempts at physical extermination to residential school imprisonment, involuntary sterilization, destruction of our food sources and land bases, gendered segregation through incarceration, and the perpetration of ethnocide. Further, settler society has prevented us from living as Indigenous Peoples on our own lands. As Indigenous Peoples, we simply cannot reproduce or continue to survive if our populations are incarcerated, sterilized, and systematically attacked and our food sources as well as air, waters, and lands are destroyed. The antidote to these violent and repressive actions requires a commitment to support Indigenous life, lands, and ways of being. This requires a reworking of the existing social order.

As Dakota people have begun to think about justice in the context of our *Minisota* homeland, we have realized that before we can move to a discussion of justice we need to bring the injustices to the forefront of public attention. This, I believe, applies to the Canadian context as well. No one will be committed to righting the wrongs if they cannot recognize and name those wrongs. Thus, the first step in working toward justice involves establishing a truth-telling forum in which Indigenous Peoples can voice our suffering from the violent effects of European, Canadian, and American invasion, genocide, land theft, and colonization.

At the conclusion of the Truth and Reconciliation Commission in South Africa, Desmond Tutu stated that "No one in South Africa could ever again be able to say, 'I did not know,' and hope to be believed.'"[2] The hope is that we would reach a point in Canada and the United States in which settler society could no longer deny the crimes (both historical and ongoing) perpetrated against Indigenous Peoples with any semblance of credibility. Thus, truth-telling efforts whether in the form of a commission, a major educational effort, or some other forum must be conducted on a massive, public scale. At that point we can ask the questions in earnest: What does recognition of genocide demand? What does recognition of land theft demand? What does recognition of colonization demand? Awareness of truth compels some kind of action.

Once settler society acknowledges injustices and demonstrates contrition, they will create a moral imperative for restorative justice. The process of restorative justice is perhaps more easily conceived in stages. Once we initiate a phase of truth-telling, it will necessarily cause us to rethink the foundations upon which the nation-state and provinces were created.

One of those foundations is that the *settlement* of Indigenous land is benign or even benevolent. When the violence and nastiness of the imperial business is unmasked, we must question the morality of continuing to celebrate the nations' imperial and colonial icons. With that unmasking, not only do we realize that we cannot celebrate those icons, but we also realize we must pursue a campaign to *TAKE DOWN THE FORT*, both literally and metaphorically. While I employed this phrase to refer most tangibly to historic Fort Snelling in the state of Minnesota (the site of the Dakota concentration camp during the winter of 1862–63), it also applies to all monuments, institutions, place names, and texts in Canada and in the United States that continue to celebrate the perpetrators of genocide or the institutions and systems that facilitated the implementation of genocidal and unjust policies. The process of taking down the fort becomes an educational venture in itself and can assist in the truth-telling process. Any time Indigenous people challenge a beloved colonial icon, it becomes apparent just how invested settler society is in maintaining the status quo. Eradicating the symbols, then, becomes an important step in the struggle for justice.

To create a moral society, Canadians and Americans must then engage the next step in the movement toward justice: land restoration and reparations. While this usually invokes tremendous fear within settler

> To create a moral society, Canadians and Americans must then engage the next step in the movement toward justice: land restoration and reparations.

The reality is that restitution for land theft—no matter how long ago the crime was perpetrated—eventually requires the return of land.

society, there are ways to conceive the return of land that do not involve current settlers relinquishing their individual property rights, unless they wish to do so in the name of justice. In the state of Minnesota, for example, we can identify more than eleven million acres currently designated as federal, state, county, or metro-commissioned lands.[3] Settler society could immediately return those millions of acres to Dakota people without touching a single acre of privately held lands. The same is true of public or Crown lands in Canada. For justice to occur, the return of all Crown lands must be a given. The reality is that restitution for land theft—no matter how long ago the crime was perpetrated—eventually requires the return of land.

The return of land alone, however, is not enough to create justice. Instead, settler society also has to restore those lands to a pristine condition. This would require extensive cleanup efforts, particularly on the part of corporations, farmers, and resource extractors that have left horrendous environmental destruction in the wake of their activities. Together, settler and Indigenous Peoples alike will need to address all of these issues systematically. In addition, non-land-based reparations will also be a necessary element in restoring justice within Indigenous homelands. For example, other reparations might include environmental cleanup, infrastructure development for sustainable living, educational opportunities, healing centres, resources for language and culture revitalization, relocation expenses for displaced Indigenous Peoples, and debt relief.

In the end, however, none of this makes sense if institutions and systems of colonization remain in place. Ultimately, if Canadians, Americans, and Indigenous Peoples are going to create a peaceful and just society, all oppression must cease. Colonization, by its very nature, is antithetical to justice. Therefore, complete decolonization is a necessary end goal for a peaceful and just society. This would entail overturning the institutions, systems, and ideologies of colonialism that continue to affect every aspect of Indigenous life. In a nutshell, we must all rethink our ways of being and interacting in this world to create a sustainable, healthy, and peaceful co-existence with one another and with the natural world. While this may seem an impossibility given the sense of permanency we associate with the existing nation-states, the reality is that human beings are on the cusp of a great world change. The flourishing of empire has advanced societal models based on principles of domination, exploitation, and violence. This has served to harm human beings, plants, and animals as well as the air, lands, and waters thereby pushing us into a planetary crisis. Today we are witnessing the beginning of catastrophic collapses of the existing systems, both natural and man-made, as empire is ultimately self-destructive.

But, we have a choice. Author David Korten relates that this transformation "can play out in the mode of Empire, as a violent, self-destructive, last-man-standing competition for individual advantage. Or it can play out in the mode of Earth Community, as a cooperative effort to rebuild community; to learn the arts of sufficiency, sharing, and peaceful conflict resolution; and to marshal our human creativity to grow the generative potential of the whole."[4] I, for one, would prefer the latter option. If Canadians and Americans choose Earth Community, it will require all of us to rework the existing social order and to adopt a new set of values based on mutual respect and sustainability.

Contemplating this future requires expansive thinking from all of us. For non-Indigenous people, it asks that you challenge, re-examine, and reject the racist and colonialist programming to which you have grown accustomed. It also asks that you rethink the values of domination, consumption, and exploitation that have become a part of Canadian and American societies. For Indigenous Peoples, it requires that we awaken our consciousness to the potential for liberation. Most importantly, however, it requires all of us to move beyond a simple re-education and acknowledgement of past harms. It requires action that will fundamentally alter the current power imbalance. It requires action that will serve to ensure justice to the Original Peoples of this continent.

These questions are being raised at a time when the international community is beginning to address both the historical harms perpetrated against Indigenous Peoples globally and the contemporary harms we suffer because of ongoing subjugation and oppression. On 13 September 2007, the General Assembly of the United Nations adopted the *Declaration on the Rights of Indigenous Peoples* with an overwhelming majority. This declaration affirms both the individual and collective rights of Indigenous Peoples as a way to promote justice and peace for all human beings throughout the world without discrimination. Article

I understand the tragic history between the United States and Tribal Nations. And we've got to acknowledge that truth if we are going to move forward in a fair and honest way.

Barack Obama's Message for First Americans 24 October 2008

8 of the *Declaration* is particularly relevant to the discussion of how a state addresses tremendous crimes against humanity:

1. Indigenous Peoples and individuals have the right not to be subjected to forced assimilation or destruction of their culture.

2. States shall provide effective mechanisms for prevention of, and redress for:

   (*a*) Any action which has the aim or effect of depriving them of their integrity as distinct peoples, or of their cultural values or ethnic identities;

   (*b*) Any action which has the aim or effect of dispossessing them of their lands, territories or resources;

   (*c*) Any form of forced population transfer which has the aim or effect of violating or undermining any of their rights;

   (*d*) Any form of forced assimilation or integration;

   (*e*) Any form of propaganda designed to promote or incite racial or ethnic discrimination directed against them.[5]

Certainly, the Canadian government and its citizens are guilty of perpetrating every one of these internationally recognized crimes, as is the United States government. By eliminating or severely debilitating the original owners of the land and its resources, colonial powers have ensured that Indigenous Peoples could no longer threaten the genocidal and exploitative policies that would continue to enrich them and other citizens.

Article 8 of the *Declaration* directly dictates that both Canada and the United States have an obligation to acknowledge and offer redress for these harms. Reparations are not simply a potential option, they are a settler obligation and an Indigenous right.

NOTES

[1] This essay is adapted from the introductory chapter, "Envisioning Justice in Minnesota," in Waziyatawin (2008). *What Does Justice Look Like? The Struggle for Liberation in Dakota Homeland*. St. Paul, MN: Living Justice Press. For further information, visit: www.livingjusticepress.org

[2] Tutu, Desmond M. (1999:120). *No Future Without Forgiveness*. New York, NY: Doubleday.

[3] Minnesota Department of Natural Resources (2000). *Public Land and Mineral Ownership in Minnesota: A Guide for Teachers*. Revised May 2000. Retrieved 27 November 2008 from: http://files.dnr.state.mn.us/lands_minerals/PLteachersguide.pdf

[4] Korten, David (2006:63). *The Great Turning: From Empire to Earth Community*. San Francisco, CA: Berrett-Koehler Publishers, Inc.

[5] United Nations (2008:5). *United Nations Declaration on the Rights of Indigenous Peoples*. Retrieved 24 November 2008 from: http://www.un.org/esa/socdev/unpfii/documents/DRIPS_en.pdf

Sisters outside the Pukatawagan day school
with a group of boys wearing Plains Indian-style headdresses made from paper, circa 1960
Attributed to sister Liliane
National Archives of Canada, PA-195120

[Reprinted from the Legacy of Hope Foundation's *Where Are the Children?* exhibit catalogue (2003)]

David Hollinsworth

David Hollinsworth has worked with Aboriginal people since 1968 as both an activist and an academic. David taught Aboriginal Studies at Flinders University and at the University of South Australia (1972–1997). David is an Adjunct Professor at the University of Queensland and the University of the Sunshine Coast. David also works as a consultant in anti-racism and Indigenous affairs for the Commonwealth and various state governments as well as Aboriginal organizations. David was a founding member of the Stolen Generations Alliance (SGA) and has served as National Secretary and is now National Non-indigenous Co-Chair of the SGA. He was a founding member and delegate of the previous organization, the National Sorry Day Committee.

David's curriculum design, teaching, and publications focus on the history of the Stolen Generations and the intergenerational impact of government policies of child removal.

He has published widely on Aboriginal history and politics, Indigenous health, and on representations of Aboriginality. Major works include *Race and Racism in Australia, Third Edition* (2006) and *They Took the Children* (2003), which won the 2004 NSW Premier's Young People's History Award. David has an international reputation for his work on Australian racism and effective anti-racism strategies.

BEYOND SORRY:
MAKING THE APOLOGY
GENUINELY MEANINGFUL IN AUSTRALIA?

After many years of struggle by members of the Stolen Generations, Australian Prime Minister Kevin Rudd gave the Apology on the 13 February 2008. This apology was "for the laws and policies of successive Parliaments and governments"[1] and offers a watershed in relations between the government and Indigenous peoples, especially the Stolen Generations and their families. This national apology was a fundamental element in the 54 recommendations of the *Bringing Them Home (BTH)* report of the National Inquiry into the Separation of Aboriginal and Torres Strait Islander Children from Their Families conducted by the Human Rights and Equal Opportunity Commission between 1995 and 1997. Because the *BTH* report was released on the 26 May 1997, this date is commemorated as National Sorry Day, although its name and focus may change in the light of the apology having been made.

Between 1998 and 2003, all states and territories had made some form of acknowledgement and apology.[2] So too had most churches, some police departments, social workers, and more than one million individual Australians.[3] The Howard Government received the *BTH* report from co-chairs Sir Ronald Wilson and Mick Dodson, but refused to make an apology, supposedly because an apology would admit legal liability and because present-day Australians could not be expected to apologize for something "in the past" that they did not do. Prime Minister John Howard and Minister John Herron were adamant that what was done had no relevance to today, even claiming that the term "stolen generations" was a misnomer in that no entire generation was ever removed.[4] Reactions to this intransigence by members of the Stolen Generations were mixed.[5] Many felt that an apology was tenuous coming after a decade of rule by the Howard Government. Others stated that the delay meant they had to make their own peace rather than wait for others to recognize their claim. Yet the fact that there had been no national recognition and apology meant that healing could not commence for many.

In 2007, then opposition leader Kevin Rudd committed to making an apology as one of his first actions if he were to be elected prime minister

Strong commitment to the apology from Kevin Rudd turned around public opinion, but at the same time the Rudd Government ruled out compensation.

for the next government. After the election of the Rudd Government, Indigenous Affairs Minister Jenny Macklin moved quickly to consult with both peak organizations, the Stolen Generations Alliance and the National Sorry Day Committee (NSDC). Some members of the organizations favoured the 26 May (Sorry Day) as the logical choice for the apology as well as giving time to foster broader community support. In the end, the government opted to make the apology the first formal item of business for the 42nd Parliament on the 13 February 2008.

PUBLIC OPINION AND THE APOLOGY

As a result of the Howard Government's criticisms of the *BTH* report, public opinion polls indicated that 57 per cent were opposed to an apology while 40 per cent agreed: "Australians today weren't responsible for what happened in the past."[6] The Labor Party's preparedness to act was strengthened by effective campaigns by lobby groups, including Australians for Native Title and Reconciliation (ANTaR), Reconciliation Australia (RA), and especially GetUp! Action for Australia. In a poll released on the 7 February 2008, 55 per cent agreed and 36 per cent disagreed with the decision to apologize.[7] In the poll held immediately after the apology, these results had improved to sixty-eight per cent approval and twenty-two per cent disapproval.[8]

Such shifts in public opinion show the influence of political leadership (or its absence) can be significant. More than a decade of anti-Aboriginal rights rhetoric had severely eroded popular support built up in the pre-Mabo period.[9] Denial of the Stolen Generations and denigration of the *BTH* report was a key component of that campaign.[10] Strong commitment to the apology from Kevin Rudd turned around public opinion, but at the same time the Rudd Government ruled out compensation. Public opposition to monetary compensation is consistent with widely held beliefs that Indigenous people receive "special treatment" and unearned benefits from government.[11]

THE NEED FOR FULL REPARATIONS

A key component of the *BTH* report was measures to make reparations according to the van Boven principles,[12] including an acknowledgement and apology, recorded testimonies, guarantees against repetition through community education and appropriate legislation, and measures for rehabilitation, including language and cultural centres, family tracing and reunion services, assistance with identification as Aboriginal or Torres Strait Islander, and protection and access to records. The Report also called for measures for restitution: counselling services, Indigenous control of the welfare of Indigenous children, and monetary compensation for those directly affected by forcible removals for economically assessable damage, for example, for physical and mental harm, loss of opportunities, and loss of culture and land rights.[13]

The Howard Government response was limited within an individualized health and welfare framework to counselling and assistance for family tracing and reunions, but there was little support for group compensation measures and no monetary compensation.[14] The Rudd Government supports a much broader approach to the *BTH* recommendations, signalled in part by the involvement of the Department of Families, Housing, Community Services and Indigenous Affairs as well as the Department of Health and Ageing, and by a willingness to involve the SGA and the NSDC in developing and implementing the *BTH* program. The prime minister has firmly located this new approach within a determination "to close the gap that lies between us [Indigenous and non-Indigenous Australians] in life expectancy, educational achievement and economic opportunity."[15] Prime Minister Rudd recognized that without such practical actions, the apology could remain just a "moment of mere sentimental reflection."[16] In negotiations with the SGA, Minister Macklin continues to reject individual compensation despite this broader vision.

THE NEED FOR A NATIONAL COMPENSATION FUND

The *BTH* recommended a non-adversarial national compensation fund administered by an independent board and funded by all Australian governments. The fund would provide a lump sum in compensation to any person "who was removed from his or her family [unless the responsible government] can establish that removal was in the best interests of the child."[17] In addition, the fund should award extra compensation for specific harm and/or loss resulting from removal. Compensation was to be awarded under the following heads:

1. Racial discrimination.
2. Arbitrary deprivation of liberty.
3. Pain and suffering.
4. Abuse, including physical, sexual and emotional abuse.
5. Disruption of family life.
6. Loss of cultural rights and fulfilment.
7. Loss of native title rights.
8. Labour exploitation.
9. Economic loss.
10. Loss of opportunities.[18]

It is important to note that the proposed statutory compensation mechanism was not intended to displace the claimant's common law rights to seek damages.[19]

These are difficult issues, but the fundamental need for an accessible and affordable compensatory mechanism that minimizes the degree of re-traumatization of claimants is undeniable.[20] The extent of the harm and/or loss resulting from removals, however "well intentioned," was shown in the evidence to the National Inquiry.[21] It was reiterated in the 2006 Ministerial Council for ATSI Affairs' *Bringing them home report on the economic and social characteristics of those impacted on by past policies of forcible removal of children*, which compared various health and welfare outcomes for those removed to those who were not. This report found:

> •Higher rates of people with a disability or long-term health condition (68.8 per cent compared to 55.3 per cent)
> •Lower rates of completion of Year 10 – 12 schooling (28.5 per cent compared to 38.5 per cent)
> •Lower rates of living in owner occupied housing (16.9 per cent compared to 28.3 per cent)
> •Higher rates of being a victim of physical or threatened violence (33.5 per cent compared to 18.1 per cent)
> •Lower rates of retention to Year 10 (28.5 per cent compared to 38.5 per cent)
> •Lower rates of participation in sport or physical recreation activities (35.4 per cent compared to 47.0 per cent)
> •Higher rates of smoking (70.5 per cent compared to 51.2 per cent)

◆Higher rates of being arrested more than once in a five year period (14.6 per cent compared to 8.8 per cent)
◆Lower rates of full-time employment (17.8 per cent compared to 24.8 per cent).[22]

It is probably obvious that the hurt, loss, and trauma for many of those removed and for the families they left behind can never be adequately compensated. It will be difficult to assess such harms and find appropriate forms of compensation to individuals, to families, and to communities. However, one crucial element of a comprehensive compensation process is the official acknowledgement and recognition. One of those who received compensation under the Tasmanian State (provincial) scheme is Deb Hocking, a long-time activist for the Stolen Generations. Deb has stated:

> I think that a huge component of the healing process for Stolen Generations is acknowledgement of the pain and suffering that has taken place due to government processes, policies, or laws. The wording of this letter was extremely honest and heartfelt. Monetary compensation is one thing, however big or small, but to have recognition of acceptance of blame and a heartfelt apology has not only allowed me to begin my healing processes, but also been a huge step forward for Reconciliation in Tasmania.[23]

The alternative of refusing to provide a non-adversarial compensation mechanism will be hundreds of extremely expensive and traumatic civil litigations. There are plenty of lawyers who will work *pro bono*, but will take sizable percentages of any eventual payments. Class actions have already commenced in several states, yet this approach is inhumane, immoral, and likely to cost much more than a basic compensation scheme. In the most relevant case, after 13 years of struggle, Bruce Trevorrow received compensation of $450,000 for injuries and losses suffered, a further $75,000 in damages for his unlawful removal and false imprisonment, and $250,000 in lieu of interest.[24] Less than a year after his victory Bruce passed away, as have so many of those who deserve recognition and compensation.

Where possible, the Australian Government encourages land use and ownership issues to be resolved through mediation and negotiation rather than litigation. The ownership and management of land gives Indigenous Australians the capacity to forge new partnerships and pursue economic development.

Jenny Macklin
Indigenous Affairs Minister
Parliament House
Canberra, Australia
3 April 2009

Cunneen and Grix[25] have documented the many legal obstacles to successful litigation of Stolen Generations cases. These include:

* the problems Indigenous people have in overcoming statutory limitation periods, when these events occurred many decades ago;
* the difficulty of locating evidence, particularly when governments were lax in recording matters involving Indigenous people;
* the emotional and psychological trauma experienced by claimants in the hostile environment of an adversarial court system;
* the enormous financial cost;
* the length of time involved before the outcome of litigation is finalized;
* the problem of establishing specific liability for harms that have been caused; and
* overcoming the judicial view that 'standards of the time' justified removal in the best interests of the child.[26]

Australian courts have consistently favoured official documents over oral testimony, ignoring the obvious tendency to suppress negative information and to present positive accounts of government actions.[27] There is also the irony of having to prove in a court of law the actual harm from removal and detention, and then have the court dismiss that information and make the claimant a poor witness and the evidence suspect. The case for an alternative statutory compensation tribunal that could avoid re-traumatizing claimants is clear.[28]

WAYS FORWARD TO HEALING

While the need for adequate and accessible reparations is central, there are myriad needs in relation to healing of the hurt and harm done to members of the Stolen Generations, their families, and communities. As previously noted, members of the Stolen Generations and their families have higher than average poor physical and mental health. Some people cannot access Aboriginal medical services because they lack the necessary means of identification. Some find the available services and programs (including mainstream services) unsuitable or inappropriate. A national

Aboriginal and Torres Strait Islander healing foundation is needed to complement the work of the compensation tribunal. Such a foundation controlled by members of the Stolen Generations with expertise could establish best practice healing programs, advise governments and Indigenous health services on policies and programs, and develop and provide specific educational and training programs for Indigenous and non-Indigenous health practitioners. Members of Stolen Generations groups have visited Canada and strongly support the Aboriginal Healing Foundation model. The SGA is currently researching Canadian and Australian models of best practice to assist the Rudd Government to develop effective and comprehensive healing policies and programs.

An Australian Aboriginal and Torres Strait Islander healing foundation could provide seed funding to Stolen Generations healing circles and conduct research and policy work. It could also provide (perhaps in partnership with universities) pre-service and in-service training for health professionals and others whose work involves the families of Stolen Generations people. In partnership with the relevant government departments, it could oversee and support the existing family tracing and reunion (Link-Up) services. In the spirit of the *BTH* recommendations, the healing foundation could guide the provision of government and private sector services to the Stolen Generations and their families according to principles of self-determination and self-reliance.

CLOSE THE GAP

Prime Minister Rudd made an eloquent and powerful statement in the apology on the 13 February 2008. He rightly linked the symbolic significance of the apology to the need for practical steps to "close the gap" and to bring about the long overdue healing. We can only hope that this magnificent beginning is realized in a comprehensive program designed to implement all 54 recommendations of the *Bringing Them Home* report, including genuine reparations and healing for all those damaged by past policies and practices.

Notes

[1] Rudd, The Honourable Kevin (2008). *Prime Minister of Australia Speech Apology to Australia's Indigenous Peoples.* House of Representatives, Parliament House, 13 February 2008. Canberra, AU: Prime Minister of Australia (see Appendix 6). Retrieved 21 August 2008 from: http://www.pm.gov.au/media/Speech/2008/speech_0073.cfm

[2] Human Rights and Equal Opportunity Commission [HREOC] (no date). Content of apologies by State and Territory Parliaments. Retrieved 21 August 2008 from: http://www.hreoc.gov.au/social_justice/bth_report/apologies_states.html

[3] Australian Institute of Aboriginal and Torres Strait Islander Studies [AIATSIS] (no date). *Sorry Books: An Online Exhibition* (retrieved 21 August 2008 from: http://www1.aiatsis.gov.au/exhibitions/sorrybooks/sorrybooks_hm.htm); Senate Legal and Constitutional References Committee [SLCRC] (2000). *Healing: A Legacy of Generations.* Canberra, AU: Commonwealth of Australia (retrieved 21 August 2008 from: http://www.aph.gov.au/SENATE/COMMITTEE/legcon_ctte/completed_inquiries/1999-02/stolen/report/index.htm).

[4] *See* SLCRC (2000:292); *see also* Herron, John (2000:18). *Federal Government Submission: "Inquiry into the Stolen Generation" to the Senate Legal and Constitutional References Committee,* presented by Senator the Hon. John Herron, Minister for Aboriginal and Torres Strait Islander Affairs, March 2000.

[5] As a Founding Member of the National Sorry Day Committee (1998 to 2004) and a Founding Member of the Stolen Generations Alliance from 2007, I have had the privilege of shared conversations with hundreds of members of the stolen generations and their families. For privacy reasons, individuals are not identified. The views expressed in this article are mine, and not officially those of the SGA.

[6] Newspoll, Saulwick & Muller and Hugh Mackay (2000:34). Public Opinion on Reconciliation: Snap Shot, Close Focus, Long Lens. In Grattan, Michelle (ed.), *Reconciliation: Essays on Australian Reconciliation.* Melbourne, AU: Black Inc.

[7] GetUp! Action for Australia (2008). *Press Release* - Majority of Australians support apology for Stolen Generations: first poll in 11 years. Retrieved 21 August 2008 from: http://www.getup.org.au/files/media/getupreleasessorrypoll.pdf?dc=259,360455

[8] Metherell, M. (2008). PM said sorry - and so said more of us. *Sydney Morning Herald*, 18 February 2008, page 4. Retrieved 5 November 2008 from: http://www.smh.com.au/text/articles/2008/02/17/1203190653987.html

9 Markus, A. (2002). *Race: John Howard and the Remaking of Australia*. Sydney, AU: Allen and Unwin; Dodson, M. (2004). Indigenous Australians. In R. Manne (ed.), The Howard Years. Melbourne, AU: Black Inc: 119–143.

10 Manne, R. (2001). In denial: The stolen generations and the right. *Australian Quarterly Essay* 1.

11 Mickler, S. (1998). *The Myth of Privilege: Aboriginal Status, Media Visions, Public Ideas*. Fremantle, WA: Fremantle Arts Centre Press; Neill, R. (2002). *White Out: How politics is killing Black Australia*. Sydney, AU: Allen and Unwin.

12 The van Boven Principles include rights to restitution, compensation, and rehabilitation for victims who have had their human rights and fundamental freedoms violated. These principles were revised to ensure that domestic law is consistent with international legal obligations as well as to ensure that victims are compensated for a State's violation of international human rights and humanitarian law norms. The United Nations General Assembly adopted the revised version, the *Basic Principles and Guidelines on the Right to Reparation for Victims of Gross Violations of Human Rights and Humanitarian Law*, also known as the Van Boven/Bassiouni Principles on 16 December 2005. Retrieved 29 April 2009 from: http://www.unhchr.ch/Huridocda/Huridoca.nsf/0/85787a1b2be8a169802566aa00377f26?Opendocument

13 HREOC (1997). *Bringing Them Home: National Inquiry into the Separation of Aboriginal and Torres Strait Islander Children from Their Families*. Sydney, AU: Commonwealth of Australia.

14 Dodson, M. (1999). We all bear the cost if the apology is not paid. In B. Attwood and A. Markus (eds.), *The Struggle for Aboriginal Rights: A Documentary History*. Sydney, AU: Allen and Unwin: 352–354.

15 Rudd (2008:para. 1).

16 Rudd (2008: para. 26).

17 HREOC (1997:312).

18 HREOC (1997:304).

19 HREOC (1997).

20 HREOC, Aboriginal and Torres Strait Islander Commission [ATSIC], and Public Interest Advocacy Centre [PIAC] (2001). *Moving Forward: achieving reparations for the stolen generations*. A national conference held 15–16 August 2001 in Sydney, Australia (retrieved 26 February 2009 from: http://www.hreoc.gov.au/social_justice/conference/movingforward/); Cunneen, C. (2005). Colonialism and historical injustice: reparations for Indigenous peoples. *Social Semiotics* 15(1):59–80.

21 HREOC, 1997.

[22] Ministerial Council for ATSI Affairs (2006:9). *Bringing them home: A Report on the economic and social characteristics of those impacted on by past policies of forcible removal of children.* Retrieved 21 August 2008 from:http://www.mcatsia.gov.au/cproot/593/4318/Bringing%20Them%20Home%20Baseline%20Report.pdf

[23] Personal communication, 8 May 2008.

[24] Lower, Gavin and Mark Dunn (2008). Stolen generation victim wins $250,000 more. *Herald Sun*, 2 February 2008. Retrieved 21 August 2008 from: http://www.news.com.au/heraldsun/story/0,21985,23146298-2862,00.html

[25] Cuneen, C. and J. Grix (2004). *The Limitations of Litigation in Stolen Generations Cases.* Research Discussion Paper 15. Canberra, AU: Australian Institute of Aboriginal and Torres Strait Islander Studies.

[26] Cunneen (2005:68).

[27] Cunneen and Grix (2004).

[28] PIAC (2000). *PIAC Submission to the Senate Legal and Constitutional References Committee Inquiry into the Stolen Generation.* Retrieved 21 August 2008 from: http://www.austlii.edu.au/au/journals/AILR/2000/37.html

Boys on the dock from the
Spanish Indian Residential School
Courtesy of Father William Maurice, S.J. Collection – The Shingwauk Project

Roland Chrisjohn is a member of the Oneida Nation of the Confederacy of the Haudenausaunee (Iroquois). He received his doctorate in Personality and Psychometrics from the University of Western Ontario, following which he obtained his certification as a clinical psychologist in 1986. Roland has been active in issues involving Aboriginal people in Canada for over 40 years. He has worked with Aboriginal young offenders, women's organizations, prisoners' associations, family and children services, and suicide intervention programs. He has taught such courses as personality, statistics, multivariate analysis, Native studies, world history, and education courses at six different universities in Canada. Roland is currently the director of the Native Studies program at St. Thomas University in Fredericton, New Brunswick. He has written more than 50 articles on a variety of subjects, and is the principal author of *The Circle Game: Shadows and Substance in the Indian Residential School Experience in Canada* (1997).

Tanya Wasacase is a Cree woman from Saskatchewan. She received her bachelor's degree from St. Thomas University (Fredericton, New Brunswick) and her master's degree from the University of New Brunswick where she is currently pursuing her doctorate. She is part-time faculty working in the Native Studies program at St. Thomas University. Tanya's areas of interest are Indigenous peoples and public health, education, and social policy issues. She is currently engaged in the critical examination of social science research and is working to expose Western assumptions, prejudices, and biases underlying explanations of drug and alcohol abuse among North American Indigenous peoples. Central to her work is the development of an alternative historical materialist framework for understanding and treating drug and alcohol abuse in Indigenous communities.

HALF-TRUTHS AND WHOLE LIES:
RHETORIC IN THE "APOLOGY" AND
THE TRUTH AND RECONCILIATION COMMISSION

INTRODUCTION

Along with many of our colleagues, we have not been at all hesitant in making known our objections both to the pronouncement made in June 2008 by Canadian Prime Minister Stephen Harper (we believe the term "apology" is inappropriate) and to the Truth and Reconciliation Commission (TRC) installed by his government. However, apart from some television, radio, and newspaper coverage immediately after his statement, and several invited addresses since then, we have had little opportunity to expand upon our concerns.[1] Consequently, we appreciate this chance to set forth our position (or op-position). The fact that our objections can be stated, regardless of whether or not our arguments influence anyone, shows an encouraging current willingness to listen; in the past, governments, government agencies, and churches have silenced their critics by pretending not to hear them. We will focus our comments here as much as possible on the TRC. Anyone wishing to see the continuity between these remarks and those we made concerning Harper's statement may consult the document cited.

THE REALITY OF RHETORIC

If nothing else, the history of Canadian governmental policies toward Indigenous peoples should have taught us long ago to take their initiatives with a block of salt. We therefore find it troubling that so many people have embraced the government's own characterization of their words ("truth," "reconciliation," "apology," and so on) and deeds ("mistakes," "forging a new partnership," et cetera) at face value. Harper's government is the ideological, legal, ethical, and political successor to those governments that created residential schools in the first place. These successive governments recruited the churches of Canada to collude in their operation of these schools; maintained the institution for over 100 years regardless of any change in the nominal form of the government; accommodated, rather than investigated and litigated, criminal actions on the part of church and bureaucratic officials; ignored, denied, and then minimized the depredations recounted; and initiated a series of irrelevant temporizing maneuvers (public relations campaigns denigrating Aboriginal claims, public squabbles with churches over relative liability, alternative dispute resolutions, and so on) rather than deal squarely with issues. These are just a few of the many deeds that we could recount.

We must also bear in mind that the residential school system was only one aspect of a range of policies aimed toward Aboriginal peoples that similarly could and should be condemned.[2] All this happened, we have charged,[3] with the government's full knowledge that the policy created and supported was utterly in violation of the international law Canada had helped bring about but had contrived in such a way as to suit its own agenda. Consequently, are caution and skepticism not the most reasonable reactions to the June 2008 pronouncement emerging from this shameful record of transgression and evasion? It was not incidental that the campaign to frame the pronouncement as an apology began months before it was made, and remember that a year and a half earlier the Parliament of this government publicly considered, in all seriousness, the invention of a "new kind of apology" that would vacate any possibility of liability being attached to it. They did not consider at the same time a new kind of marriage proposal that committed neither party to marriage, a new kind of tax that gave back money to Canadians, or a new kind of truth that would not have to correspond to facts. What Indigenous peoples and Canadians-at-large have been subjected to in the entire run-up to the apology for residential schools and the creation of the Truth and Reconciliation Commission has been *rhetoric*, a concerted effort to manipulate our perception and understanding of what is happening. Formally, rhetoric is *persuasive*, rather than *correct*, argumentation (not that a correct argument cannot be persuasive) and, as such, is a form of discourse similar to political campaigning, advertising, spin-doctoring, and other situations where the sizzle is more important than the (possibly non-existent) steak.

At one time, an introduction to rhetoric was part of high school-level education, then it became a requirement of first-year university schooling, and now it is an increasingly difficult-to-find option for generalized, liberal arts programs. Only prospective lawyers and marketers can count on an introduction to the ins and outs of rhetoric. While we were suspicious of how the marginalization of rhetoric has coincided with the rise of unchallenged ridiculous ideation (for example, the suggestion that the purchase of an expensive pair of sneakers will transform you into a local version of a millionaire professional basketball player), at least we have asked how is it that the individual capacity to evaluate the quality of arguments has gradually become so irrelevant. On the face of it, an introduction to rhetoric seems (to us, anyway) as useful and as important as it ever was. Whatever the story behind the decline of rhetoric, it is its current absence that concerns us here; and, rather than complain about its passing we will endeavour to clarify exactly what its proper use can give us when applied to the instance of the TRC. We will take the two foundational terms, "truth" and "reconciliation," in reverse order.

TWO SHIPS THAT CRASH IN THE NIGHT

The term "reconciliation" has been attached to issues of Indian residential schooling from the first inklings of the range of church offenses.[4] It was an obvious attempt to connect what should happen in Canada with what had happened in South Africa, after Apartheid, but problems with its application were noted even then. To put it simply, before two parties can *reconcile* they must, at some earlier time, have been *conciled*; that is, two distinct parties, independent and moving in their own directions for their own reasons, meet, share, and decide to make their independent ways forward into a single, combined effort.

The classic exemplar of this has been when a woman and a man (nowadays the sex of the parties involved has become irrelevant) meet and decide to become joined in matrimony. Of course, the path of true love rarely runs smoothly, and the union may be dissolved for one reason or another. There is and has been for centuries any number of interventions (for example, clerical counselling, marriage consultation, and mediation by friends and/or family) aimed at healing the rift, whatever its basis. *Reconciliation*, then, is the success of these enterprises, a restoration to the earlier condition of a single, shared and combined effort.

This, of course, puts the lie to the application of this term to the relation between Indigenous peoples and the mainstream Canadian populace and polity. The consistent feature of policies considered, established, and maintained by Canada with respect to Indigenous peoples has

> To put it simply, before two parties can *reconcile* they must, at some earlier time, have been *conciled* ...

been our termination.[5] The consistent feature of our reaction to those policies has been resistance (passive and otherwise). This should all be completely obvious, but it should be recalled that the word was, indeed, similarly misused in the hearings held after Apartheid was vacated,[6] but nobody (of consequence, anyhow) complained about it here. How did this slip by critical sensibilities? *Reconciliation* is an expression that is both warm and fuzzy; it is, after all, such a relief to an extended family and community when a warring married couple, both parties of which are generally esteemed by all concerned, return to a prior happy state.

Reconciliation, then, is an attempt to insinuate a revised and bogus history of Indian/non-Indian relations in Canada. It implies that, once upon a time, Indigenous peoples and settlers lived in peace and harmony, working collaboratively toward shared long-term goals, only to have residential schooling (which began with only the best of intentions) rear its ugly head and drive a wedge between Canadians and Indigenous peoples. The job of the Truth and Reconciliation Commission, like that of a good marital therapist or (more appropriately in this instance) a concerned priest, is to mend the rift, heal the split, and make two conjoin again as one. It is an interesting fable, but there is more history to *Star Wars* than to this scenario. The (ex)termination of Indigenous peoples and their unsurrendered pre-existing title to land and resources is central to the political economy of Canada; was, is, and will continue to be.

"DRAW A LION INCOMPLETELY..."

As bad as reconciliation fares under examination, truth does even worse. As we charged in our response to Harper's statement:

> This commission can (1) subpoena no witnesses, (2) compel no testimony, (3) requisition no document. It cannot find, charge, fine, or imprison. Thus far, the only ones lining up to testify are members of groups who have already testified (the Royal Commission on Aboriginal Peoples generated thousands of pages of testimony from school survivors, a corpus, we must add, that has not in the slightest way entered into the consciousness of the average Canadian in the 12 years since its publication) and those who still maintain sufficient plausible deniability to publicly defend its inactions (the RCMP, for example). Those

most obviously culpable have already stated their intentions *not* to bother showing up.[7]

Nothing whatsoever has changed with respect to these charges, now that the Commission is in (sort of) operation. It may be claimed that we are insulting the Survivors of residential schooling who are now coming forward to make their stories known. Insulting may well be going on, but it is not us who are doing it. The header for this part of our presentation is taken from an old Chinese proverb: "Draw a lion incompletely, and it looks like a dog." Its meaning is that an incomplete picture will be mistaken for something it is not; and a lion and a dog are significantly different enough for the difference to be important. Will the testimony of Survivors be sufficient to draw the picture of the truth of Indian residential schooling in Canada? Even after a moment's reflection, it is obvious that Survivors' testimonies *cannot* bring retribution or compensation for crimes committed and/or resolve the following injustices and:

1. Murders, abortions, suspicious deaths, and so on have always been a part of an undercurrent of charges concerning residential schools.[8] What does the government and the churches know about these crimes? Who committed them? Who were the victims? Where are the bodies of the victims? Where are those who are criminally responsible, either directly or indirectly? How much was known of the circumstances at the time of commission? Why has the government not acted as yet upon this information?

2. Children in residential schools were experimented upon by mainstream Canadian researchers, with the permission and cooperation of officials charged with the children's well-being. Experiments in dental deterioration and tracking the spread of deliberately induced tuberculosis have already been made public.[9] Who performed them? Who approved them? Where are those who are criminally responsible, either directly or indirectly? Why did Canada flout the Nuremberg Code of responsible research and informed consent? Why has the government not acted thus far upon this information?

> Will the testimony of Survivors be sufficient to draw the picture of the truth of Indian residential schooling in Canada?

3. Sub-lethal criminal actions (rapes, torture, deprivation, and so on) have already been stipulated to in several criminal proceedings.[10] Has the full range of these actions been revealed? Have the perpetrators been identified? Has the full range of the victims of these perpetrators been acknowledged? Has the government cooperated fully with investigations of these crimes? If so, why does nothing seem to be happening? If not, why not, by what authority, and for what purpose?

4. As already noted, the government and churches have engaged in a long series of irrelevant reactions to the increasing number of revelations on residential schools, starting with simply ignoring them and culminating in the current Truth and Reconciliation Commission. What is the internal record of these reactions? Who fashioned them and to what end? How much taxpayer money has been spent trying to evade legitimate grievances of abused individuals instead of admitting guilt? How much taxpayer money has been saved by the expedience of waiting for Survivors of residential schools to die?

5. We have also charged that Indigenous peoples (ex)termination has been consistent government policy since Confederation. Is there an internal paper trail, including Cabinet documents, that would either substantiate or refute this charge? What has been the ideological force behind the charge if it is substantiated within Canada's own internal documents? What is the true explanation behind such an unwavering series of catastrophic policies and programs if the charge is refuted?

6. Covering up a crime is itself a crime.[11] Who has been responsible in the governments, bureaucracies, and institutions in operation since the closure of the last residential school in fashioning this cover-up? How has the cooperation of supposedly independent parties (child welfare agencies, newspapers, police forces, judges, and so on) been coordinated? Who crafted the evasions in Canadian law necessary to mis-define genocide and remove any chance of an Indigenous person ever bringing a charge against a Canadian authority or official?

We could generate more questions, especially if we were able to sift deeper through the facts with more finely gauged questions in our search for truth. What should be clear, however, is that those who have and will testify can only do so with respect to their personal experiences. As pointed out at the start of this section, the Commission is *structurally enjoined* from pursuing any matter that is deeper than this, regardless of how important such inquiries are thought to be. We have no doubt that the Indigenous people who testify at the forthcoming sessions will be telling the truth, and nothing but the truth.[12] They cannot, however, tell the *whole* truth, which resides, in our best guess, in Cabinet documents, memoranda of agreement, consultation documents, and the minds and hearts of people who cannot be compelled to be open and honest. And, if our readers find the citation of an old Chinese proverb too obscure, perhaps a Yiddish one will resonate more: "A half-truth is a whole lie."

Truth and Reconciliation Conjoined

Truth and reconciliation thus seem remote, to us anyway, from anything this Commission, however well-intentioned, is capable of producing. The question of what the Commission is designed to do thus must be addressed: what is a succession of individuals testifying publicly about painful personal memories actually aimed at accomplishing?

First, it should be pointed out that this format of one group of people (the Survivors) complaining publicly about the actions of another group of people (their oppressors) is what the oppressors, the historic mission churches, already sentenced themselves to back in 1993.[13] The scandal breaking then of sexual abuse, degradation, racism, and genocide even before the range and extent of crimes (against individuals and against humanity) became known could be expiated, they proclaimed, by forcing themselves to "listen to the complaints of their victims." In the intervening time since we first encountered this assertion it has not become any more sensible. In general, the perpetrators of a crime do not get to enforce their own sentence unless, of course, the victims are Indigenous people and the perpetrators are anyone else. Even if genocide is taken off the list of offenses it makes no difference. Would "having to listen to the victim" be sufficient castigation for rape, child abuse, enslavement, or other more specific abuses associated with residential schooling? In our view, it is no more than for bank robbery, insider trading, or forcible confinement. The very inclusion of such a suggested restitution for the crimes of residential schooling, much less its elevation to the only form of redress now guaranteed to residential school Survivors, bespeaks that there are factors lurking behind such an obvious dodge. We will mention two.

First is the obvious ritual, religious form of talking to clergymen about unspeakable sins. It looks and sounds like some bizarre confessional, where one confesses what was done to him or her, instead of what he or she did, and, in a further perversion, confesses to representatives of those who committed the original offenses. Somehow, the crimes of clergy are absolved, not by them accepting responsibility for their actions, but by listening (if they so choose) to victims accuse them of those actions. At least those testifying at the Commission hearings are not going to be sent away with acts of penance to perform.

Second, and even more objectionable, is the latent suggestion that public testimony will bring about some kind of *catharsis*: a discharge, as it were, of accumulated negative psychic energy, as if that release is therapeutic. Thus, in short, the healing agenda that we have already criticized at length[14] has returned, and there are no longer any paradigms to rival it. Somehow, excoriating one's oppressors in public (even if they are not there) will feel good and validate the marginalized lives the victims of the abuse of Indian residential school have had to live.

We suppose that raging at one's oppressor (even if it is only shouting down a well) could possibly feel good for a time; but establishing that such actions have long-term therapeutic benefit beyond what one could obtain from a placebo[15] has yet to be demonstrated. How many days or how many hours will it be before those who testify find themselves back where they started, with the additional task of having to face the enormity of the realization that public castigation of an identified personal oppressor has not only done nothing to resolve personal issues, but it has let the offending party and the institution standing behind him or her off the hook?

Let us be clear: *the crimes of the Indian residential school system are not reduced to the individual injuries experienced by those compelled to suffer them. Even if Bill, Dave, Ann, and Elizabeth feel better by publicly charging their tormentors and even if those feelings prove to be long-lasting and bring personal peace and tranquility to their lives for the first time, the crimes have not been undone. The schools were not created to destroy the lives of Bill,*

Dave, Ann, and Elizabeth but to destroy forms of life that were surviving and growing within them. Making individuals whole does not thereby reconstitute the Indigenous forms of life residential schooling was mandated to destroy.

CONCLUSIONS

A significant omission in everything we have read about the Truth and Reconciliation Commission is the fact that there is already in existence considerable literature on previous similar commissions convened in other countries.[16] It seems to us a natural first step to review what has happened before, with the aim (if nothing more) of seeing what problems arose previously in an effort to avoid them this time. It was our initial intention to provide such a review in this paper, but we have already far out-written our welcome. If the current Commission is not going to include such a review, we would welcome an opportunity to undertake it in a future contribution.

Nevertheless, we will finish this piece by summarizing what such a review would tell us. To put it simply, while truth and reconciliation have, at best, only problematically been either revealed or brought about in such proceedings, what, in retrospect, the victims have discovered they desired most, what they might consider most important, was not only ignored but is completely absent in any findings of any truth and reconciliation commission: *justice*. Our critique can be reduced to exactly this: truth and reconciliation are not justice, and the Commission will not produce justice even if successful in its mandate (which, we have argued, is a task it cannot achieve). The people who are coming forward to testify before the Commission are doing so in good faith. It does them no service to embroil them in a dismissible process that resolves nothing, clarifies nothing, and permits the offenders yet another layer of obscurantism. Rather than a new beginning, the Truth and Reconciliation Commission has become the same old song. Residential school Survivors deserve better.

NOTES

[1] Chrisjohn, Roland, Andrea Bear Nicholas, Karen Stote, James Craven, Tanya Wasacase, Pierre Loiselle, and Andrea O. Smith (2008). An Historic Non-Aplogy, Completely and Utterly Not Accepted. Retrieved 17 December 2008 from: http://www.marxmail.org/ApologyNotAccepted.htm (Reprinted later in *The St'át'imc Runner* July 2008:3–8).

[2] The "60s Scoop;" the loss of status by Native women; the treatment of Native veterans; discriminatory hiring practices; health care (or its absence); housing (or its absence); water; failure in fiduciary responsibility; the list seems endless.

[3] Chrisjohn, R., T. Wasacase, L. Nussey, A. Smith, M. Legault, P. Loiselle, and M. Bourgeois (2002). Genocide and Indian Residential Schooling: The Past is Present. In R. Wiggers and A. Griffiths (eds.), *Canada and International Humanitarian Law: Peacekeeping and War Crimes in the Modern Era*. Halifax, NS: Centre for Foreign Policy Studies, Dalhousie University: 229–266.

[4] Chrisjohn, R. and S. Young (1994). *The Circle Game: Shadow and Substance in the Indian Residential School Experience in Canada*. Unpublished draft research report commissioned by the Royal Commission on Aboriginal Peoples and submitted October 1994.

[5] Chrisjohn, R. and S. Young (1997). *The Circle Game: Shadow and Substance in the Indian Residential School Experience in Canada*. Penticton, BC: Theytus Press.

[6] Hamber, B. (2002). 'Ere their story die': Truth, justice and reconciliation in South Africa. *Race and Class* 44(1):61–79.

[7] See note #1.

[8] Mallinder, Lorraine (2009). Playground bones force Canada to face genocide of Indian children. *NEWS.scotsman.com*. Retrieved 23 April 2009 from: http://news.scotsman.com/latestnews/Playground-bones--force-Canada.4845558.jp

[9] Napier, David (2000). Ottawa experimented on Native kids. *Anglican Journal* May 2000 (retrieved 23 April 2009 from: http://www.anglicanjournal.com/issues/2000/126/may/05/article/ottawa-experimented-on-native-kids/?cHash=a96ff05573). Some of Napier's claims have been disputed (*see* John Siebert, *Anglican Journal*, November 2000), but it makes no difference whether you side with the original charges or with those who dispute them; (1) most of Napier's claims (and the more serious ones, like violating the Nuremburg Code and failing to act in the best interest of the child) have not been disputed but remain unaddressed, and (2) Napier makes no claim that his investigation of experimental abuses was comprehensive (that is, the possibility of additional, perhaps even more serious abuses remain). The existence of controversy here

at all makes our point: there are compelling grounds for proper authority to investigate the competing claims and interests.

[10] A sample list of criminal cases involving institutional child abuse, including those involving Indian residential schools, can be found in: Shea, Goldie M. (1999). *Institutional Child Abuse in Canada: Criminal Cases*. Prepared for the Law Commission of Canada [unpublished]. Retrieved 5 January 2009 from: https://dalspace1.library.dal.ca/dspace/bitstream/handle/10222/10442/She a%20Research%20Criminal%20Cases%20EN.pdf?sequence=1

[11] Nixon, we should remember, was indicted for covering up the Watergate crimes, not authorizing them.

[12] This is an attitude, however, that the non-Indigenous Canadian public as a whole is in no way obliged to share. They do not even need to bother paying any attention to the proceedings (unlike, say, in Germany, where the genocide of Jews is mandated in the curriculum right through to high school graduation). We predict here (and assert our right to an enormous "I told you so" in due course) that, to the extent testimony and Commission findings are noted at all in the mainstream, large parts of such acknowledgements will directly or indirectly impugn the testimony provided by Survivors.

[13] Royal Commission on Aboriginal Peoples Public Hearings Round IV: Historic Mission Churches Special Consultations. Ottawa, ON, November 8 and 9, 1993. In CD-ROM *For Seven Generations: An Information Legacy of the Royal Commission on Aboriginal Peoples*. Ottawa, ON: Libraxus Inc.

[14] See note #5.

[15] Jopling, David A. (2008). *Talking Cures and Placebo Effects*. London, UK: Oxford University Press.

[16] Barkan, Elazar (2000). *The Guilt of Nations: Restitution and Negotiating Historical Injustices*. New York, NY: W.W. Norton & Company, Inc.; Rotberg, R. and D. Thompson (2000). *Truth v. Justice: The Morality of Truth Commissions*. Princeton, NJ: Princeton University Press; Hayner, Priscilla (2002). *Unspeakable Truths: Facing the Challenge of Truth Commissions*. New York, NY: Routledge; Rolston, Bill (2002). Why Truth? Why Now? *Race & Class* 44(1):v–vi; Cobban, Helena (2007). *Amnesty after Atrocity? Healing Nations after Genocide and War Crimes*. London, UK: Paradigm Publications.

SECTION 3

TOMORROW'S HISTORY

Photographer: Allen Deleary

FRED HILTZ

Fredrick James Hiltz is the thirteenth Primate of the Anglican Church of Canada. Born in Dartmouth, Nova Scotia, in 1953, Fred has lived most of his life by the Atlantic Ocean. Many of the churches he has served have been within a stone's throw of the coast. Fred grew up in an Anglican family in Dartmouth and was baptized into the church at the age of four. Fred holds a Bachelor of Science degree from Dalhousie University, specializing in biology, and a Master of Divinity at the Atlantic School of Theology.

After being ordained in 1978, Fred ministered in small communities in Nova Scotia, including Sydney, Melford-Guysborough, and Timberlea-Lakeside. This is where he cultivated his love for parish ministry, specifically for supporting people in times of difficulty and celebration. In 1984, Fred became the assistant priest at the Cathedral Church of All Saints in Halifax and, in 1987, became the director of the Anglican Formation Program at the Atlantic School of Theology. In 1988, he was appointed Rector of the historic St. John's Anglican Church in Lunenburg. In 1995, he was elected Suffragan Bishop of the diocese of Nova Scotia and Prince Edward Island and, later, in 2002, elected Diocesan Bishop. In July 2007, Fred was elected to the office of Primate.

As chief pastor of the Anglican Church of Canada, Fred takes great joy in visiting what he calls "our beloved church." He enjoys spending time with parishes and dioceses across Canada and supporting ministry on the ground. He is also committed to supporting the work of other bishops. Fred is also passionate about cultivating Anglican-Lutheran relations, both in Canada and internationally. Since 2006, Fred has co-chaired the Anglican-Lutheran International Commission. Now, as Primate, he actively works with the Evangelical Lutheran Church in Canada, a full communion partner of the Anglican Church of Canada. In January 2008, Fred took on an active role in the Primate's World Relief and Development Fund (PWRDF) when he became the first Primate to be elected president of its board. Fred is committed to promoting this Anglican social justice and development organization, which he believes is a witness to Christ's compassion. He is a strong advocate for mission initiatives in the service of the Gospel within the Anglican Church of Canada and our worldwide Communion.

REMEMBERING THE CHILDREN:
THE CHURCH AND ABORIGINAL LEADERS TOUR

The following are the remarks made by the Most Reverend Fred Hiltz, Primate of the Anglican Church of Canada, in Ottawa, Ontario on 2 March 2008 during the Church and Aboriginal Leaders Tour.

Today marks the beginning of an Aboriginal and Church Leaders Tour with stops in Ottawa, Vancouver, Saskatoon, and Winnipeg to promote awareness and anticipation of the Truth and Reconciliation Commission to be established by the federal government in consultation with the Assembly of First Nations.

In a recently published volume, *From Truth to Reconciliation: Transforming the Legacy of Residential Schools* (produced by the Aboriginal Healing Foundation Research Series), we read in the introduction:

> Aggressive civilization to accomplish colonial goals was thought to be futile in the case of adults. Residential schooling was the policy of choice to reshape the identity and consciousness of First Nations, Inuit, and Métis children. The persistence of colonial notions of superiority is evidenced in the fact that residential schooling ... punished the expression of Aboriginal languages, spirituality, and life ways and attempted to instill a Euro-Canadian identity in Aboriginal children.[1]

This policy of assimilation had its origin in *The Gradual Civilization Act* of 1857. It was reinforced by *The Indian Act* of 1876 and sanctioned by successive Canadian Parliaments. The language used to describe this policy was itself disturbing, for it spoke of removing children from their "evil" surroundings. Simply stated, the "savage" child would be remade into a "civilized" adult.

The Church had a significant role in this program of assimilation in that we provided the teaching staff and supervised a number of the residential schools. The Anglican Church of Canada, which I represent, ran 24 of these schools concurrently through the 1920s. Over time, we ran 36.[2]

The theme of the walk we begin today is "Remembering the Children." They were taken far from home and family and then denied their language and culture as we went about remaking them in our image. The children were punished for speaking their language. They were abused physically, emotionally, and sexually. Many were scarred for life. Many survived their experiences. Many others went missing. Many died.

As churches we have *so much* for which to be *so sorry*.

In August 1993, Archbishop Michael Peers offered an apology to Aboriginal peoples on behalf of the Anglican Church of Canada at the National Native Convocation in Minaki, Ontario. His apology included the following statement:

> I know how often you have heard words which have been empty because they have not been accompanied by actions. I pledge to you my best efforts, and the efforts of our church at the national level, to walk with you along the path of God's healing.[3]

Fifteen years later, the Anglican Church of Canada, along with other churches, views the establishing of the Truth and Reconciliation Commission as a very significant step along the long road toward the healing of which Archbishop Peers spoke.

The Truth and Reconciliation Commission will provide an opportunity for survivors of the residential schools to tell their stories. It will enable those who listen to grieve with them as they speak of how they were robbed of their language and culture, how their dignity was diminished, how their bodies were abused, and how their spirits were broken. It will enable Canadians to begin coming to terms with the long-term impact of the residential schools. It will enable Canada to compile an honest, accurate, public, and permanent record of the residential schools. At a January 2008 gathering of Anglicans involved with work arising from the legacy of abuse in residential schools, Esther Wesley (co-ordinator for the Anglican Indigenous Healing Fund) spoke of the need for a Truth and Reconciliation Commission clearly and directly. She said, "This is a history that belongs to all of us. It belongs to all Canadians and we need to know our history to prevent it from ever happening again."

When the truth has been told and the truth received, when the truth has been borne and properly recorded, then we shall be much further along the path of understanding that will lead to reconciliation and a renewed national resolve to respect the dignity of every human being.

As church leaders, we welcome the news of the establishing of the Truth and Reconciliation Commission, and we eagerly anticipate the appointment of the commissioners. We are committed to the truth-telling the Commission calls for, and we pledge our best efforts to continue raising the profile of the Commission's work over the next five years. We recognize that the road to healing and reconciliation is a long one, and we remain committed, hand in hand, to see this journey through.

In this sacred work of "Remembering the Children," we ask for the Creator's blessing and guidance.

Notes

[1] Castellano, Marlene Brant, Linda Archibald, and Mike Degagné (2008:1–2). Introduction. In *From Truth to Reconciliation: Transforming the Legacy of Residential Schools*. Ottawa, ON: Aboriginal Healing Foundation: 1–8.

[2] Between 1820 and 1969, the Anglican Church ran a total of 36 schools, with its peak involvement occurring in the late 1920s, during which the Church had concurrently operated 24 schools.

[3] Peers, Michael (1993). *A message from the Primate, Archbishop Michael Peers, to the National Native Convocation Minaki, Ontario*, Friday, August 6, 1993 (*see* Appendix 3). Retrieved 26 November 2008 from: http://www2.anglican.ca/rs/apology/apology.htm

Photographer: Jane Hubbard

VALERIE GALLEY

Valerie Galley is of Ojibwa and Canadian ancestry and a member of the Nipissing First Nation. She maintains ties with her mother's home and with a large extended family in northern Ontario. In 2005, she graduated from Trent University with her Master of Arts degree in Canadian Studies and Native Studies.

Over the past two decades, she has worked as a policy analyst, researcher, and writer on Aboriginal issues in policy and program implementation at the local, regional, and national levels. In the early 1990s, she worked with the Kwak'waka'wakw, Nuu-chah-nulth, and Coast Salish peoples on their welcoming ceremony for the XV Commonwealth Games in Victoria—a hands-on experience learning about their protocol, ceremonies, languages, and histories. Also in the 1990s, Valerie was honoured to work on the team that implemented the Aboriginal Head Start Urban and Northern Initiative, an early childhood education program with a culture and language component. She has also researched and written presentations and policy papers for various national Aboriginal organizations on topics such as partnership approaches with the Government of Canada and matrimonial real property rights. She held a position at Indian Residential Schools Resolution Canada during the launch of its alternative dispute resolution option for former students of Indian residential schools. In April 2008, Valerie co-wrote the Indigenous women's caucus statements about Indigenous language revitalization for the United Nations Permanent Forum on Indigenous Issues in New York City. Currently, she is an independent researcher and writer.

In 2000, the Assembly of First Nations awarded Valerie with the Tommy Prince Award for merit in Native Studies. Her formal education, the guidance of Elders, her participation in ceremonies, and her childhood experiences have made Valerie a woman determined to contribute to Indigenous cultural and language revitalization.

RECONCILIATION AND THE REVITALIZATION OF INDIGENOUS LANGUAGES

[T]he loss of Aboriginal languages was not a product of Aboriginal indifference to their languages, but the result of systematic efforts by governments to discourage their use ... The present state of affairs is bleak testimony to the efficacy of those policies. This reality generates special duties on governments to help undo what they have done.[1]

One way of getting rid of a language is to get rid of all the speakers.[2] The governments in Canada had launched efforts to do just that—get rid of all the speakers—from the late 1800s until the 1950s, and this has become a widely accepted fact among Aboriginal peoples, Aboriginal studies scholars, and proponents of social justice, among countless others, over the past 40 years. The Indian residential school system was one of the most profound programs that governments undertook with the co-operation of the churches—namely, Roman Catholic, Anglican, United, and Presbyterian—to rid Indigenous peoples in Canada of their languages and cultural practices. Despite these efforts, the belief of some Indigenous people in themselves, their cultural practices, and their languages remained of paramount importance to them. Some children grew to be adults who spoke their Indigenous language,[3] but most others did not. While the deliberate actions of state and church for over 70 years did not obliterate Indigenous languages completely, it did have a dramatic, negative impact on the natural way in which parents and grandparents pass on their languages to their children and grandchildren that resulted in a significant overall decline in their use.

Today, there is neither a piece of federal statutory legislation nor an overarching federal policy for the recognition and revitalization of Indigenous languages in Canada; there were no laws, policies, or programs that could have guaranteed Indigenous languages their rightful place within Canada despite the 1960s movement supporting bilingualism and multiculturalism, the devolution of programs in the 1980s and 1990s, and the 2005 report by the Task Force on Aboriginal Languages and Cultures.[4] In 2008, the Government of Canada issued an historic apology to the former students of residential schools. Conservative Prime Minister Stephen Harper said:

> First Nations, Inuit and Métis languages and cultural practices were prohibited in these schools. Tragically, some of these children died while attending residential schools and others never returned home.
>
> The government now recognizes that the consequences of the Indian Residential Schools policy were profoundly negative and that this policy has had a lasting and damaging impact on Aboriginal culture, heritage and language ... We now recognize that it was wrong to separate children from rich and vibrant cultures and traditions that it created a void in many lives and communities, and we apologize for having done this.[5]

The responses of Aboriginal leaders and people alike have been pretty consistent—the Apology will be rendered meaningless without the appropriate actions on the part of the Government of Canada. The fact that Aboriginal people have been compelling the Canadian government to recognize and support the revitalization of Indigenous languages for years is a clear indication of the commitment to ensure that future generations converse in their own languages. The government's acknowledgement that they are culpable in this matter demands that appropriate redress for the effects of residential schools on languages and cultures is given. Since it has still not done so, the time for the Government of Canada to rethink and transform its legislative and policy approaches to Indigenous languages is now. Language restoration should be a key component of reconciliation within the work of the Truth and Reconciliation Commission (TRC).

Precedents for language policy in Canada were established prior to Confederation by governments, churches, missionary societies, and companies. In Canada, issues of language have been addressed in public policy since the eighteenth century when the *Québec Act* of 1774 explicitly recognized the official use of both French and English within the province of Quebec.[6] The fact that language choice is explicitly stated in this statute makes it unique as one of the first pieces of legislation in modern history recognizing specific languages for public use.[7] Further, the *Québec Act's* recognition of French and English also sets a precedent for the recognition of only two founding languages in Canada with no mention of the 50 or more Indigenous languages being spoken at that time.[8] The churches operated the residential schools according to the implicit assumption that Euro-Canadian languages—French and English—and cultural practices would replace Indigenous ones.[9] Ironically, the Hudson Bay Company (HBC) is the one institution that had a formal language policy during pre-Confederation times. In 1828, HBC incorporated a ruling into the *Rules and Regulations of the Northern Department* of the Hudson's Bay requiring "mothers and children" (who were usually Indian) to converse in either English or French and the "father" (who was usually a Hudson Bay employee of European ancestry) to teach them their alphabet and catechism.[10] The reality was that language policy in Canada was destined to focus on English and French.

In the late 1940s, the Government of Canada began to formally consult with Indians when it held the Special Joint Senate and House of Commons Committee on the Indian Act in response to pressure from veterans' organizations and church groups that had brought attention to the deplorable conditions on reserves.[11] Revisions to the *Indian Act* were made based upon these hearings, which then resulted in the revised *Indian Act*, 1951. This version of the *Act*, similar to its previous ones, did not address Indian languages; however, it did recommend that Indian children be educated with non-Indian children, clearing the path for their integration into Canadian society.[12] No recognition of the diversity of Indian languages was reflected in this legislative change; integration was the objective.

By the late 1960s, attitudes toward Indigenous languages in Canada had not changed. From 1963 to 1967, the Royal Commission on Bilingualism and Biculturalism undertook its work. While its final report mentions Indigenous languages, it merely clarifies that the examination of the Indigenous language question is outside the scope of their mandate, justifying why their inquiry focused upon the "two founding peoples"— English and French.[13]

In 1966, the *Hawthorn Report* was released. This report was a national survey designed to uncover how Indians could best achieve parity with other Canadians. The report advocated that Indians be "citizens plus":

"They speak of 'two founding races,' namely Canadians of British and French origin, and 'other ethnic groups,' but mention neither the Indians nor the Eskimos. Since it is obvious that these two groups do not form part of the 'founding races,' as the phrase is used in the terms of reference, it would logically be necessary to include them under the heading 'other ethnic groups.' Yet it is clear that the term 'other ethnic groups' means those peoples of diverse origins who came to Canada during or after the founding of the Canadian state and that it does not include the first inhabitants of this country."[14]

Canadian citizens with special rights within the Canadian state.[15] *Plus* referred to "ongoing entitlements, some of which flowed from existing treaties, while others were to be worked out in the political processes of the future, which would identify the Indian peoples as deserving possessors of an additional category of rights based on historical priority."[16] The Government of Canada's policy on the conservation of Indian languages lacked clarity, and this was mentioned in the second volume of the report in which integration remained an overarching theme. The report recommended that Indian children be actively integrated into English and French schools. Only one recommendation out of 60 relates to Indian languages, which called for the preparation of pedagogical tools relevant to Indian languages.[17] As the groundwork was being laid for official bilingualism and multiculturalism in Canada, the focus remained on integrating Indians into Canadian society. No formal acknowledgement of Indigenous languages was even being entertained by the Liberal governments of the 1960s who, in fact, attempted to formalize integration into policy.

In 1969, the Government of Canada (a narrow Liberal majority government) tabled the *White Paper*, which proposed the termination of special rights for Indians. It also proposed the *Indian Act* be repealed so that services for Indians could come through the same channels and government agencies as they do for other Canadians.[18] Coming from the premise that "ethnic-specific institutions endanger the integrity of the state,"[19] Prime Minister Trudeau argued that Indigenous peoples should not be afforded special rights in Canada, a modern society.[20] While Indian people did not wish to be governed by the *Indian Act*, they also did not like the *White Paper*, mainly because of three main issues:[21] first, the federal government had secretly written the paper and disregarded Indian input,[22] (not only had Trudeau disregarded Indian input, but he had ignored the *Hawthorn Report's* recommendation to afford special status to Indians); second, the policy could affect the loss of lands and reserves; and three, the administration of Indians, notably in the education sector, by the provinces was proposed. In the *White Paper*, the responsibility of language and cultural preservation was to be left solely to the Indian peoples:

> Indian culture also lives through Indian speech and thought.
> The Indian languages are unique and valuable assets.

Recognizing their value is not a matter of preserving ancient ways as fossils, but of ensuring the continuity of a people by encouraging and assisting them to work at the continuing development of their inheritance in the context of the present-day world. Culture lives and develops in the daily life of people, in their communities and in their other associations, and the Indian culture can be preserved, perpetuated and developed only by the Indian people themselves.[23]

Ironically, this reflects the reasons why Indigenous peoples are fighting for language preservation. The careful wording about Indian languages in the *White Paper* suggests that the Government of Canada was going to tolerate Indian languages, but would make no formal commitment to preserve them, as this could be done only by Indian people themselves. This is not justifiable given that the Indian residential school system, in which many Indians of that time had been schooled, had actively promoted cultural assimilation. Support from the federal government would be needed in order for Indigenous languages to be languages of daily life, business, service delivery, and education.

A commitment to preserve Indian languages was one of the things that the Indian leadership wanted. In 1970, an organized protest in opposition to the *White Paper* followed. The Indian Association of Alberta presented the *Red Paper*, officially entitled *Citizens Plus; a presentation by the Indian Chiefs of Alberta to the Right Honourable P.E. Trudeau, Prime Minister, and the Government of Canada*. This was spearheaded by Harold Cardinal (Cree), board member for the National Indian Brotherhood (NIB) and President of the Indian Association of Alberta. The NIB adopted this as its official response to the *White Paper*. The *Red Paper* focused its proposals regarding Indian language education on the establishment of an Alberta Indian education centre that would feature the best aspects of traditional Western education and Indian education and develop and maintain Indian languages throughout its program.[24] Here, the *Red Paper*'s proposal where languages are concerned is clear; the Indian leadership wanted the Government of Canada to ensure the survival of Indian languages.

In 1972, under the leadership of National Chief George Manuel, the NIB hosted a workshop on education, resulting in a paper called *Indian*

I'll create opportunities for tribal citizens to become teachers, so you can be free to teach your children the way you know best. I'll increase funding to tribal colleges. And I will make Native language education and preservation a priority.

Barack Obama's Message for First Americans 24 October 2008

Control of Indian Education that contained proposed goals for language and cultural programs, consistent with those in the *Red Paper*, which stated that Indian children should learn the languages, cultures, and histories of their peoples. In response to this paper, the federal government began to turn over partial administrative responsibility for education to band councils. At the same time, the government began to fund programs for language and culture preservation through the Department of the Secretary of State.[25] Grants began to filter into representative Aboriginal organizations in 1971 totalling $1.9 million. Grant dollars increased for the next several years, some providing financial aid to regionally based Aboriginal communications entities for newspapers, community radio, and media training. In 1972, the Native Friendship Centres program began to assist Aboriginal people in urban centres and provide bilingual services in various Indigenous languages, as well as English and French. By 1975, expenditures increased to $11.3 million,[26] with $1.2 million spent on native communications societies and newspapers. In 1976, a program for social and cultural development aimed at cultural expression through cultural festivals, exhibitions, theatre, educational programs, and Aboriginal history and culture also began. This infusion of federal monies into Aboriginal communities was wanted and needed.

While the preservation and revitalization of Indigenous languages have not been advanced through public policy at a federal level, it is useful to highlight some of the Government of Quebec's actions. In February 1983, the Quebec Provincial Cabinet adopted 15 principles prior to the first Constitutional Conference of First Ministers, in which two of the principles explicitly refer to Indigenous languages: Principle 1 recognizes Indigenous peoples as distinct nations with the right to their languages and cultures and to determine their collective identities; and, Principle 7 recognizes the right of Indigenous peoples to administer institutions in areas of culture, education, and language.[27] In 1985, the Quebec National Assembly passed the *Motion for the recognition of aboriginal rights in Québec*, which had been tabled by the Parti Québecois despite objections by the Aboriginal Task Force members who had co-developed the principles.[28] In June 1989, a working paper was written emphasizing the importance of Indigenous languages and recommending that the Québec government adopt a favourable position toward Indigenous language development; however, funding for Indigenous language projects in the early 1990s remained scarce in Québec.[29] Regardless, the motion recognizing the importance of Indigenous languages in Québec provided a beginning from which legislation and policy could be developed, which was a welcome but modest initiative.

The Government of the Northwest Territories has undertaken more bold legislative measures. In their 1990 *Official Languages Act,* six Indigenous languages were granted official status: Chipewyan, Cree, Dogrib, Gwich'in, Inuktitut, and Slavey.[30] In the absence of federal legislative recognition, provincial and territorial measures are possible with federal fiscal support. In 1985, the Government of Canada, through the Department of the Secretary of State, began administering a funding agreement that allowed for government services in the legislatively recognized languages and for the development of each of the NWT official languages as working languages.[31] The initial five-year agreement, beginning in 1985, was for $16 million and was renewed for $17 million. Then, in 1994, the five-year agreement was renewed once again for $30 million, representing a relatively substantial federal investment into Indigenous languages, albeit for one territory.

In 1982, Canada repatriated the Constitution. While existing Aboriginal and treaty rights were enshrined in Section 35, the meaning of this section remained undefined. The national First Nations, Métis, and Inuit organizations were, therefore, promised four First Ministers' Conferences to work out the meaning of Section 35. While all the conferences did occur, none had resolved the outstanding constitutional questions.

In 1988, the Assembly of First Nations held a national conference on Aboriginal language policy, which was funded by the Department of the Secretary of State, and adopted two resolutions: first, Indigenous languages should be granted official status in the Constitution; and second, the federal government should place Indigenous languages on par with French where budget allocations were concerned. The resolve of the Assembly of First Nations, however, was met unfavourably by the Government of Canada's position for Canada as a multicultural society. Instead of approving these resolutions, the government announced plans for a National Institute of Ancestral Languages and further tabled an *Act Establishing the Canadian Institute of Heritage Languages,* which never came to fruition.[32] Although the *Canadian Multiculturalism Act* (Bill C-93) of 1988 contains sections that could be deemed favourable to Indigenous languages, it is still legislation that fails to recognize Indigenous languages as the first languages of Canada and thereby place them on an equal footing with French and English.

Also in 1988, the Assembly of First Nations finalized a *Proposal for an Aboriginal Languages Policy* and its accompanying *Implementation Policy* for the Department of the Secretary of State. According to their research, a total of $6,286,000 had been expended on Aboriginal Language Retention programs from 1983 to 1988 from federal, provincial, and territorial departments such as the Department of the Secretary of State, Indian and Northern Affairs Canada, Canada Employment and Immigration Commission, and Health and Welfare Canada and from private entities.[33] Further, Jamieson projected that $15 million would be needed annually and over the long-term to adequately support language retention for organizations throughout Canada. In 1988, Verna Kirkness developed a report on *Aboriginal Languages Foundation* where she recommended that a $100 million endowment fund be established to protect and revitalize Aboriginal languages. Explicitly stated was the Assembly of First Nations' position that First Nations being subsumed into the multicultural mosaic of language policy and funding was an option they were unwilling to entertain at the expense of asserting the distinct place of First Nations within Canada. To ensure language revitalization for all Indigenous language groups, the proposed price was very big. The fact that it was not paid is regrettable given the endangered state of Indigenous languages today.

The Assembly of First Nations persevered with its language revitalization efforts despite the federal government's insistence on subsuming Indigenous languages into multicultural policies and programs. In 1989, *Bill C-269 Constituting the Foundation for Aboriginal Languages* was tabled for first reading in the House of Commons. In this bill, the governance structure, administrative structure, mission, and mandate were outlined. In addition, it proposed that the foundation garner additional financing from gifts, donations, and bequests. This bill, however, met with an unfavourable response in the House. In the late 1980s, the Government of Canada, lead by the Mulroney Progressive Conservatives, did not advance the prospects for Indigenous language revitalization nationally. Despite the national dialogue on Aboriginal rights fuelled by the First Ministers' meetings, the federal government advanced its multicultural

> First Nations being subsumed into the multicultural mosaic of language policy and funding was an option they were unwilling to entertain ...

policies and gave no credence to the policy and program proposals put forth by the Assembly of First Nations. It is virtually impossible to quantify the cost of doing nothing in the 1980s; however, it is more than plausible that the eventual costs of the inaction will be high.

In December 1990, the Standing Committee on Aboriginal Affairs released its fourth report entitled, *"You Took My Talk": Aboriginal Literacy and Empowerment*. In this report, the Standing Committee acknowledges Indigenous languages as "irreplaceable cultural resources"[34] and advocates for literacy programs in Indigenous languages as well as in one or both of Canada's official languages. Three recommendations focus on Indigenous language issues:

1) advocacy for the federal, provincial, and territorial governments to support Indigenous language literacy and impart this to the Council of Ministers of Education;

2) an institution be established to promote the survival, development, and use of Indigenous languages; and

3) Indigenous language versions of self-government legislation be published "along with" the English and French versions.

While this report reinforces the rationale for Indigenous language literacy and upholds the fundamental recommendations of First Nations, it did not aspire to create the institution that Kirkness had proposed a few years earlier.

In the late 1990s, the Liberal government of Jean Chretien responded to the *Final Report of the Royal Commission on Aboriginal Peoples* (RCAP). Released in November 1996, the five-volume, 3,500-page report contains analyses of research studies and Aboriginal perspectives assembled as a vision for Aboriginal peoples in Canada. *Gathering Strength, Canada's Aboriginal Action Plan* was announced in January 1998 as the federal government's response to RCAP's report. Suggesting a number of programs and structures that were informed by RCAP's research, *Gathering Strength* addresses all Aboriginal peoples—First Nations, Métis, and Inuit. A First Nations-specific action plan was developed in collaboration with the Assembly of First Nations and the federal government.[35] Its main objectives support a renewed relationship between First Nations and the Government of Canada.

Gathering Strength is a plan that outlines roles for several federal departments, including the Department of Canadian Heritage, for language, heritage, and culture initiatives. The *Statement of Reconciliation* is included among the initiatives to renew the partnership between First Nations and the federal government by affirming treaty relationships; establishing mechanisms for decision making; establishing mechanisms for regional protocols; healing from the intergenerational effects of Indian residential schools (i.e., the Aboriginal Healing Foundation); and building support for languages, heritage, culture, and communications in the form of public education. *Gathering Strength* created a common agenda for First Nations that crossed departmental lines, which signified the commitment of First Nations, other Aboriginal groups, and the federal government to engage in a renewed relationship.

In June 1998, the Minister of Canadian Heritage announced the creation of a four-year Aboriginal languages initiative for the preservation, protection, and teaching of Aboriginal languages in Aboriginal communities and homes. A total of $20 million was made available, which meant that each year $5 million was distributed for First Nations languages (receiving 75%), Michif (receiving 10%), and Inuktitut dialects (receiving 15%). This funding allowed for a range of activities from the development of language strategies and plans to language resources creation and to the instruction of students in Indigenous languages. In its 2003 evaluation of the Aboriginal Languages Initiative, the Department of Canadian Heritage states "Expected long-term outcomes include the preservation and revitalization of Aboriginal languages. This goal will take considerable time and more funds than are now available through the program."[36]

During the late 1990s until the time the *Indian Residential Schools Settlement Agreement* was ratified, the federal government was addressing the mounting cases of former students for physical and sexual abuse they experienced while attending residential schools. While legal, policy, and programs were being explored toward the legal resolution of abuse issues, the federal government was developing a "programmatic response," a form of restitution for the loss of language and culture. Indian Residential

Schools Resolution Canada (which has been subsequently subsumed into Indian and Northern Affairs Canada) and the Department of Canadian Heritage were partnering on this initiative. The buzz, within the federal government at least, was that a programmatic response would be forthcoming following the finalization of the report by the Task Force on Aboriginal Languages and Cultures,[37] which was released in June 2005.

Written in the wake of the settlement process for legal claims by former students of Indian residential schools, the Task Force proposed a national strategy to preserve, revitalize, and promote Indigenous languages and cultures within Canada. Needless to say, the Task Force was comprised of First Nations, Inuit, and Métis. In 2002, while the Task Force's work was underway, the Liberal government committed $172.7 million over 11 years towards the revitalization and preservation of Aboriginal languages and cultures. This meant that more than $15 million per year would have been available for language revitalization over the course of 11 years, which would have made this the largest federal allocation in history for Indigenous languages in Canada. The change in political leadership within Parliament meant that this allocation would not come to fruition. In December of 2006, the new, Conservative Minister of Canadian Heritage, Bev Oda, announced that the allocation of $160 million had been removed from the fiscal framework. This removal was so untimely given the critical state of Indigenous languages.

Hope for the revitalization of Indigenous languages in Canada lies in the potential of the TRC. The *Settlement Agreement* was approved on 10 May 2006 by all parties involved—Government of Canada, legal counsel of the former students, churches, Assembly of First Nations, and Inuit representatives—and is the largest class-action settlement in Canadian history. The TRC is the companion piece to the common experience payment (CEP), independent assessment process (IAP), commemoration activities, and health and healing support measures as part of the *Settlement Agreement*. The Commission's goals embody the commitment to reveal the many truths about the Indian residential school system and its impacts upon not only the former students, but their children and grandchildren and possibly Canadian society-at-large. Granted, former students have been receiving monetary compensation through the CEP and IAP programs. Will this monetary compensation

We are instructed to speak in our language when we are saying words that are important because it's a spiritual way of speaking.

The centre of our being is within the element of language, and it's the dimension in which our existence is most fully accomplished. We do not create a language, but are created within it.

Mary Lou Fox
Elder
Speaking at the public hearings of the Royal Commission on Aboriginal Peoples in Ottawa, Ontario 11 May 1992

being given to individuals fuel the revitalization of Indigenous languages? It is unreasonable to expect that monetary compensation for individuals be spent on collective interests such as language and cultural revitalization initiatives. Besides the federal government's obligation to *undo what it has done*, is it reasonable to expect that funds for language and cultural revitalization reflect the amount of money invested by the Government of Canada to remove Indigenous languages from the Canadian landscape for more than 70 years remain?

Canadian politicians created the expectation for reconciliation in 2008 when they apologized for the Indian residential school system and its legacy. The words of the Official Leader of the Opposition and then leader of the Liberal Party, the Honourable Stéphane Dion, merit some attention:

> For too long, Canadian governments chose denial over truth, and when confronted with the weight of truth, chose silence. For too long, Canadian governments refused to acknowledge their direct role in creating the residential schools system and perpetrating their dark and insidious goal of wiping out aboriginal identity and culture ... As the leader of the Liberal Party of Canada, a party that was in government for more than 70 years in the 20th century, I acknowledge our role and our shared responsibility in this tragedy. I am deeply sorry. I apologize.[38]

The fact that the Liberal leader acknowledged the significance of his party's role in perpetuating the Indian residential school system, and all that it did, is encouraging. Let us work together to remind the Prime Minister and the opposition party leaders of their words of apology, regardless of which party forms the Canadian government. Addressing the issues at hand, particularly language revitalization, must remain at the forefront.

Canada cannot undo what it has done as it gears up a reconciliation process while gearing down funding efforts to revitalize languages. A substantial long-term and sustained investment for language revitalization would be in keeping with the spirit of reconciliation as would official recognition in the form of federal statutory legislation. This preliminary examination reveals that, primarily, there has been a lack of long-term sustainable federal legislative, policy, and program initiatives for Indigenous language revitalization. In the context of reconciliation, it is unconscionable that any government in Canada would continue to oppose these substantive initiatives.

Garnering support of the Canadian public, politicians, and public servants requires widespread public education so that they may learn the history of residential schools and what their legacy means, not only for Aboriginal people, but for Canadian society as well. What lies before Canada through the TRC is the opportunity to reveal the truth of the Indian residential school system with respect to Indigenous languages and to make corresponding recommendations for revitalization. Granted, the prediction of Indigenous language extinction is one of a number of concurrent challenges now being faced in the aftermath of the Survivors' experiences. What is known is that the abuses were inflicted in a system designed to rid Canada of Indians. Nevertheless, the historical realities and the recent apology necessitate the appropriate redress by the federal government. One major appropriate action to be undertaken as strongly and as swiftly as possible is to revitalize Indigenous languages. Let us continue to work together to transform the discord between Canada and its Original Peoples.

NOTES

[1] MacMillan, Michael C. (1998:185). *The Practice of Language Rights in Canada*. Toronto, ON: University of Toronto Press [endnote removed]. MacMillan references Peter Christmas (1989) in "How Can We Preserve Our Native Language?" *Canadian Issues* 9:172. The widespread adoption of such goals in various nations is documented in Skutnabb-Kangas, Tove and Robert Phillipson (1989). *Wanted! Linguistic Human Rights*. ROLiG-papir 44. Roskilde, DEN: Roskilde Universitetcenter, Lingvistgruppen.

[2] Walsh, Michael (2005). Will Indigenous Languages Survive? *The Annual Review of Anthropology* 34:293–315.

[3] *See:* Mary Jane Norris (2007). Aboriginal Languages in Canada: Trends and Perspectives on Maintenance and Revitalization in Jerry P. White, Susan Wingert, Dan Beavon, and Paul Maxim (eds.), *Aboriginal Policy Research: Moving Forward, Making a Difference, Volume III*. Toronto, ON: Thompson Educational Publishing, Inc.: 197–226.

[4] The *Official Languages Act* was first adopted by Parliament in 1969, making English and French the two official languages of Canada. In 1971, Prime Minister Pierre Trudeau announced in the House of Commons that Canada was adopting a multiculturalism policy. The *Canadian Multiculturalism Act* was later adopted by Parliament in 1988, which acknowledges that "the Constitution of Canada and the *Official Languages Act* provide that English and French are the official languages of Canada and neither abrogates nor derogates from any rights or privileges acquired or enjoyed with respect to any other language ... that Canada is a party to the *International Convention on the Elimination of All Forms of Racial Discrimination*, which Convention recognizes that all human beings are equal before the law,... and to the *International Covenant on Civil and Political Rights*, which Covenant provides that persons belonging to ethnic, religious or linguistic minorities shall not be denied the right to enjoy their own culture, to profess and practise their own religion or to use their own language." While this *Act* allows for equality in the use of languages other than English and French, the Indigenous languages of Canada's First Nations, Inuit, and Métis do not enjoy the official status that English and French have under the *Official Languages Act*.

[5] Harper, Stephen (2008). *Prime Minister Harper offers full apology on behalf of Canadians for the Indian Residential Schools system*. Retrieved 18 February 2009 from: http://pm.gc.ca/eng/media.asp?id=2149

[6] The *Québec Act* of 1774 states the following: "*Provided always, and be it enacted*, That nothing in this Act contained shall extend, or be construed to extend, to make void, or to vary or alter any Right, Title, or Possession, derived under any Grant, Conveyance, or otherwise."

[7] Battarbee, Keith (2007). Aboriginal Languages in 21st-Century Canada. In Martin Howard (ed.), *Language Issues in Canada: multidisciplinary perspectives*. Newcastle, UK: Cambridge Scholars Publishing: 40–63.

[8] The Task Force on Aboriginal Languages and Cultures recognizes that there are 53 Indigenous languages groups in Canada; see note 6.

[9] Milloy, John S. (1999). *A National Crime: The Canadian Government and the Residential School System • 1879 to 1986*. Winnipeg, MB: The University of Manitoba Press.

[10] The Champlain Society (1940). *The Publications of the Champlain Society: Minutes of Council Northern Department of Rupert Land 1821—1831*. Toronto, ON: The Champlain Society.

[11] Special Joint Committee of the Senate and the House of Commons Appointed to Examine and Consider the Indian Act (1946). *Minutes of Proceedings and Evidence: Vol. 1-21*. Ottawa, ON: Edmond Cloutier, Printer to the King's Most Excellent Majesty Controller of Stationery; Dickason, Olive Patricia (2002). *Canada's First Nations: A History of Founding Peoples from Earliest Times* (Third Edition). Toronto, ON: Oxford University Press.

[12] *Indian Act*, 1951, c. 29, s. 1.

[13] Royal Commission on Bilingualism and Biculturalism (1967:xxii, xxvi). *Report of the Royal Commission on Bilingualism and Biculturalism, Book I: The Official Languages*. Ottawa, ON: Queen's Printer and Controller of Stationery.

[14] Royal Commission on Bilingualism and Biculturalism (1967:xxvi).

[15] Hawthorn, H.B. (ed.) (1966). *A Survey of the Contemporary Indians of Canada: A Report on Economic, Political, Educational Needs and Policies In Two Volumes*. Ottawa, ON: Queen's Printer and Controller of Stationery.

[16] Cairns, Alan C. (2000:12). *Citizens Plus: Aboriginal Peoples and the Canadian State*. Vancouver, BC: University of British Columbia Press.

[17] Hawthorn, H.B. (ed.) (1967). *A Survey of the Contemporary Indians of Canada: A Report on Economic, Political, Educational Needs and Policies, Part 2*. Ottawa, ON: Queen's Printer and Controller of Stationery.

[18] Government of Canada (1969). *Statement of the Government of Canada on Indian Policy, 1969* (The White Paper, 1969). Presented to the First Session of the Twenty-eighth Parliament by the Honourable Jean Chrétien, Minister of Indian Affairs and Northern Development, Ottawa, ON.

[19] Weaver, Sally M. (1984:217). A Commentary on the Penner Report. *Canadian Public Policy* 10(2):215–220.

[20] Weaver, Sally M. (1981). *Making Canadian Indian Policy: The Hidden Agenda 1968-1970*. Toronto, ON: University of Toronto Press, *see page 179*.

[21] Weaver (1981).

[22] Manuel, George and Michael Posluns (1974). *The Fourth World, An Indian Reality*. Don Mills, ON: Collier-Macmillan Canada, see pages 168–69.

[23] Government of Canada (1969:14–15), see note # 17.

[24] Indian Chiefs of Alberta (1970). *Citizens Plus; a presentation by the Indian Chiefs of Alberta to the Right Honourable P.E. Trudeau, Prime Minister, and the Government of Canada* [unpublished document].

[25] Trudel, François (1996). Aboriginal Language Policies of the Canadian and Quebec Governments. In Jacques Maurais (ed.), *Quebec's Aboriginal Languages: History, Planning and Development*. Toronto, ON: Multilingual Matters Ltd.: 100–128.

[26] Secretary of State (1975). Annual Report for the year ending March 31, 1975. Ottawa, ON: Secretary of State.

[27] SAGMAI [Secrétariat des activités gouvernementales en milieu amérindien et inuit] (1981). Vers des négociations avec les Indiens attikameks et montagnais. *SAGMAI Rencontre* 2(2):4.

[28] Joffe, Paul (2000). The 1985 Québec National Assembly Resolution on Aboriginal Rights: A Brief Commentary. Submitted to the Aboriginal Justice Implementation Commission.

[29] Trudel (1996), see note # 24.

[30] *Official Languages Act*, R.S.N.W.T. 1988, c. O-1.

[31] Trudel (1996), see note # 24.

[32] Trudel (1996), see note # 24.

[33] Jamieson, Mary E. (1988). *The Aboriginal Language Policy Study, Phase II: Implementation Mechanism*. Ottawa, ON: Assembly of First Nations.

[34] Standing Committee on Aboriginal Affairs (1990:iv). *"You Took My Talk": Aboriginal Literacy and Empowerment: Fourth Report of the Standing Committee on Aboriginal Affairs*. Ottawa, ON: Queen's Printer for Canada.

[35] Indian and Northern Affairs (1998). *Agenda for Action with First Nations*. Ottawa, ON: Minister of Public Works and Government Services Canada.

[36] Consilium (2003:5). *Aboriginal Languages Initiative (ALI) Evaluation Final Report*, prepared for Department of Canadian Heritage. Ottawa, ON: Department of Canadian Heritage.

[37] These were my observations while working on contract with Indian Residential Schools Resolution Canada in 2003.

[38] Dion, Stéphane (2008). Leader of the Official Opposition Residential School Apology. Retrieved 18 February 2009 from: http://www.liberal.ca/story_14080_e.aspx

Photographer: Fred Cattroll

MARI TANAKA

Mari Tanaka is a 26 year-old undergraduate student in the Department of Cultural Studies at UBC Okanagan. Her research interests include popular media, language education, intercultural communication, and constructions of identity. Upon completing her undergraduate degree, she plans to further her studies at the graduate level. She was born in Fukuoka, Japan and moved to Vancouver, British Columbia in 1991.

THE INHERITED LEGACY: AS A *HYPHEN* CANADIAN

As an immigrant to this country, I was bombarded with everything and anything that was associated with Canadian-*ness*. Canadians were painted as nice, accepting, culturally diverse, nature-loving hockey players and peacekeepers. The perception of a Canadian identity is associated with only positive images; this picture seems to be incomplete. I was raised with the notion that I have to fully comprehend my family and national histories in order to understand who I am and where I come from. Also, my family always encourages me to have a comprehensive understanding of world histories, particularly those that affect my own personal identity. In my opinion, a self-identity cannot be whole without understanding and accepting both the positive and negative legacies of past generations.

Throughout the mid-1800s to the late-1900s, the Canadian government, in conjunction with the Church (Catholic as well as other sects of Christianity), stole generations of Indigenous children from their homes, families, elders, and communities. The children were taught to be ashamed of who they are and were physically, mentally, and sexually abused. This was an attempt at cultural genocide. The children who attended these schools were never meant to thrive. Countless many lost their lives at these schools and many more would lose their way long after they had left the school walls. Residential schools are not a historical event buried in the past; they are still happening and will continue to affect the future if they are not addressed now. Those who attended are not the only ones that have been lost; the generations that came after and those yet to come have inherited this experience. Canada has a history of refusing to acknowledge its own colonialist policies, and residential schools have been disguised, spun, denied, dismissed, and swept under the carpet. Many, if not most Canadians today, do not recognize the impacts of residential schools.

Reconciliation will be difficult and will not occur without acknowledgement of what took place. The hope is that the Truth and Reconciliation Commission (TRC) will finally give people the chance to not forget, but to move past it. Reconciliation presents an opportunity for all parties—including the Canadian government, all sects of the

> Residential schools are not a historical event buried in the past; they are still happening and will continue to affect the future if they are not addressed now. Those who attended are not the only ones that have been lost; the generations that came after and those yet to come have inherited this experience.

Today, our children are taught that Canada is a land of freedom for the oppressed. What they are not taught, is Canada, in the past has sought to destroy their culture, religion, history and language. We must correct this and promote the real truths of our people.

Mary Guilbeault
Vice-Chairperson
Aboriginal Council of Winnipeg
Speaking at the public hearings of the Royal Commission on Aboriginal Peoples Winnipeg, Manitoba 22 April 1992

Church, federally recognized Aboriginal organizations, the victims and their families, and the Canadian public in general—to work with one another, to address each other, and to come to terms with what happened. The TRC should provide a safe and culturally relevant forum for victims and their families to tell their stories and to be finally acknowledged. These stories will have a profound impact on the collective memory of all Canadians.

Indigenous people for their part can also take this opportunity to send a message to the world that *never again* will such a racist agenda be tolerated in Canada. Residential schools happened. Why are so many Canadians unaware of that? It does not get taught in public schools, not even as a part of what is commonly referred to as the "black pages"[1] of Canadian history. It comes as a shock to many people when they do learn about this colonial practice as they arrive at post-secondary institutions. I have often heard from many of my fellow students of being shocked that they were not taught this part of history before leaving high school. That shock is often followed by guilt and shame and often leads to denial. This guilt, shame, and denial hinder people from engaging in dialogue with each other. What can be said about the Canadian moral code when people are dragged out of a church in handcuffs by police for protesting against the denial of thousands of residential school deaths, as was the case in Vancouver in early 2008.[2]

As part of the Awareness for Diversity Week in March 2008 at University of British Columbia Okanagan, members of the organizing committee made and planted window shutters around campus grounds. Students could open up the shutters and see a display of information on various issues, including residential schools. The point being made was that many of these issues are hidden or covered up. There were some angry responses to the window shutter revealing information about residential school practices in British Columbia. The complaints included: the statistics were made up, no one died, the Church had good intentions, it paints Christians in a bad light, only a small percentage of the students who attended were ever abused, and the racist attitudes and policies of the time do not exist anymore, so therefore we should not bother with it now.

I was startled by the complaints, since this was the only shutter to receive any negative feedback, but I was not surprised. I was, however, shocked by the number of people who were learning about residential schools for the first time in their lives, particularly because there had been several of these schools in this region. These complaints illustrate the lack of awareness and understanding of the history of Canada. Colonization is not over for this nation and it is not a relic of the past. People are either still benefiting or are still being victimized by the inherited legacy of Canada's colonial history. There needs to be an opportunity for discussion so that we can come to terms with what being a Canadian means to each of us. If the TRC is what it should be, it will be an opportunity to accomplish just that. Canadians can no longer choose to look the other way.

Canada's TRC will be slightly different from other TRCs that have been conducted in other countries, such as in South Africa, in that any information provided by the perpetrators, the government and churches in this case, will be provided on a voluntary basis. We will see in the coming years how forthcoming these organizations will be with information regarding their involvement, since they will still have control over what gets revealed. In order for this commission to be successful, victims and their families are being asked to relive their experiences and to share it with the general public. It is a lot to ask of people who have lived through such traumatic experiences. Although it may be therapeutic for some to share their stories, for others, the residential school settlement process and the TRC may become yet another traumatic experience in itself. There needs to be complete transparency on the participation of the government and the churches if they are to participate fully in the process. The lack of this transparency will make the creation of a *truthful* and *unbiased* historical account more difficult for the Commission. I believe the success of the TRC relies on genuine co-operation on the part of the government, the churches, and the Canadian public. Hopefully, the next five years will prove to be successful.

Compiling a truthful account of history is only one small step toward reconciliation. The abuse at residential schools has been denied for a long time. There needs to be acknowledgement so that the policies and racist discourses that lead to such blatant violation of human rights can be changed. To say "it happened so long ago, just get over it" dismisses the

My experiences of being both Canadian and Japanese—and at times having those identities denied ...

experiences of the victims and their families that are still being affected by what happened. The traumatic memories are intergenerational and have been inherited even by those who have never set foot inside these schools; so many of the social issues that Aboriginal communities face today stems from the practice of residential schools. The effects must be fully understood and recognized if we are meant to move past it, as nations.

I am a product of the inherited experiences, thoughts, wisdoms, and philosophies of all those who came before me. Representing multiple national identities meant coming to terms with those legacies, whether they were positive or negative. My experiences of being both Canadian and Japanese—and at times having those identities denied—have given me a deeper understanding of my *self* and what I represent. In order to have a full and complete understanding of our national identities, we need to have a comprehensive awareness of where we come from, and I do not believe that most Canadians today have this insight. Perhaps, as an immigrant, I have had more opportunities to question what it means to be Canadian. It is my hope that the TRC will be an opportunity for many other Canadians to do the same, and perhaps for some, for the first time in their lives. The TRC can truly be an opportunity for reconciliation, but it is up to this generation to make it so.

NOTES

[1] The phrase "black pages" (short for "universal black pages") refers to the untold negative history of Canada's treatment of blacks living within a section of Halifax, Nova Scotia, commonly referred to as Africville. See page 241in Bradford W. Morse (2007). Reconciliation Possible? Reparations Essential. In Castellano, Marlene Brant, Linda Archibald, and Mike DeGagné (eds.), *From Truth to Reconciliation: Transforming the Legacy of Residential Schools.* Ottawa, ON: Aboriginal Healing Foundation: 233–256.

[2] Webb, Kate (2008). Native protest disrupts mass: Churches accused of 'genocide' over TB deaths. *The Province*, Monday, March 24, 2008. Retrieved 5 March 2009 from: http://www2.canada.com/theprovince/news/story.html?id=5790d241-b4c4-48cf-ac75-7cf7d1ee0b7d&k=25804

Photo: Courtesy of Legacy of Hope Foundation

Erin Wolski

Erin Wolski is a member of the Chapleau Cree First Nation. She was born and raised in Mushkegowuk Territory, Treaty 9. Erin has an undergraduate degree in Environmental Health from Ryerson University. She has spent the last decade working in Ottawa at various national Aboriginal organizations and is currently Director of Health at Native Women's Association of Canada. A passionate advocate for Aboriginal women's equality rights, she focuses much of her attention to health research and policy analysis. Her work on culturally relevant gender-based analysis frameworks has contributed to the pool of knowledge nationally.

The Role of Culturally Relevant
Gender-based Analysis in Reconciliation

This article is intended to generate knowledge of gender balance and to insist its inclusion in the truth and reconciliation process. The Native Women's Association of Canada (NWAC) promotes the use of a culturally relevant gender-based analysis (CRGBA) by the men and women involved in forging a renewed relationship between Aboriginal and Canadian peoples. In *Culturally Relevant Gender-based Analysis: tool to promote equity*, we contend that NWAC's CRGBA framework is:

> a learning tool for use by anyone involved in policy, program or project development; it is intended to broaden perspectives and deepen knowledge of colonization and its outcomes. In particular, it is intended to improve Aboriginal women's health and well-being. Over 40% of Aboriginal women live in poverty, for example, and Aboriginal women are three times more likely than non-Aboriginal women to suffer violence.[1]

CRGBA development has been motivated by the total failure within current policy and decision-making processes to meet Aboriginal women's needs. Both Aboriginal and non-Aboriginal societies are guilty of not only marginalizing, but completely discounting the value Aboriginal women bring to these processes. It is our goal to see that the Truth and Reconciliation Commission equally value Aboriginal women's roles and meet their needs, from beginning to end. We have witnessed the outcomes of devaluation and imbalance, such as poorer overall health status, disproportionate incarceration rates, suicide, addiction, chronic disease, violence, and death among Aboriginal people, especially among Aboriginal women. The pursuit of truth and reconciliation must strive to impact these outcomes.

The Role of NWAC

NWAC is one of five federally recognized national Aboriginal organizations and is the only one that represents the interests of Aboriginal women. NWAC came about during a time when both Aboriginal and women's issues were at the forefront of change.

Movements that had their genesis during the 1970s were responsible for creating a political conscience unlike any other time in our history. While there have been attempts over the years to incorporate the Aboriginal world view into research and policy development processes, there has yet to be an effective, broadly accepted tool to facilitate this. It is acknowledged, however, that a holistic perspective allows for more inclusive, comprehensive approaches to issues. It is also acknowledged that the Aboriginal woman's perspective brings traditional ways of being into current ways of thinking and revitalizes matriarchy as a more viable, long-term solution to the many problems faced by Aboriginal peoples.[2]

Aboriginal issues are some of the most complex; resolution involves comprehension and respect. Prior to contact with Europeans, Aboriginal people were already rich in a long history of cultural traditions and self-governance:

> Prior to first contact, many Aboriginal societies were ... [matriarchal] in nature and focused on family, community and the continuity of tradition, culture and language; Aboriginal women were central to all of this as teachers, healers, and givers of life. While Aboriginal men and women had distinct roles, their roles were equally valued.[3]

Aboriginal society has become patriarchal. We have embraced a set of values that were once foreign. However, it should be known that the imposition of patriarchal laws, structures, and institutions has had severe, negative, and lasting impacts. We need to reflect on this and ask ourselves who is benefitting. An honest assessment of this will assist us in creating change. "The need to restore the value of Aboriginal gendered roles has motivated the development of culturally relevant gender-based analysis, or CRGBA."[4]

NWAC works to promote increased awareness of the Aboriginal woman's reality and, in the Aboriginal Healing Foundation's publication *From Truth to Reconciliation: Transforming the Legacy of Residential Schools*, NWAC President Beverley Jacobs and co-author Andrea William's submission details the linkages between the current and historical, social, and economic environments in Canada and the abhorrent trends within, specifically missing and murdered Aboriginal women. While

Aboriginal society has become patriarchal. We have embraced a set of values that were once foreign. However, it should be known that the imposition of patriarchal laws, structures, and institutions has had severe, negative, and lasting impacts.

NWAC is credited with raising the profile of violence against Aboriginal women nationally and internationally, the organization has also accepted responsibility for identifying ways to create change. The ultimate goal is to eliminate violence against Aboriginal women and it is understood that this can only come about by exposing the avenues from which it is perpetuated. NWAC views colonialism and patriarchy as underlying root causes that perpetuate racialized gender-targeted violence.

CRGBA has become a critical piece of work within Aboriginal organizations, many having developed their own frameworks to suit their own purposes. Several of these were showcased at the National Aboriginal Women's Summit in Yellowknife, Northwest Territories (NWT) in July 2008, co-hosted by the Government of the NWT and NWAC. At this event, Aboriginal women from across Canada had an opportunity to learn about CRGBA before developing action-oriented recommendations for the federal government.

COLONIZATION OF ROLES

It is well-established that the legacy of colonization changed Aboriginal people's roles in society; however, it can be argued that Aboriginal women's fall from grace was more devastating and widespread. Colonial laws and genocidal policies,[5] while impacting the delicate balance between the genders, specifically targeted Aboriginal women and their roles as family anchors. As Pertice Moffitt stated "Aboriginal women were closely linked to the land, and because land acquisition became the goal of the colonizers, Aboriginal women became the target."[6] The descent was swift and saw gendered roles changed forever. With colonization came a systematic overhaul of the value of the roles each member played within family, community, and nations.

It is a long-standing goal of Aboriginal women's organizations like NWAC to drive shifts in policy priorities that will see substantive change to the realities experienced by Aboriginal women; to see the value of Aboriginal women's roles elevated and balance restored.

As women we do have responsibilities. We are the keepers of our culture and we are the teachers of our children. I would just like to say that for our men that we don't want to walk behind you. We want to walk beside you. We want to heal with you and we want to help you make those decisions that are needing to be made for the future of our people and that we walk together.

Lillian Sanderson
La Ronge Native Women's
Council
Speaking at the public hearings of the Royal Commission on Aboriginal Peoples La Ronge, Saskatchewan 28 May 1992

CRGBA

The CRGBA framework is:

> a "living" document and will change over time. Elements of the framework have been gleaned from the work that NWAC and others have done on gender-based analysis. The Bureau of Women's Health and Gender Analysis at Health Canada, for example, helped initiate the process and provided background and support to NWAC in the development of the framework.... NWAC sees the framework as a founding document for all research and policy areas within the organization, grounding all of our research and policy work.... The goal of the framework is to facilitate the application of this knowledge within a current context. Applying CRGBA has the potential to move policy, programs and legislation toward achieving more equitable health outcomes.[7]

CRGBA is a learning tool intended to broaden perspectives and knowledge. The genocidal agenda implemented over a century ago is entrenched in current legislation, and in order to fully comprehend the legacy of impacts, preconceived notions of gendered Aboriginality must be abandoned:

> Historically, Aboriginal women have been portrayed in derogatory terms. Through [the imposition of] various laws, regulations, policies and Christian edicts, a demeaning and demoralizing portrayal became the identity of the Aboriginal woman in Canada, forcing them into an oppressed position in society, which are serious mitigating factors as to their poor health of today.[8]

The CRGBA should allow the application of new knowledge and the development of more relevant public policy within both Aboriginal and non-Aboriginal society. Once it is understood how the denial of Aboriginal identity in Canada is linked to poor health, users will begin to understand why CRGBA is so important.[9]

The policy shifts expected by implementing CRGBA will be particularly relevant as the truth and reconciliation process begins its nationwide activities and events. True reconciliation should see the development and use of Aboriginal-driven mechanisms of change. NWAC envisions the Truth and Reconciliation Commission as a critical link to health and healing in Aboriginal communities and views the Commission as an opportunity to create real change. The CRGBA is offered as a tool of change; its use will bring about more comprehensive, inclusive policy and decision-making processes.

GBA vs. CRGBA

If conventional gender-based analysis (GBA) tools are intended to address gender bias, the objective of a culturally relevant gender-based analysis is to broaden current approaches and to incorporate Aboriginal world views. Conventional GBAs are limited in scope and fail to meet the needs of Aboriginal women; CRGBA sets the bar higher contextually and requires the user to question basic assumptions and prejudices.

Colonization, for example, is perceived by many to be an historical event; however, it must be understood as a current phenomenon. CRGBA users will understand that a very real legacy of colonization continues today through policies such as those in the judicial and educational systems, through the socio-economic environments within both Aboriginal and non-Aboriginal society, and through legislation such as the *Indian Act*, the *Canadian Human Rights Act*, and the *Family Homes on Reserves and Matrimonial Interests or Rights Act* at the national level and through band membership codes at the local level.

NWAC CRGBA

The NWAC CRGBA is versatile and can be incorporated into any phase of the policy development process: planning, implementation, and/or monitoring. The indicators used to evaluate the policy (or program) in question are intended to measure the level to which a defined set of criteria is met. For example, if the desired outcome is the application of CRGBA, the level to which this is achieved can be measured by the extent to which Aboriginal women were part of the process. The tool will help the user determine why the methods used to engage Aboriginal women were unsuccessful. The following excerpt from NWAC's CRGBA framework illustrates how engagement is evaluated:[10]

Desired Outcomes	Performance Measures (Indicators)	Measurement Tools
All national Aboriginal organizations, non-governmental organizations and provincial, territorial, federal, and Aboriginal governments apply a culturally relevant, gender-based analysis so that Aboriginal women are well served in all legislative, policy, and programming initiatives affecting Aboriginal individuals and peoples.	The number and type of reasons (gender-related obstacles) for non-participation in research, consultation, communication, and design that were identified and addressed.	Assess the methods used to gain participation that ensures representation and quality participation through surveys, interviews, and questionnaires. Track the number and types of obstacles to access identified through CRGBA and the number of obstacles eliminated.

The template can be used to measure the application and incorporation of CRGBA throughout the life of the policy and should be revisited to ensure consistent and continued application. This means that Aboriginal women's roles must be maintained through all phases of the process and that Aboriginal women's perspectives must be reflected in the outcomes.

NWAC's CRGBA specifically focuses on revitalizing Aboriginal women's roles because of the long-standing imbalance, and the differential impacts Aboriginal women have experienced. However, elevating the importance of Aboriginal women and their roles does not discount the importance of Aboriginal men and their roles. Establishing and maintaining a balance between the two is also important.

There are many practical examples of the CRGBA that generate new knowledge and the potential for more sustainable solutions to Aboriginal issues. NWAC has begun to gather case studies to demonstrate how culture and gendered perspectives can shed new light on issues. Areas of particular interest are economic development, justice, violence, and health.

Aboriginal people experience disproportionate rates of many chronic illnesses. Diabetes, for example, was virtually unknown less than 50 years ago, but today the prevalence is three to five times higher than in the general population. Older Aboriginal women aged 65 years and over experience diabetes at higher rates (one in four) compared to Aboriginal men (one in five). Also, there is a special concern for the rate of growth among Aboriginal children and women of child-bearing years.[11] Therefore, Aboriginal women should be central in the development of diabetes policy and programming, locally and nationally.

When a cultural lens is applied to health, diabetes in particular, a clearer picture emerges that can broaden understanding and perhaps trigger the development of more sustainable solutions. By applying the CRGBA, more facts emerge that can explain how and why Aboriginal women in particular are predisposed to experiencing such high rates of the disease. The CRGBA will point to systemic discrimination, gendered racism, and other phenomena that perpetuate Aboriginal women's realities.[12]

The same is true of the reconciliation process. Aboriginal women's roles are critical at all levels because they have been differentially impacted by colonization. The Native Women's Association of Canada invites the Commission to use the CRGBA framework to expose the truth, to generate systemic, long-lasting change, and to revitalize gender balance.

CONCLUSION

NWAC's CRGBA framework is a living document. Since the initial drafting of this article, the framework has changed. The newest version of the CRGBA incorporates the grassroots perspective and, as such, is more easily incorporated into existing policy and decision-making processes. We feel we have succeeded in developing a simplified, more user-friendly version of the framework and offer it for use by the Commission with the understanding that by adopting the CRGBA principles, outcomes will better reflect the needs of all those who participated in the process.

Native women have been bearing tremendous burdens in their family, in the home, as well as outside the home, in the workplace and in the political arenas of this country. In order to eliminate the sexism and the racism that is directed at Aboriginal women, we have to see a concerted effort on the part of Native male leadership in this country.

Brenda Small
Speaking at the public hearings of the
Royal Commission on Aboriginal Peoples
Moose Factory, Ontario
9 June 1992

NOTES

[1] Wolski, Erin (2008/09:26). Culturally Relevant Gender-based Analysis: A tool to promote equity. *Network* 11(1):26–27. Retrieved 7 April 2009 from: http://www.cwhn.ca/network-reseau/11-1/NETWORK.eng.fallwinter08.pdf

[2] Wolski (2008/09).

[3] Wolski (2008/09:26).

[4] Wolski (2008/09:26).

[5] Jacobs, Beverley and Andrea Williams (2008). Legacy of Residential Schools: Missing and Murdered Aboriginal Women. In Marlene Brant Castellano, Linda Archibald, and Mike DeGagné (eds.), *From Truth to Reconciliation: Transforming the Legacy of Residential Schools*. Ottawa, ON: Aboriginal Healing Foundation: 119–140. This can also be retrieved in PDF format from: http://www.ahf.ca/publications/research-series

[6] Moffitt, Pertice (2004:325). Colonialization: A Health Determinant for Pregnant Dogrib Women. *Journal of Transcultural Nursing* 15(4):323–330.

[7] Wolski (2008/09:26). A large number of documents were reviewed in the creation of this CRGBA template, but most notably the following were relied upon: NWAC (2007) *Culturally Relevant Gender Based Analysis: An Issue Paper*. Prepared for the National Aboriginal Women's Summit, June 20-22, 2007, Corner Brook, NL (retrieved 9 April 2009 from: http://www.nwac-hq.org/en/documents/nwac.crgba.june1707.pdf); Status of Women Canada (2003). *Gender-Based Analysis (GBA): Performance Measurement of its Application*. Ottawa, ON: Status of Women Canada (retrieved 20 October 2008 from: http://www.swc-cfc.gc.ca/pubs/gbaperformance/index_e.html); Wolski, Erin (2007). *The Aboriginal-Driven Gender Based Analysis Framework*. August 2007 Background Paper #1. Vancouver, BC: Aboriginal Women's Health and Healing Research Group (retrieved 20 October 2008 from: http://www.awhhrg.ca/what/documents/GBABackgroundPaper1.pdf); AFN Women's Council (2007). *Draft Framework "Gender Balancing: Restoring Our Sacred Circle"*. Ottawa, ON: Assembly of First Nations (retrieved 20 October 2008 from: http://www.afn.ca/cmslib/general/AFN's%20Gender%20Re-Balancing%20Framework_EN.pdf); Wolski, Erin (2007). *Towards the Reconstruction of a Gendered Aboriginal Identity*. August 2007 Background Paper #2. Vancouver, BC: Aboriginal Women's Health and Healing Research Group (retrieved 20 October 2008 from: http://www.awhhrg.ca/what/documents/GBABackgroundPaper2.pdf); Wolski, Erin (2007). *Exploring the relevance of Gender Based Analysis to Indigenous realities in Canada: A comparative analysis, Gender Based Analysis, Phase II*. Vancouver, BC: Aboriginal Women's Health and Healing Research Group (retrieved 20 October 2008 from: http://www.

awhhrg.ca/what/documents/IndigenousGBAcomparison.pdf); Health Canada (2000). *Health Canada's Gender-based Analysis Policy*. Ottawa, ON: Health Canada (retrieved 20 October 2008 from: http://www.hc-sc.gc.ca/hl-vs/alt_formats/hpb-dgps/pdf/gba-eng.pdf); NWAC (no date). *Native Women's Association of Canada-Aboriginal Health Indicators Framework* [unpublished draft document]; Indian and Northern Affairs Canada (1999/2006). *Gender-Based Analysis Policy*. Ottawa, ON: Minister of Public Works and Government Services Canada (retrieved 20 October 2008 from: http://www.ainc-inac.gc.ca/pr/pub/eql/eql_e.pdf); Health Canada (2003). *Exploring Concepts of Gender and Health*. Ottawa, ON: Health Canada (retrieved 20 October 2008 from: http://www.hc-sc.gc.ca/hl-vs/alt_formats/hpb-dgps/pdf/exploring_concepts.pdf); and NWAC (no date). *Native Women's Association of Canada Sisters in Spirit Initiative* [unpublished draft document]. For more information contact the Native Women's Association Health Unit Director, Erin Wolski at ewolski@nwac-hq.org or at 613-722-3033, extension 229.

[8] Native Women's Association of Canada [NWAC] (2008:8–9) [footnotes removed]. *Culturally Relevant Gender Based Analysis and Assessment Tool For Health Canada Aboriginal Health Transition fund 2007-08*. Ottawa, ON: Native Women's Association of Canada [unpublished document].

[9] The NWAC Health Unit will promote CRGBA through regional outreach and through both mainstream and Aboriginal publications; excerpts in this article may be found in other publicly available documents, such as: Canadian Women's Health Network's *Brigit's Notes* Summer 2008 edition (see: http://www.cwhn.ca/brigit/notes_aug08.htm); and the National Aboriginal Women's Summit II, held in Yellowknife, NWT on 29–31 July 2008 (see: http://www.naws-sfna.ca/english/policy_papers/index.shtml). We anticipate that this will only be the beginning of CRGBA promotion in Canada.

[10] NWAC (2008:17–18), see note #8.

[11] Health Canada (no date). Aboriginal Diabetes Initiative (ADI). Retrieved 14 April 2009 from: http://www.hc-sc.gc.ca/ahc-asc/activit/marketsoc/camp/adi-ida-eng.php

[12] See Native Women's Association of Canada's website for more information at: http://www.nwac-hq.org/en/index.html

Courtesy of Janice Longboat

Natalie A. Chambers is an English immigrant who has lived in Canada for twelve years. She currently lives with her *Sqilx^w* husband, two children, and three stepchildren on the Okanagan Indian Band reserve in Vernon, British Columbia. Her children and stepchildren attend the Band language nest and language and cultural immersion elementary school, which are transformative community projects active in revitalizing the Nsxilcen language.

Natalie is currently working on a doctorate in Interdisciplinary Studies at the University of British Columbia Okanagan. She conducted her master's research on Indian residential schooling, which engaged six intergenerational Survivors of Indian residential schools and First Nations educators, counsellors, and advocates to reflect on the implications of a textual dialogue with former Indian residential school staff and then analyze staff stories. In her work, Natalie draws parallels between dialogues that have taken place between former Holocaust survivors and their perpetrators to explore possibilities for similar dialogues that may engage Indigenous and colonial peoples in Canada in the examination of cultural genocide.

As a researcher, Natalie has also worked extensively with immigrants and refugees, particularly in the area of cross-cultural caring. She co-edited a manual in this area entitled, *Cross-Cross-Cultural Caring: A Handbook for Health Professionals* (2005).

Note: The term *Sqilx^w* refers to Okanagan peoples in the Nsxilcen language.

Truth and Reconciliation:
A "dangerous opportunity"
to unsettle ourselves

Un-settling ourselves

> In Chinese, the pictogram for the word *crisis* is 'dangerous opportunity.' The two words are joined, 'danger' and 'opportunity.'
>
> In sometimes mysterious ways, a crisis creates the tension point from which we act. The purpose of a crisis is to point us in a direction, to show us the danger and to point us to an opportunity. There are actions we would not take unless faced with a problem ... If a crisis represents a specific event, a certain dangerous opportunity, chaos is the non-specific accumulation of crises ... We are being called upon to re-make our consciousness ... Our consciousness creates our culture, it creates the way that we see the world. Our world view, our values and beliefs combine to create our institutions, our political, economic and social systems.[1]

As non-Indigenous peoples—descendants of the early colonialists to the most recent newcomers—like myself, what is our emotional investment in the truth and reconciliation process with the Indigenous peoples whose homeland we call Canada? What does truth and reconciliation mean to you, your families, your communities, your children, and your grandchildren? For those of you who have no knowledge of, no daily interactions with, and no personal connections to the Indigenous peoples on whose territory you have made your homes, truth and reconciliation may lack value and meaning to you, your families, and your communities.

I address this paper largely to non-Indigenous peoples in Canada because, as a newcomer, a white immigrant woman from England, over the last twelve years I have sensed that many non-Indigenous peoples regard the issues facing Indigenous peoples to be largely irrelevant to the lives, health, and happiness of themselves and their children. On many occasions I have encountered a deep resistance among non-

Indigenous peoples to engage in discussions on the struggles that face Indigenous peoples—daily realities of oppression and systemic racism that our ancestors created and that we, sometimes passively, sometimes actively, accept and reproduce. For this reason, I ask Indigenous readers to bear with me while I demand non-Indigenous readers to look deep within ourselves and to reflect on Youngblood Henderson's critical question: "why [has] Eurocentric thought ... devoted so few resources to studying the violence inflicted on Aboriginal people after 400 years of colonization"? One must consider his theory that obviously we in the dominant society "remain anxious about the possibility of impending chaos."[2]

Fred Kelly, an Indigenous man and member of the Anishinaabe Nation, describes truth and reconciliation as a process of regaining peace with oneself and a collective process "that brings adversaries to rebuild peaceful relations and a new future together."[3] However, for settler peoples and their descendants to authentically participate and respond to the call for truth and reconciliation, we need to look, in all honesty, at our complicity in maintaining the status quo—the hegemonic colonial paradigms that historically, and in the present day, perpetrate unequal power relationships through the systemic privileging of settler peoples' knowledge, languages, and values.

Has the subjugation of Indigenous peoples become so intrinsic in maintaining the values and beliefs that support the economic, religious, and cultural institutions and systems that give meaning to our lives that we are unable to imagine how things could have been different? Truth and reconciliation, then, offers a dangerous opportunity to settler peoples to examine our values and beliefs in which colonizing Indigenous peoples plays such a significant role. In so doing, we may then begin to authentically respond to the painful legacy of Indian residential schools.

Many non-Indigenous peoples know very little or almost nothing about the Original Peoples of this land. It is important for us to acknowledge this so that we may begin to examine our own cultural and social positioning, risk feelings of discomfort and unease by participating in Indigenous peoples lives and communities, (for example, by attending local First Nations events that are open to the public), and opening our hearts and minds to truly listen to and learn from the experiences of

Indigenous peoples. The process of unsettling ourselves in truth and reconciliation may stir up powerful negative emotions such as resistance, defensiveness, and denial and feelings of paralysis. However, by practicing self-acceptance and being patient with the process, these emotions may shift to feelings of anger, then grief and sadness, as we come to understand and see for ourselves how colonization is experienced as cultural genocide by Indigenous peoples. When we feel a sense of profound loss, then, and only then, our hearts may be at a place where we can authentically participate in truth and reconciliation with Indigenous peoples.

As an immigrant to Canada and from a number of years doing research and interviewing many immigrant and refugee peoples, I have observed that thoughts of our displacement from our original homelands often evoke powerful and painful emotions. Whether we or our ancestors immigrated with the hope of creating a better life or out of necessity for survival (as with refugees), burying fond memories of our homelands and the loved ones we have left behind often becomes a survival strategy necessary to our adaptation to the new society and environment around us. However, as immigrant peoples strive to forget our original displacement and our original fear of the unknown, a societal collective amnesia develops to protect us from chaos—created by guilt, grief, insecurity, and dislocation.

As an Indigenous woman living on the land of her ancestors, Okanagan activist and traditional knowledge keeper Jeanette Armstrong has described us, the settler peoples, in her father's words, as "dangerous; they are all insane ... It's because they are wild and scatter anywhere."[4] She speaks about discord in the community, within hers and elsewhere globally, caused by growing technology in our daily lives to create depersonalization and disorder—"people without hearts." She further explains:

> Translation is difficult, but an interpretation in English might be 'people without hearts' - people who have lost the capacity to experience the deep generational bond to other humans and to their surroundings. It refers to collective disharmony and alienation from land. It refers to those whose emotion is narrowly focused on their individual sense of well-being without regard to the well-being of others in the collective.[5]

Our way of life is so different. The two lives—the Native life and the white life—are different.

Tonena McKay
Big Trout Lake First Nation
Speaking at the public
hearings of the
Royal Commission on
Aboriginal Peoples
Big Trout Lake, Ontario
3 December 1992

For the health and happiness of my children, my stepchildren, and my future grandchildren, I am emotionally deeply invested in the process of creating, restoring, and nurturing meaningful relationships with Indigenous peoples based on our shared humanness and compassion. Living in a *Sqilx^w* reserve community as a mother and stepmother to *Sqilx^w* children and as a wife to a *Sqilx^w* community educator and artist, I write from cultural borderlands as an "outsider within"[6] the First Nations reserve community that I call home. In attempting to share what truth and reconciliation looks like through the eyes of an immigrant newcomer who is forever tied to an Indigenous family and community, I will describe my views from the two worlds in which I live and work, worlds that at times seem vastly disconnected. I will also share some insights that I gained when I conducted research with First Nations intergenerational Survivors and Indian residential school staff in the hope of encouraging other non-Indigenous peoples to examine themselves, their own location and positioning in Canadian society, and to reconsider their own relationships (or lack of) with Indigenous peoples.

A VIEW FROM CULTURAL BORDERLANDS

I grew up in the crowded, at times, chaotic and dirty metropolis of London, England. When I left for Canada in the 1990s, the population of Greater London had reached seven million people. I was raised in a small nuclear family that spent little time with extended family members. My mother's parents, both from the working classes in the East End of London, had been raised in an orphanage where they had met one another as children. According to family myth, my great grandmother and her sisters would socialize with the Chinese dockworkers near her home in the slums, which is how she met my great grandfather, a Chinese sailor who came to England with the East India Company.

When my great grandmother passed away shortly afterwards, my great grandfather remarried and gave the children up to the orphanage. (The orphanage was actually an industrial school model.) My grandfather was just five years old. My grandmother's story is similar. At the tender age of three, she was given up to the orphanage by her father after her mother passed away as a young woman. No other extended family members were able or offered to keep the children with their own families. My grandparents' family relationships were fragmented; sisters and brothers had been separated into different houses at the school and had little time to bond and develop nurturing relationships. This is all I have gleaned about my mother's family history.

As a child I was fascinated with learning more about my ancestry, perhaps because we knew so very little and no one ever really wanted to talk about what we did know. However, growing up I always wanted to know more about the industrial school my grandparents attended. I found it so strange to think that I would never know anything about the adults that raised my grandparents. Time and time again I would ask about the strangers—the school staff—that raised them, and usually my incessant child's questioning would be met with awkward silence. Even as a child I sensed that the past seemed to carry too much hurt and shame.

I know even less about my father's family simply because he never showed much interest in talking about them, and we spent very little time in their company. As far as I can recall, my father's parents were also from the working classes in London. I believe that my grandfather was a carpenter and my grandmother was a seamstress. Consequently, my family tree has very short branches.

As a child, I promised my mother that I would live with her forever, but throughout my teen years I yearned for a cleaner, more rural setting in which to live my life. I intensely disliked the gray skies and dirty, littered gray sidewalks, and I felt trapped inside what I experienced as a busy, overcrowded, concrete, artificial world. As a young woman, I felt profoundly separate, alienated, and therefore vulnerable within my own society and on my own land. So, at age 21, I came to Canada by myself, looking for a sense of community.

In my first four years here as an international exchange student and then as a young master's student, I spent most of my time living in artificially constructed communities on university campuses. During the last eight years, I have lived within reserve communities. Consequently, I have never really experienced immersion into mainstream Euro-Canadian society.

From my perspective as an immigrant coming from the imperial centre, there was no disputing that Indigenous peoples all over Canada had been subjected to the outright theft of their lands and resources. I found this shameful, and my sense of indignation motivated me to learn as much as I could about Canada's colonial history.

As a newcomer to Canada, I found it very challenging to develop friendships when, as I and other immigrants quickly discovered, it seemed you need to book an appointment to simply get together. This was a little unusual for me and, in fact, after I met my husband and began living in reserve communities, I found social relationships a lot more relaxed, and it was easy to develop genuine friendships. By contrast, non-Indigenous peoples seemed to lack a sense of community. Abdullah states that the "dominant consciousness paradigm of our [Western] society is 'I Am Separate,'"[7] and this was evident in the lay out of the communities, towns, and cities. Never before had I been so dependent on a vehicle to get everywhere—to connect with other people or simply purchase basic groceries.

As an exchange student, I selected classes where I could learn more about colonization. Within a year of coming to Canada I had learned about the *Indian Act* and the long history of legislation enacted to appropriate Indigenous peoples' lands and resources, remove children from their families, reduce the number of individuals qualifying for official Indian status, and many other oppressive forms of public policy.

As an Englishwoman who was raised in London, the imperial centre, I felt a sense of obligation to learn about the actions and attitudes of the many British explorers, merchants, missionaries, and settlers that had come to Canada before me. From my perspective as an immigrant coming from the imperial centre, there was no disputing that Indigenous peoples all over Canada had been subjected to the outright theft of their lands and resources. I found this shameful, and my sense of indignation motivated me to learn as much as I could about Canada's colonial history.

I made a conscious effort to find books and articles written by Indigenous scholars and I began attending events that were hosted by local Aboriginal organizations and the First Nations Student Centre at the university, including conferences, forums, urban powwows. I also signed up as a volunteer to help cook dinner and serve at a local Community Action Program for Aboriginal children and their families. In these social settings, I was usually a minority. With my strong English accent, I stood out like a sore thumb, but I was always made to feel welcome. People seemed surprised that I did not seem to have any preconceived ideas and that I was interested to listen to their stories and experiences of living in

Canada as Indigenous peoples. I often did not say too much as it soon became apparent that I did not know very much, had a lot to learn, and would gain more from listening. In these settings, I experienced a sense of authentically connecting to people that seemed to be lacking at the university and other non-Indigenous social settings.

These early experiences as a newcomer motivated me to enroll as a graduate student in a master's program, as I wanted to learn more about the Indian residential schools that so many of the First Nations people I had come to know had described attending as children. Perhaps because my own grandparents were raised by strangers in positions of authority at an industrial school in England, I grew up with some level of emotional sensitivity regarding the institutionalization of infants and children and the profound intergenerational consequences of the separation and alienation of sibling relationships, the loss of parenting role models, and the lack of emotional support and unconditional love and acceptance.

Maybe for these reasons I listened attentively when I heard the testimonies of the many Indigenous peoples in Canada who courageously tell of their experiences of compulsory attendance at Indian residential schools and of their families and communities who, reeling from the devastating effects of whole generations of children, tell of losing the opportunity to love, nurture, and educate their own children.

When First Nations Survivors would talk about their experiences in the Indian residential schools, I wondered, "Who were the people who raised these little children? Where are they now? As they look back in the present day, what do they now think of the schools? How do they process present day critiques of the schools, and what ways do these critiques impact on their lives and sense of self? Do they understand these critiques? These are the kind of questions that motivated me to initiate a research project that would involve interviewing Anglo-Canadian former school staff.

I was struck by how distinctly Indian residential school policies violated the UN *Convention on Genocide*.[8] Notwithstanding even the violent, physically abusive character that was an integral part of the culture of the schools, the prohibition of language, culture, and Indigenous identity profoundly struck me as practices of cultural genocide. Yet, the government, the public-at-large and even the media that has extensively reported the testimonies of First Nations Survivors appear resolute in avoiding discussions of cultural genocide.

As the standard response was to stonewall First Nations peoples demands for public inquiries and concrete responses to accusations of cultural genocide, I wondered where all the retired Indian agents, church and government bureaucrats, missionaries, school teachers, dormitory supervisors, and other colonial employees with living memories were and whether they talked to their children and grandchildren about their experiences. What stories would they tell? I also wondered how First Nations Survivors, their families, and their communities would feel if former colonial agents began sharing their perspectives and telling their stories. Would a project proposing to interview former staff be experienced and perceived as furthering injustice?

With these thoughts in mind, I developed a participatory research project that included interviews with six Aboriginal people to elicit their views on why we might ask former Indian residential school staff about their experiences of working in the schools and how these stories may further Indigenous and non-Indigenous peoples' understandings of the Indian residential school system and colonialism in the present day. I questioned as to what extent an opportunity to develop interview questions for former staff might be welcomed by Indigenous peoples, and would this be perceived and experienced as a potentially beneficial method of addressing social injustice and of initiating new relationships founded upon dialogue and respect.

EXPLORING ETHICAL SPACES IN INDIAN RESIDENTIAL SCHOOL RESEARCH

History has attested to the usefulness of dialogue between oppressed individuals and their oppressor groups as a continuing effort towards achieving social justice. My research approach parallels extensive dialogues that have taken place between the children of former Holocaust survivors and Nazi perpetrators, written in several books that have explored these interpersonal and textual dialogues. These research studies explore issues of social justice (including interpersonal and intergenerational justice) and, in doing this kind of research, ask critical questions that are of significance to discussions on the roles of colonial actors in facilitating injustice through the support of Indian residential schools. Some of these critical questions include:

+ How are we to understand the mechanisms that lead ordinary people to be complicit in facilitating social injustice on a grand scale?

+ Who are those people exactly?

+ Do they feel accountable for the wrong they have done?

+ Can good or ordinary people pursue heinous acts?

+ Can individuals belonging to oppressor groups understand and acknowledge the roots of pain that are experienced by survivors of oppression?

+ Can (children of) survivors understand and acknowledge the viewpoints of the (children of) perpetrators?

+ To what extent may resentment and indignation stand as fatal obstacles to restoring equal, moral relationships between an oppressor and the oppressed social groups?[9]

These studies also emphasize the profound impact of genocide on the descendants of survivors and perpetrators as they struggle to understand how to live their lives "in the shadow" of genocide and make sense of their present-day roles in relation to the burdens of history that they have inherited.[10]

The issues that face present-day Germans, including the children of Nazis, Nazi sympathizers, and the passive bystanders of genocide could provide great insights to non-Indigenous Canadians who are struggling to reconcile their national image with a violent history of oppression and cultural genocide. In post-war Germany and post-apartheid South Africa, silence and denial characterized the responses of perpetrators of oppression, as well as the responses of bystanders.

In similar ways, colonial societies such as in Australia, New Zealand, and Canada have been characterized by an active resistance to acknowledging the oppression of Indigenous peoples. "Settlement as forgetting," Stephen Turner explains, is "a condition of [and intrinsic to colonial] culture" and enables settler societies "to live ahistorically."[11] Everett Worthington notes that "the perpetrators in atrocities almost never apologize to the victims," and if they do "admit to their deeds, they usually do not express regret and remorse, but rather justify and excuse their acts." He adds, "In genocide and mass killing, both victim and perpetrator are wounded. However, they are wounded in different ways ... Even though victims and perpetrators are wounded in different ways and pass those wounds on to subsequent generations, it is difficult for the perpetrators to admit that they are wounded."[12]

As Canadians, we may be vaguely aware of these kinds of dialogues between oppressed and oppressor groups within the context of the Holocaust or the South African Truth and Reconciliation Commission. It is only recently, with the establishment of the Indian Residential Schools Truth and Reconciliation Commission, we have had to consider how we might facilitate these kinds of dialogues between Indigenous peoples and the descendents of colonial peoples here in Canada. The Commission is resolved to include all Canadians in a process of truth-telling and healing. From their work with second generation Holocaust survivors and the Nazi perpetrators, Alan and Naomi Berger's definition of "working through" may assist non-Indigenous peoples with this process. They suggest that in working through,

> one revisits the source of pain by speaking about it, analyzing its impact on an individual's perception of psychosocial life, his/her religious perspective, and his/her view of the 'other.' In the process, one seeks to detoxify the issues involved so that further exploration and understanding can occur without the various psychic barriers that can block self-understanding ... this way of working through enables one to be in touch with the past without being paralyzed by its legacy.[13]

The six Aboriginal participants[14] who guided the development of my project on former Indian residential school staff emphasized the necessity for non-Indigenous peoples to begin working through the history and present-day colonization of Indigenous peoples. They showed great insight into the complex and painful process of listening to the experiences of former staff, individuals who may tell stories and hold onto truths that greatly contrast with the realities and truths of First Nations Survivors. Henry, an educator from the Secwepemec Nation, described how the perceptions of non-Indigenous peoples often fall dramatically short of the reality of Indigenous peoples lived experiences.

> The work that needs to happen is to understand what the process is… the colonizer must see themselves doing different work than colonizing. For example, the Minister of Indian Affairs believes that he's doing good work, but ask anyone else [Indigenous peoples] and they see them as the bad guys. So the colonizer needs to look at this.

Gord was a younger Aboriginal participant who had been removed from his Cree birth family and placed into the home of a white foster family during his childhood. His experiences of cultural alienation as a survivor of the Children's Aid Society and as a life skills counsellor working with First Nations Indian residential school Survivors led him to reflect on the experience of childhood trauma. He envisioned that former staff might have a role in healing relationships between Indigenous and non-Indigenous peoples by:

> Decycling it [the abuse] by unravelling it, by putting it in front of you and looking at it … I think a part of what the teachers themselves … need to understand is that … they need to come to an understanding within themselves and those who have decided to seek help on what they did, I think that's the only time there is going to be an opportunity to be healing for themselves, and to ask themselves their own questions, 'As a teacher, why did I do that? Who taught me that?' All these things, there are so many isolated individual situations that I think they need to face up to, to take responsibility for your actions … It's even better when they come forwards and say, 'Oh yeah, I did make a mistake and I want to come forwards and I want to do something to help heal.

Gord anticipated that former staff would have to undergo a healing journey because "trying to assimilate a human being and make them something that they are not [is a very] dysfunctional way of looking at life." He had many questions for former staff such as: "Do you feel that what you did during the residential school era made a change? Is that a

Paternalism in the last half of this century is our legacy. I see it as a refined form of colonialism which our cousins, the Indians in the south and in the west, are familiar with. Men who abuse women learn it from their fathers. Therefore, one shouldn't be surprised that some of our people practice paternalism themselves when in a position of power over others. That is why it is very important to me and my neighbours that as much self-governing power and resources as possible must be restored to the community and family levels.

Saali Peter
Big Trout Lake First Nation
Speaking at the public hearings of the Royal Commission on Aboriginal Peoples
Iqaluit, NWT
26 May 1992

healthy change for another human being? Does it contribute to another person's quality of life?"

During her life, Virginia, from the Okanagan Nation, was an outspoken Survivor of the Indian residential school system. She encouraged me to interview former staff as a means toward continued dialogue and raising awareness of the schools among the larger society. She repeatedly expressed her concern that the history of the residential schools will one day be forgotten. She felt strongly that most non-Indigenous peoples "say that us natives are just making stuff up." She shared with me painful memories of attending the Indian residential school in Cranbrook so that "people should know the truth and not hearsay." While she encouraged me to interview former staff, she felt strongly that they would be unable to, "tell you the truth. I believe deep down they won't because they themselves did a lot of harm to us. How else can they justify it? They can't. To tell you the truth I wouldn't believe their stories because I think they'll only tell you what they think you want to hear."

Many of the participants considered that it may be useful to learn about the experiences of former staff who worked in Indian residential schools and that it may also be useful to integrate these accounts into the history of the schools. However, I was advised by Erma, a teacher-in-training from the Nuu-chah-nulth Nation, to handle the perspectives and stories of colonial actors with care because "it is another perspective that hasn't been looked at. And to have the whole story, you do need other and all perspectives." All of the Aboriginal participants stressed the need for me to critically examine the values and beliefs underlying the Indian residential school stories of former employees. As Bobby and Alvin from the provincial Indian Residential School Society explained:

> Canadians cannot be persuaded that all these things could happen. We can use some of the staff members to see how people's perspectives can become so skewed. If we can persuade former employees who were there, then maybe others will also recognize.

WHAT CAN WE LEARN FROM ENGAGING IN DIALOGUE WITH COLONIAL ACTORS?

My interviews with former staff started in 2001, a full two years into my master's program. Between 1999 and 2001, I had taken a leave from my studies to accept a graduate co-op position, which coincidentally was at the En'owkin Centre, an Indigenous post-secondary institute on the Penticton Indian Band reserve that is partnered with University of British Columbia Okanagan's Indigenous Studies program. While working at the En'owkin Centre, I developed many long-lasting friendships. I also met my husband.

Consequently, by the time I began my interviews with former staff, my socio-cultural positioning had shifted considerably. Even within a short time period of living in Okanagan communities, I had heard countless painful stories told by elders, their children, and their grandchildren in which Indian residential schools seemed like prisons where children learned to live in fear of expressing themselves culturally, emotionally, and spiritually in case of punishments meted out by powerful staff members. I also, for the first time, witnessed individuals of all ages struggle to re-learn or to learn from scratch their own languages following the lasting impact of language prohibition policies in the schools. In my relationship with my husband, I also became an instant stepmother, a caretaker to three infants, and began to see the world through the eyes of children.

Before my first interviews with staff, I experienced feeling both intensely nervous and angry. It was difficult to imagine meeting individuals who had worked in the residential schools and hearing their stories from the perspective of adults in authority, when for so long I had been listening to Survivors tell their stories of how these schools and the staff looked through the eyes of vulnerable children.

I found myself experiencing alternating feelings of sadness and anger throughout the long process of doing two sets of interviews with four former staff. I also felt some anxiety and tension about going into these homes, opening my heart to experience the uniqueness of individual former staff, and taking an empathetic approach while making space for the stories of staff. I felt this would make me something of a traitor to the many First Nations Survivors and their descendants whose negative stories of schooling I had listened to over the years. Contradictorily, I also acknowledged to myself that former staff would likely assume by looking at me that this young white woman would listen without prejudging or silencing them. My dual roles offered a utility to carry out the project successfully, but created considerable inner turmoil and confusion.

The one man and three women were church-going senior citizens in their sixties and seventies. They opened their homes to me, serving me tea and cookies and, in one instance, a full meal at the dinner table. Their attitudes were welcoming, and our encounters seemed somewhat formal, with an unspoken acknowledgement that I was in their home to gather information.

While our initial encounters were a little awkward, all four of the participants appeared to open up, and they expressed a sense of relief at being offered an opportunity to work through years of silence on their perspectives and experiences at Indian residential schools. Several of the staff presented themselves as victims of silence. Beverley, a former girls' dormitory supervisor at Alberni Indian Residential School, shared "hearing about these abuses and these things that happened that were so dreadful, that I just closed up and would not speak about it, having been there or anything else."

After hearing about the court cases, Christine, a former teacher at Norway House, also, "stopped talking about having worked as a teacher for two years in an Indian residential school because I got quite uncomfortable about it. Right away the stereotype and people's minds jumped to conclusions and I thought, 'I don't need this.'" Sharing their experiences at the schools seemed to be a process of seeking validation for the four former staff.

As Jack, a former boys' dormitory supervisor at Alberni Indian residential school, stated that staff were most likely motivated to share their stories, "I guess a part of it would be to ease our conscience ... These things did happen, the schools did happen." In a separate interview, Beverley also stated, "I couldn't say, 'It didn't happen.' It happened."

Talking to former staff and hearing their stories of working in the schools was an extremely challenging process for me emotionally. I had started the project with some hope that through the process of participating in the interviews and receiving feedback on their interviews from the First Nations participants (communicated through me), would create possibilities for former staff to question their commonsensical beliefs and ideas about the cultural superiority of non-Indigenous peoples. I had hoped that the sharing of stories would help to "forge a common story that could serve as a basis for a different kind of reconstructed memory ... [an] exceptionally difficult"[15] challenge. These hopes were only partially realized. Only Christine, a former teacher, seemed deeply emotionally invested in the process of examining the values and beliefs that had led her to work in the schools, as well as her actions during her period of employment. As she shared a painful memory of slapping the face of a child, she seemed full of shame and regret. She recalled:

> Oh, you could see the anger in his eyes. And really he had every right to have hit me, when I think back, but he did not. But I knew that the hatred was there, and I lost that with him. There is no way you could ever reconnect after you've gone over that line. And I knew that was the wrong thing to do for him and for me. I've regretted that all my life.

I completed my project with former Indian residential school staff in 2003 but I am still struggling to share my work with a wider audience so that people may learn from these dialogical encounters between Indigenous peoples and colonial actors, because I am still not entirely sure what we may learn from talking with and listening to former staff and other colonial actors. Christine's emotional journey seemed to suggest that further textual dialogues between First Nations Survivors and former staff may contribute to a shift in colonial consciousness in the larger society. However, as the interviewer responsible for facilitating the process, it was difficult to consider the emotional turmoil that Christine, as a compassionate and self-critical human being, may have experienced as a result of her participation:

> I think ... see, sometimes I think I don't want to question ... Yes, I wished I hadn't started [the interviews] because I don't think I'm that useful, number one. And number two, I found it really unsettling ... First of all, I was angry at myself. Not at you, I don't think. It was at me. I thought, "Why did I ever think that I

could do this?" Then I thought, "Well, I have to think about this and not get ... what is this issue?" So after that, I sort of calmed. When I get angry I don't bawl or swear or anything. I just get turmoil inside. Then I have dreams. I didn't dream about that issue.

Observing the absence of critical self-reflection experienced by former staff was even more difficult, because it challenged me to reconsider my own ideas about how to create space for humanizing perceptions of both non-Indigenous and Indigenous peoples between both groups. Upon reading my final project, Jack's simple response evokes the paradox and ambiguity of being confronted with competing realities: "On the whole, Natalie, I feel that you have read too much into what we said. We were all just young people trying to do a job with very little support."

Textual dialogues between individuals in oppressed and oppressor groups open up space to examine the challenges that individuals in dominating groups face as they attempt to comprehend their roles in perpetuating the oppression of others in society within the complexity of creating dialogues based on mutual compassion, humanness, and respect. In my final telephone conversation with Christine, she shared having thought about the idea of setting up a workshop where dialogue might take place between First Nations Survivors and former staff. However, she concluded that she would have to "avoid this kind of situation because I'm not emotionally stable enough to do that ... I feel sad when I listen to them [Survivors], and I feel real empathy that they have that anger and sadness in them."

Many of these kinds of workshops have been utilized in facilitating dialogue between the children of Holocaust survivors and Nazi perpetrators, and perhaps these approaches would be possible with the descendants of colonial actors and First Nations Survivors. I hope that the preliminary textual dialogues shared here may offer some insights into the challenges and opportunities offered by truth and reconciliation.

WHAT CAN WE OFFER OUR CHILDREN?

You didn't do it, so why are you defending it? You don't have to because you can oppose it just as easily as you can embrace it ... You *can* separate yourself from what has been done—and what's *being* done. But first you have to be willing to call what's being done by its right name.[16]

I approached the study of the accounts of former staff of Indian residential schools with the belief that the prohibition of Indigenous cultures and languages at Indian residential schools in the past will continue to be perpetuated into the present day unless the non-Indigenous population can turn our gaze and look into the mirror to examine the colonial images of ourselves and our ancestors.

In the present day, my family and I are involved in a revitalization movement that is sweeping through the Okanagan Nation. Two of my stepchildren attend a small band-operated elementary school for elementary grades kindergarten to six that focuses on Sqilxʷ culture and language immersion. Most of the children in attendance at the school are cousins. They learn *Nxsilcen* from 9 to 12 A.M., and in the afternoons, they learn a modified version of the provincial curriculum. My toddler, goes to the daycare on-reserve and participates in a Language Nest program. Every morning, he is greeted in *Nxsilcen* by a fluent Elder and an apprentice language assistant who work in the infant toddler room.

Over the last three years, our whole family have attended (sometimes irregularly) a weekly three-hour evening language class, which is also taught by an Elder and language apprentice. Since these programs began, the desire to see our children grow up as fluent *Nxsilcen* speakers with a secure sense of their cultural identity now absorbs almost every aspect of our family's daily lives.

The responsibilities of family, the children's education, and community life leave me with little time to spend outside of the community, and I know few non-Indigenous people in the neighbouring towns. Consequently, graduate school offers a different view of the world that contrasts greatly with my everyday reality of life at home on the reserve. My unique standpoint as a white woman on the margins of an Aboriginal community provides me with an interesting view of non-Indigenous and Indigenous peoples relations. It also raises many difficult questions about how non-Indigenous peoples perceive their roles in defining and re-defining relationships with Indigenous peoples and moving towards truth and reconciliation.

In the present day, Aboriginal peoples across Canada are struggling to develop and maintain elementary and secondary schools to revitalize critically endangered languages and cultural knowledge for their children with very little awareness or support within mainstream society. The per capita allocation to operate band schools is less than the monies provided to operate public schools, even though band schools face enormous challenges in taking control of their own education and overcoming the negative historical experiences of education in Indian residential schools.[17] These challenges speak loudly to the continued lack of value placed on Indigenous languages, knowledge, and culture by the dominant society.

How may non-Indigenous peoples move towards reversing the pattern of prejudice that is entrenched in the master narrative of Canadian history and acknowledge past colonial projects as acts of cultural genocide and abuses of Indigenous people's human (and community) rights? The recent official federal government apology and appeal for forgiveness from Indigenous peoples, including demands by other government leaders of Canada to sign the *United Nations Convention on the Rights of Indigenous Peoples*, adds new weight to the necessity for non-Indigenous peoples to examine ourselves. What shift in consciousness will it take for the Canadian public to discover themselves as oppressors in the past and present day and to demonstrate solidarity with First Nations by demanding the government to provide support for Indigenous communities to revitalize their languages and cultures for future generations?

When will non-Indigenous peoples find the courage to face their own discomfort and lack of knowledge of Indigenous peoples and cultures? When will we, with open hearts and minds, initiate dialogues with Indigenous peoples and be ready and willing to listen and learn about the lived experiences and harsh realities of colonization from those whose lives continue to be shaped by oppression? When will we, the newcomers on this land, finally understand all we have taken, and continue to take, of Indigenous peoples lands, resources, languages, and knowledge? When will we open our hearts and minds so that our consciousness of colonization may grow and that we may feel some of the pain of all that has been lost to future generations? When will we look beyond ourselves to fully see how disconnected we are from this living land, recognize our lack of knowledge, and grieve?

Only when we look beyond our own limited views of ourselves that are fostered by our narrow social and cultural experiences will we be able to see and accept that not so long ago it was our own ancestors who were the Indian agents, residential school staff, church employees, and colonial bureaucrats and that, even today, ourselves, our families, and our communities are colonizers who continue to benefit from the dispossession of Indigenous peoples' lands and resources. When we see Canadian society through these new eyes, we will then begin to experience anger as we witness continued social injustice, feel resistance towards our prescribed roles as oppressors, break the silence of colonization as forgetting, and initiate new relationships with Indigenous peoples as allies, activists, and caring fellow human beings. We must continually ask ourselves: "What can I do? How can I learn more? Who and what can I influence?" In challenging ourselves in these ways, we may begin to engage in an emotional shift.

As we begin to accept our roles in perpetuating colonization and oppression, a new paradigm may begin to emerge that is based on compassion and relationships and where diversity may be embraced and cherished. My husband, Okanagan educator Bill Cohen contemplates this new paradigm where truth and reconciliation is actualized and, "perhaps generations from now, our children can eat salmon together at a feast, and peoples from diverse cultures can meet and share in the spirit of generosity and cooperation."[18]

As a parent and step-parent of children engaged in Okanagan language and cultural revitalization projects, I find my life increasingly shaped by community processes that emphasize the sharing of special skills and knowledge for the benefit of the collective. In the reserve community in which I call home, I am first and foremost a mother and a parent with responsibilities toward my children. It is from this place that I must explore possible ways to engage others through caring, sharing, respect, reciprocity, and reflexivity and, hopefully, insights into how, as a researcher, I can best contribute in the future may follow.

NOTES

[1] Abdullah, Sharif M. (1995: 6–13). *The Power of One: Authentic Leadership in Turbulent Times*. Gabriola Island, BC: New Society Publishers.

[2] Henderson, James (Sa'ke'j) Youngblood (2000:32). The context of the state of nature. In Marie Battiste (ed.), *Reclaiming Indigenous Voice and Vision*. Vancouver, BC: University of British Columbia Press: 11–38.

[3] Kelly, Fred (2008:11). Confession of a born again pagan. In Marlene Brant Castellano, Linda Archibald, and Mike DeGagné (eds.), *From Truth to Reconciliation: Transforming the Legacy of Residential Schools*. Ottawa, ON: Aboriginal Healing Foundation: 11–40.

[4] Armstrong, Jeannette C. (1997:para. 3). Sharing one skin: native Canadian Jeanette Armstrong explains how the global economy robs us of our full humanity. *New Internationalist* Jan-Feb, 1997. Retrieved 17 April 2009 from: http://findarticles.com/p/articles/mi_m0JQP/is_287/ai_30411447/

[5] Armstrong (1997:para. 4).

[6] Hill Collins, Patricia (1991:35). Learning from the outsider-within: The sociological significance of black feminist thought. In Mary Margaret Fonow and Judith A. Cook (eds.), *Beyond Methodology: Feminist Scholarship as Lived Research*. Bloomington, IN: Indiana University Press: 35–59.

[7] Abdullah (1995:14), see note #1.

[8] Article II, includes: "a) Killing members of the group [a national, ethnical, racial, or religious group, as such]; b) Causing serious bodily or mental harm to members of the group; c) Deliberately inflicting on the group conditions of life calculated to bring about its physical destruction in whole or in part; d) Imposing measures intended to prevent births within the group; e) Forcibly transferring children of the group to another group." *Convention on the Prevention and Punishment of the Crime of Genocide*, adopted by the General Asssembly of the United Nations on 9 December 1948. Retrieved 17 April 2009 from: http://www.un.org/millennium/law/iv-1.htm

[9] Weissmark, Mona Sue (2004). *Justice Matters: Legacies of the Holocaust and World War II*. New York, NY: Oxford University Press.

[10] Berger, Alan L. and Naomi Berger (eds.) (2001:1). *Second Generation Voices: Reflections by Children of Holocaust Survivors and Perpetrators*. New York, NY: Syracuse University Press.

[11] Turner, Stephen (1999:21). Settlement as forgetting. In Klaus Neumann, Nicholas Thomas, and Hilary Ericksen (eds.), *Quicksands: Foundational Histories in Australia & Aotearoa New Zealand*. Sydney, AU: University of New South Wales Press: 20–38.

[12] Worthington, Everett L., Jr. (2006:261). *Forgiveness and Reconciliation: Theory and Application*. New York, NY: Routledge.

[13] Berger and Berger (2001:6), see note #10.

[14] The following participants are indicated by first name only, and the interviews were conducted from October 2001 to July 2003.

[15] Worthington (2006:260), see note #14.

[16] Churchill, Ward (2002, 2004:163). Ward Churchill. In Derrick Jensen (ed.), *Listening to the Land: Conversations About Nature, Culture and Eros*. White River Junction, VT: Chelsea Green Publishing Company: 153–163.

[17] Personal correspondence with Bill Cohen, April 2009.

[18] Cohen (2009).

Sisters holding Aboriginal babies, circa 1960
Photographer: Sister Liliane
National Archives of Canada, PA-195122

[Reprinted from the Legacy of Hope Foundation's *Where Are the Children?* exhibit catalogue (2003)]

JOHN RALSTON SAUL

John Ralston Saul was born in Ottawa, Ontario. He studied at McGill University and at University of London, where he obtained his doctorate in 1972. A Companion in the Order of Canada (1999), he is also Chevalier (knight) in the Ordre des Arts et des Lettres (Order of Arts and Letters) of France (1996). His 14 honorary degrees have been given to him by McGill University, University of Ottawa, and Herzen State Pedagogical University in St. Petersburg, Russia, among others.

John is an award-winning essayist and novelist who has been having a growing impact on political and economic thought in many countries. John believes that Canada is influenced and shaped by Aboriginal ideas: egalitarianism, a proper balance between individual and group, and a penchant for negotiation over violence are all Aboriginal values that Canada has absorbed. Among many issues that he is particularly known for his commentaries, of note are his discussions on the nature of individualism, citizenship, and the public good and the role of freedom of speech and culture. John is presently Series Editor of Penguin's "Extraordinary Canadians" project. He is also the co-chair of the Institute for Canadian Citizenship, patron and former president of PEN Canada, founder and honorary chair of French for the Future, chair of the advisory board for the LaFontaine-Baldwin lecture series, honorary chair of the Project Advisors' Committee for Evergreen at the Brickworks, and patron of the Canadian Academy of Independent Scholars, PLAN (a cutting edge organization tied to people with disabilities), Engineers without Borders, and the Canadian Landmine Foundation.

As a writer or editor, John has had many works published, both fiction and non-fiction. His latest works include *A Fair Country: Telling Truths about Canada* (2008) and *The Collapse of Globalism and the Reinvention of the World* (2005). His works have been translated into more than a dozen languages. John has received many national and international awards for his writing, most recently the Pablo Neruda International Presidential Medal of Honour from the Chilean government. He also received the Governor General's Literary Award for non-fiction, two Gordon Montador awards, and a *Premio Lettarario Internazionale* in Italy.

RECONCILIATION: FOUR BARRIERS
TO PARADIGM SHIFTING

Reconciliation can only begin when the people of Canada collectively wish it. This proposed desire to live differently with the *other* has to be precisely that—a desire. Travelling about the country over the years and, in particular, over the last two months after publishing *A Fair Country*,[1] I have sensed that people are now ready for reconciliation. I sense this particularly from the eagerness with which many Canadians have embraced the idea that Canada is a country inspired more by Aboriginal world views than European world views. Many Aboriginal leaders have been saying this in one way or another for many years, but it has been as if non-Aboriginal people were not listening, did not know how to listen, or were intimidated by the message. Now, many are no longer intimidated by this way of thinking. How many? I sense that this is building into a new consensus; yet, a consensus can be nothing more than romanticism if people do not work out why they now feel this way and what went so wrong that it obscured our shared reality for a century and a half. I can think of four things that still stand in the way. Four barriers will have to be dealt with, and some of Canada's institutions will have to undergo paradigm shifts if any real reconciliation is to take place.

BARRIER ONE:
LACKING A PLAN FOR CHANGE

First, while non-Aboriginal people may now be ready for change, many of them still have no idea of how to go about it. This is no longer the result of ill will. They simply have little sense of what that change would look like realistically. Those who have been explaining the situation and laying out scenarios for decades—those involved with the Royal Commission on Aboriginal Peoples, for example—must be amazed at how little of this debate has made its way into the public consciousness. Each breakthrough, which ought to have been initiated immediately, has broad implications for how our society could function. Supreme Court decisions such as *Guerin* and *Delgamuukw*,[2] for example, or the Haida and Taku decisions[3] on the obligations to consult have been immediately shrunk into the narrowest possible definitions. These breakthroughs are

The *Delgamuukw v. British Columbia* court case was launched by the Gitxsan and Wet'suwet'en peoples and was intended to reclaim their land through acknowledgement of ownership, jurisdiction, and self-government of their traditional territories by the provincial and federal governments. The decision of the Supreme Court of Canada, handed down on 11 December 1997, did not settle the original claim, but it did confirm the existence of Aboriginal title in British Columbia and has since had far-reaching effects on policies, positions, mandates, and laws that impact on First Nations, especially with the treaty negotiations process. The decision also ensured that, in future trials, oral evidence would be granted as much weight as written evidence.

The Haida Nation and the Taku River Tlingit First Nation decisions provide an obligation to consult with Aboriginal communities when Aboriginal rights and title to lands and resources could be affected.

still treated as if they are exceptions to the rules of Canadian society, which they are not.

Canadians in general now seem to be ready to assume guilt or responsibility for wrongs done when it comes to questions on Aboriginal issues. But guilt and responsibility are only preliminary steps. They may clear the way for change, but they do not represent change itself. If left on their own, they can become an obstacle to change. For example, I can see a tendency in public representations of guilt and responsibility to tie both to an assumption that Aboriginal society is largely broken and irreparably dysfunctional. In other words, while the willingness to apologize is genuine, it is somehow tied to an assumption that things are really not going well among Indigenous peoples and that these problems are irresolvable.

This attitude is partly the outcome of an addiction among mainstream media to cover up what does not work in society in general. In the case of covering up stories on Aboriginal issues, this sort of tabloid populism, even in the best newspapers or on the best television programs, is not counterbalanced by any other view of Indigenous society. And so the persistent waves of dysfunctional stories represent, for most Canadians, the only stories they hear. And even the occasional positive stories—for example, that there were 27,000 Status First Nations people in post-secondary education in 1999, up from 200 in the mid-1960s[4]—are presented as an artificial lamentation that the numbers are below the national average.

In such an atmosphere, a myth—a false myth—is created, which is not so different from the myth of a century ago that Aboriginal people represented a dying civilization because they did not adapt to the modern world. Now, Aboriginal people are represented as a growing population that cannot function in contemporary society, unless of course they accept the concepts of that society, which is to say the concepts derived from Europe. In other words, the conscious intellectual concepts of many Canadians have not changed; yet other Canadians sense that these concepts do not really work for them or for Canadian society as a whole. And, of course, they do not work for Aboriginal people.

Reconciliation can only happen if these concepts are based on truth—a truth that works for all people—and clarity of understanding between people. Guilt and pity, on the other hand, destroy human relations. Of course, these very real social problems were produced by the residential schools, the lack of respect for treaties, and the long period of institutionalized racism. These cannot be solved in an atmosphere of guilt and pity. The most basic need is to obtain knowledge and therefore understanding. There is a remarkable and fast-growing new Aboriginal leadership, which has a very good understanding of both Indigenous and non-Indigenous civilizations, such as how they fit together in their historic and modern forms and how they are influenced by each other. These leaders are finding new ways to be heard by their own communities and, also, by Canadians in general. This is happening because they are novelists, playwrights, lawyers, academics, and political figures. Their influence is growing incrementally and their understanding is key to breaking the old, intellectually lazy assumptions of most Canadians. The central need is not incremental; it is for a broad understanding of what change would look and feel like for everyone. I will come back to this under the subject of language.

BARRIER TWO:
NOT HEARING TRUTHS

Now it is essential to look at the second barrier, which is how people listen to the most fundamental of truths; how they are able to hear them. The most basic of steps—moving towards reconciliation because we are able to listen to the truth—has only just begun. It will be a long process because people who have suffered have yet to be heard in any sustained way. They need to hear themselves being listened to. They need to hear others hearing them. Which others? Their families and communities, the population as a whole, the religious and civil organizations that had overseen the wrongdoing, and the governments that are ultimately responsible.

People are beginning to understand how painful this will be for both the speaker and the listener, but these truths must be spoken because healing is itself a painful process. Yet, it is meant to be a process of dignity and self-affirmation for those who suffered, not one in which guilt and pity pull everyone down. It is not meant to add to the dominant false

In *Guerin v. The Queen*, Musqueam First Nation sued the federal government for breach of trust in the lease for the Shaughnessy Heights Golf Course in south Vancouver, which was entered into by the federal government on behalf of Musqueam First Nation. When disclosed, the actual terms of the lease were much less favourable than the terms discussed with the Department of Indian Affairs when the First Nation agreed to surrender the land. The decision of the Supreme Court, handed down in 1984, recognized the Crown's fiduciary relationship with First Nations. It established that the Crown would be held to a rigorous standard of loyalty toward First Nations when dealing with First Nations' interests in land. Ten million dollars in damages were awarded in favour of Musqueam First Nation.

myth of Aboriginal society being dysfunctional in the modern world. It is meant to be a humanizing process in which people who were not the victims learn to understand the dehumanizing nature of suffering. Suffering does not disappear simply because it has been evoked. That long experience of being heard and of hearing is meant to bring people through their suffering and their guilt to a new shared dignity.

BARRIER THREE:
NEEDING A COMMON LANGUAGE

The third barrier brings us back to language. Reconciliation is neither romantic nor easy. It can only happen if people share a language that they feel to be true. What I mean by *language* is a way to evoke and share an understanding. This is where the greatest difficulty lies. The language by which Canada most commonly functions remains passively derivative of nineteenth century British and French concepts. As we have slipped closer to the United States, our dysfunctional language has been increasingly adapted to reflect the US version of the same European ideas.

This Euro-American way of expressing relationships and situations is tied to the old concepts of the monolithic, Westphalian nation-state, which assumes that there will be a centralized mythology, a natural majority of citizens, probably with some racial foundation, and a form of loyalty based on the habits of that majority. Yet, Canada is not monolithic, it is not at all Westphalian, and it does not have a centralized mythology or a natural majority in its citizenry. Loyalty cannot therefore be based on the habits of a majority. Loyalty here could perhaps be based upon shared ethics or a sense of place or of inclusion—something that resembles an Aboriginal world view of the circle. As for the possibility of racial loyalty, it does not even make pseudo-sense as a Canadian concept.

If a country persists in using a false language, it will not be able to function. In the case of reconciliation, each time an Aboriginal leader uses terms such as *self-government*, *sovereignty*, or *nation*, the non-Aboriginal listener hears these terms in the Euro-US sense—quite a different sense than how Aboriginal listeners perceive these terms. Georges Erasmus talked about this at length in his LaFontaine-Baldwin lecture: "even when we used the same words, Aboriginal people and government representatives

> Suffering does not disappear simply because it has been evoked. That long experience of being heard and of hearing is meant to bring people through their suffering and their guilt to a new shared dignity.

were often talking about different things."[5] He was referring partly to the in-depth research by the Royal Commission on Aboriginal Peoples into language, meaning, and the possibility of understanding; but also to the legacy of misunderstanding that has stonewalled discourses between Aboriginal and Canadian people for the last three centuries and into the new millennium.

What I have argued in *A Fair Country* is that most Canadians are confused by what they actually mean when they write or speak. Why? It is because they remain chained to Euro-US meanings, as if Canada were a culture inspired by and derived from Britain, France, and the United States and from European ideas of philosophy, politics, and law in general. There is influence of course, but if this approach does not ease and strengthen in the way we deal with ourselves and with others, then that influence cannot be as profound as we think. It is a more meaningful interpretation to see ourselves as a civilization inspired by Aboriginal world views. The way we act at our best makes sense when it is traced to Aboriginal language, meaning, and concepts coming out of the shared experiences of the seventeenth, eighteenth, and early nineteenth centuries. Again, as Georges Erasmus puts it: "This is how Canada came to be a 'peaceable kingdom,' not one born of violence and conquest."[6] For me, this explains the instinctive, positive reaction I have continually heard when I evoke the concept of inspiration based on Aboriginal world views for the whole civilization, whether from old-stock immigrants or new arrivals.

If this idea of a more accurate inspiration is accepted, then it becomes quite easy to develop a language of meaning that works on all sides. It is a matter of education. This means rethinking the way in which we teach philosophy, law, literature, political science, and so on. Today, they are all taught as if there was no reality here, as if everything important begins elsewhere. While it is good to have specializations and therefore good to concentrate on Aboriginal law or literature, this should not mean that Aboriginal world views are sidelined as a closed shop specialty. These ideas also need to be built into the heart of how we all think about philosophy, politics, and literature. That is how you construct the language of understanding and reconciliation. To be precise, if the Aboriginal concept of the circle is the basis of the Canadian approach towards citizenship, immigration, and federalism, we make a terrible mistake in acting as if the sources for these things were mysteriously found in the Enlightenment, in the Westphalian nation-state model, or in early European democracy.

There are three obvious examples of how faulty this approach can be, and they lie in 1) the status of *Delgamuukw*, 2) the treatment of Aboriginal languages, and 3) the federal government's approach to Northern sovereignty.

Delgamuukw represented an important breakthrough in the formal indigenization of Canadian law, not simply in the treatment of indigenous oral memory. Of course, the legal recognition of oral memory was a revolution in the interpretation of this case and of other related cases. But Canada is, in general, a far more oral culture than any other Western democracy. This orality is constantly being enriched by the strengthening of Aboriginal society and its role in Canada and by the continuing arrival of immigrants—soon to be citizens—whose first language is neither English nor French. For the whole life of these new first-generation citizens, their relationship with Canada will be primarily oral. If this works in a way that is not so easily done in other countries, it is because there is a strong inheritance of Aboriginal orality, very much alive and powerful, upon which new Canadians can build. This Aboriginal-immigrant relationship should be one of the most important relationships in Canadian society. Yet, the mainstream structures seem to stand in the way of what could be the single most important conversation inside our society—between Aboriginal people and new Canadians. This is a missing conversation central to any real reconciliation. Few efforts are being made to encourage it, yet there is no history of antagonism or betrayal between Aboriginal people and new Canadians. Without slipping into generalizations, many of the latter are simply confused by a debate from which they feel excluded.

The precise comment that can be made on *Delgamuukw* is that it could be used as a broad principle throughout governmental legal debates with Aboriginal people and throughout Canadian law in general. *Delgamuukw* represents a partial normalization of the indigenous roots of Canadian law. Perhaps this reality is being ignored by most of the legal community because it threatens their Euro-US-derived state of mind. But that is their problem. It should not be ours. The concept of orality in Canadian civilization, with its inspiration and roots derived from Aboriginal world views, could be a valuable tool in altering the nature of our shared conversations, in indigenizing them and, therefore, in opening another path to a deeper sort of reconciliation. English and French aside, there are more than fifty surviving languages indigenous to this place. Each of them belongs to a particular people that are also part of the complex Canadian texture. The large majority of these languages are in danger of extinction.[7] That is a tragedy for their particular nation, but it is also a tragic loss for all Aboriginal and non-Aboriginal people in Canada. A language lost represents the closing of a door on our ability to understand ourselves in this place. Not to understand this is to reveal a deep dependence on the colonial model of imported cultures as the root of Canadian civilization. How can we talk of reconciliation when the Government of Canada is still dragging its feet to support the teaching of these languages? They are an essential part of the shared collective unconscious.

The current anxiety over Canadian sovereignty in the Arctic echoes the colonial mindset. Our claims are based on a legal thread leading from unsuccessful British explorers—trying to get through the Arctic to somewhere else—to British ownership, and from there to Canadian ownership. You would have thought that a simpler and far stronger legal argument would have been that Canadians have been living in the Arctic for thousands of years. They are Inuit. We are attempting to make our shaky British-derived claim through the Law of the Sea arguments, but this law is based on a European legal idea of water—a few hundred years old—as something that separates land and is susceptible to penetration by enemies. The Inuit-based idea—thousands of years old—is that water and ice join land, and it is this idea that constitutes the principal means of communication for Inuit. We would do far better to advance this concept. That would mean describing Canada as a country indigenous to this place, and that would mean the development of a language of reconciliation.

What I am arguing here is that a mass of Aboriginal words and concepts exists that presents the world and our existence in a very different way than that of standard European concepts. There is an urgent need to bring those words and concepts into a broad public place. If we do so and talk among ourselves about their full meaning, I believe that we will

We are treaty people. Our nations entered into a treaty relationship with your Crown, with your sovereign. We agreed to share our lands and territories with the Crown. We did not sell or give up our rights to our land and territories. We agreed to share our custodial responsibility for the land with the Crown. We did not abdicate it to the Crown. We agreed to maintain peace and friendship among ourselves and with the Crown.

Chief George Desjarlais
West Moberly First Nation
Speaking at the public hearings of the Royal Commission on Aboriginal Peoples
Fort St. John, British Columbia
20 November 1992

discover both the roots of our shared civilizations and the fundamental language of reconciliation.

BARRIER FOUR:
ABSENCE OF SHARED PUBLIC MECHANISMS

The fourth barrier to this reconciliation is the absence of the practical, shared public mechanisms from which we can all work. Some of these are painfully obvious. As long as the treaty and other related negotiations are dragged out, it will remain impossible for everyone to move towards a constructive relationship. As long as most non-Aboriginal people in Canada do not understand the role and implications of the treaties, let alone understand that they too are treaty people, the negotiations will drag on in a modern facsimile of the old ways. The life of endless legal details does nothing for anyone except for those who are paid to drag out the process. Meanwhile, the lives of Aboriginal leaders are marginalized by their need to concentrate on treaty battles rather than on broader social construction and reconciliation. For years now, good people have tried to get this message of waste across to the population at large. Banal though it is to say, but as long as treaty-related negotiations are not finished, reconciliation will not happen. The mechanisms of delay, being as deeply anchored as they are in our governmental and legal systems, means that only pressure from the broad population can speed up government action.

PARADIGM SHIFTING

Of course, the process of treaty negotiations will continue, yet I cannot help but think that a very precise strategy is needed to change education across the country. Some provinces have already begun building the Aboriginal pillar into their teaching of history to classes that are largely non-Aboriginal. The challenges are only partly about history and geography, they are also about ideas central to the way in which we all imagine ourselves. Our civics courses need to build ideas from Indigenous world views into the primary explanations of our democracy. Our literature courses, still structured as if we were colonial outcroppings of Britain and France, need to be radically changed. Philosophy and ethics are taught in our high schools as if Canada did not exist, let alone the Aboriginal civilizations that shaped Canada.

I believe Treaty commitments are paramount law.

Barack Obama's
Message for First Americans
24 October 2008

In other words, there is an urgent need to go to the provincial ministers of education in order to propose how curricula could be changed. Equally, there is a need to attack our university systems in a highly strategic way. Environmental studies need to be attacked for their artificially value-free approach and their avoidance of an Aboriginal concept of humanity's integrated *place* in the process. Philosophy departments have to be pushed to change their narrow and derivative European approach. Our whole concept of Northern studies illustrates the basic problem. We are the only circumpolar country without a university in the Arctic. We have three colleges. The southern universities have a monopoly on Northern studies. Their professors and students come up in the summer to study and observe. They head back home for winter in the South. There is no buildup of wealth of Northern studies in the North, let alone investment in the communities. A three-campus Northern university with four research chairs at each would radically change the way everyone thinks about the Arctic, the Inuit, and the northern environment. There would be a long-term opportunity for Inuit and other Aboriginal and non-Aboriginal professors to develop real northern study centres in the North, attracting young Inuit and other Canadians.

At the heart of all that I am describing lies the gradual slippage of Canadians moving away from the idea that citizens—Aboriginal or not—can be part of modernity if they live in smaller isolated communities. The truth is that Canada cannot exist if we think of it as merely a southern, urban reality. What then becomes of the physical country and the necessary balance between place and people? Over half of the 1.2 million Aboriginal people in Canada live at least part of the year in cities,[8] but Canada only makes sense as a country if its whole physical reality works. This means seeing the non-urban country—that is, most of our non-Westphalian nation-state—as a positive force that must be strengthened. That means treating the non-urban country not as a costly appendage and realizing that these hundreds of communities need to be seen as filled with purpose—another sort of purpose—which makes the whole country make sense. The idea of Canada as a place tied to a deeply non-urban and non-rural civilization is key to understanding ourselves and therefore understanding what reconciliation might feel like.

All of this is part of the idea that people can only discover and live reconciliation if they understand what it would look like and feel like. It means to think of themselves in a different way—a way that is not European derived. If non-Aboriginal people in Canada begin to see themselves as being from here in the sense that they are inspired by ideas proper to this place and to the peoples of this place, then reconciliation will make sense to them.

Notes

[1] Saul, John Ralston (2008). *A Fair Country: Telling Truths about Canada.* Toronto, ON: Viking Canada.

[2] *Delgamuukw v. British Columbia*, [1997] 3 S.C.R. 1010; and *Guerin v. The Queen* [1984] 2 S.C.R. 335.

[3] *Haida Nation v. British Columbia (Minister of Forests)*, 2004 SCC 73; and *Taku River Tlingit First Nation v. British Columbia (Project Assessment Director)*, 2004 SCC 74. For a good review of these decisions, *see*: Olynyk, John (2005). The Haida Nation and Taku River Tlingit Decisions: Clarifying Roles and Responsibilities for Aboriginal Consultation and Accommodation. *The Negotiator* (April 2005):2–7.

[4] Lumb, Lionel (2006). Closing the gap in First Nations Education Will 'Transformative Change' Really Happen? *The Teacher* (March 2006):5.

[5] *Cited in*: Saul, John Ralston, Alain Dubuc, and Georges Erasmus (2002:101). *The LaFontaine-Baldwin Lectures: A Dialogue on Democracy in Canada.* Edited by Rudyard Griffiths. Toronto, ON: Penguin Canada.

[6] *Cited in*: Saul, Dubuc, and Erasmus (2002:106).

[7] *See*: Canadian Heritage (no date). *Aboriginal Languages Initiative (ALI) Evaluation.* Retrieved 2 December 2008 from: http://www.pch.gc.ca/progs/em-cr/eval/2003/2003_01/tdm_e.cfm

[8] Statistics Canada (2008). *Aboriginal Peoples in Canada in 2006: Inuit, Métis and First Nations, 2006 Census.* Ottawa, ON: Minister of Industry.

Spanish Indian Residential School
Courtesy of S.J. Collection – The Shingwauk Project

GREGORY YOUNGING

Gregory Younging is a member of Opsakwayak Cree Nation in Northern Manitoba. He holds a Master of Arts degree from the Institute of Canadian Studies at Carleton University and a Master of Publishing degree from the Canadian Centre for Studies in Publishing at Simon Fraser University. He received his doctoral degree from the Department of Educational Studies at University of British Columbia.

Gregory has worked for the Royal Commission on Aboriginal Peoples, Assembly of First Nations, and Native Women's Association of Canada. From 1990 to 2003, he was Managing Editor of Theytus Books. He is now Coordinator of the Indigenous Studies Program at University of British Columbia Okanagan in Kelowna. Gregory is a former member of Canada Council's Aboriginal Arts Advisory Committee (1997–2001) and the British Columbia Arts Council (1999–2001). He is Chair of the Indigenous Peoples Caucus of Creator's Rights Alliance (2002– present).

Some of his articles have been published in Australian Canadian Studies Journal (1996), Prairie Fire Literary Journal (2001), Indigenous Affairs Journal (2003), (Ad)Dressing Our Words: Aboriginal Perspectives on Aboriginal Literature (2001), and most recently, Aboriginal Oral Traditions: Theory, Practice, Ethics (2008). He has edited or co-edited the Gatherings series now in its tenth volume. Gregory has also published a book of poems, The Random Flow of Blood and Flowers (1997).

INHERITED HISTORY, INTERNATIONAL LAW, AND THE UN DECLARATION

Now the apology done applause can begin
Now the apologies done applause begins
If it bleeds it leads If it cries it flies ...

Now the struggle has a
name ...

Some truth some reconciliation and gone with the wind
If it feeds the need If it dies it dies[1]

INHERITED HISTORY

My own understanding of the immense impact of the residential school system came as a gradual realization. My family members who attended residential schools either sheltered me from, and/or sheltered themselves from the reliving by telling about, the experience. The generation of our parents, aunts, and uncles did their best to grow up together on Beatlemania and Trudeaumania after *the experience*. My cousins and I later found out that our parents would sometimes seek condolence among each other. (In the knowledge that they were the last generation to go through the experience first-hand, they did not want to burden us with it.) As for me and my cousins, we listened to The Guess Who as kids and, then later, watched Gretzky (yes, I dreamed that one day I would play like him). Although most of my female cousins preferred The Carpenters and Rod Stewart (and maybe were not so much into hockey), we tried to blend in and be good little Canadian kids; but it never really worked. As teenagers, we all retreated into our own self-reflections each in our own way, sometimes supporting each other, and we came out with a collective stark discovery: "Something is wrong here!"

As we became young adults, some of the residential school stories started to slip out. And when they did, in what I recall as my darkest moments, my cousins would share them with me. *"Do you know how Uncle lost a finger?" "Did you ever wonder why they all speak Cree and they didn't teach us?" "This is hard, but do you know what happened to your mom?"* In a way, it was perhaps good that we were on a slow learning curve about what happened (just like Canada is now). There was usually plenty of time between the unceremonious unveilings of our family's residential school experience to slowly contemplate what it might mean. Yet even so, I now realize that I blocked out parts of this second-hand knowledge of our family history. On some level of my consciousness, I did not or do not want to know. Indeed, this realization has helped me understand why the generations before us blocked out the first-hand knowledge and did not want us to know.

My mother was one of the many residential school Survivors who did not make it through high school. She recalls that, as a middle-aged adult, she visited a friend who was taking university courses and saw coursebooks on the table and told her friend, "I have read those books so maybe I could go to university someday." Soon after, she entered an upgrading program and then started taking university night courses. She became the first Survivor to do her master's and doctoral research on the residential school system. *Dealing with the Shame and Unresolved Trauma: Residential School and Its Impact on the 2nd and 3rd Generation Adults* is Dr. Rosalyn Ing's (my mother) 1990 University of British Columbia Ph.D. thesis. Due to my mother's extensive research on the multi-generational impacts of residential schools, I have been made acutely aware of myself and my cousins as second-generation Survivors and my daughter, nieces, and nephews as third-generation Survivors, although the impact on us could never measure up to that of the generations before us.

I will never forget the profound experience I had at The Banff Centre for the Arts Publishing Workshop in 1991. All of the workshop participants formed imaginary publishing companies and developed book project ideas to promote at a mock book fair. My book concept was a book on residential schools (in the back of my mind it was my mother's research). I stood up to introduce my book to the booksellers and book sales agents at the pretend book fair—who were actually real publishers, booksellers, and book sales agents and some were of the best in the business—and started to tell them about how "it is time for a book about this dark chapter in Canadian history to be published." As I continued, trying to impress my high-profile audience, my voice began to crack, and then I was suddenly overcome with tears. I backed away for a few moments to regain my composure. I tried to continue my presentation, but the tears flowed even harder. I tried again, but I just could not do it. In the end,

I had to walk away thinking to myself "what is this I just experienced?" *There's that word again:* "experience."

Our generation inherited this family history by just being who we are—part of the continuum of our ancestors' legacy right through to the few generations that preceded us. This was not by our own choice, and certainly this was not by our parents' choice as they attempted to shelter us from it, but the truth eventually prevails. Indigenous peoples often refer to our "blood memory," meaning that the experience of those that have gone before us is embedded in our physical and psychological being. What happened to me at The Banff Centre in 1991 was that the pain of my family, those who went to residential school, was being channelled through me, and I was experiencing it as my own pain. Blood memory is also closely linked to the Indigenous precept of the present generation being the transition between the past and future generations; thus, we carry the responsibilities of honouring our ancestors' legacy and safeguarding the rights and well-being of future generations.

The blood memory state of being is not exclusive to Indigenous peoples, although it is certainly more prevalent in Indigenous existence. In order for this grand concept of reconciliation to work, Canadian people, too, need to inherit the history of those that have gone before them if they are to forge a better path into the future.

> The neo-conservative right, in both Canada and Australia, relies for its arguments on historical revisionism or denial. They claim that Aboriginal poverty and ill health are the result of the failure of contemporary policies rather than the product of hundreds of years of colonialism and that any moral wrongs occurred as part of colonial history.[2]

Apart from their relationship with Indigenous peoples, Canadians first need to undergo a type of micro-reconciliation within themselves. In so doing, the present generation of Canadians need to face up to what has been done in their name, and they must own it as being part of who they are. Canadians need to play catch-up in the big reconciliation game, because Indigenous people have already done that. Canadian reconciliation must begin with: 1) throwing out all the historical disassociations and denials, and 2) getting out of the prevailing generation-centric headspace. As

Indigenous peoples often refer to our "blood memory," meaning that the experience of those that have gone before us is embedded in our physical and psychological being.

we attempt to venture down the road toward reconciliation, Canadians would probably benefit a lot by learning from, and viewing the world like, Indigenous peoples; not vice versa.

THE DOCUMENTED, IGNORED HISTORY

Canada's unknown history is well-documented and goes back to the early foundations of international law governing interactions and agreements between nations. The principles of international law were expressed by the British Crown in the *Royal Proclamation of 1763*, which stated "that the several Nations or Tribes of Indians with whom We are connected … should not be molested or disturbed in the Possession of such Parts of Our Dominions and Territories as, not having been ceded to or purchased by Us, are reserved to them."[3] The Upper and Lower Canada acts of 1850, one being *An Act for the Better Protection of the Lands and Property of Indians in Lower Canada* and the other *An Act where the Better Protection of Indians in Upper Canada imposition, the property occupied or enjoyed by them from trespass and injury*, further recognized these principles within their titles.

The *British North America Act* of 1867 also acknowledged the responsibilities of the *Royal Proclamation* and upheld the honour of the Crown in Section 91(24), stating that "It shall be lawful for the Queen … to make Laws for the Peace, Order, and good Government of Canada, in relation to … Indians and Lands reserved for the Indians."[4] It was on the basis of international law and treaty processes established in Europe that treaties were signed between the British Crown and the Indigenous nations from 1871 to 1921 in the territory that became known as Canada. These treaties involved two categories of lands: 1) unsurrendered Indigenous territories, which would remain under Indigenous control, and 2) land bases that were for British settlement. This is why Canadians need to recognize that they too are treaty people.[5]

This early history of the relationship between Britain/Canada and Indigenous peoples is based on international law, nation-to-nation negotiations, and mutual consent. However, towards the end of the treaty period, Canada began to stray down a path leading away from international law to an adversarial and hostile relationship with Indigenous peoples. This era, which continues through to today, includes

We need a nation-to-nation relationship.

Barack Obama's Message for First Americans 24 October 2008

the residential school system and several other breeches of international law that was later developed through the United Nations. With *An Act to encourage the gradual Civilization of the Indian Tribes in this Province, and to amend the Laws respecting Indians* of 1857 and *An Act to amend and consolidate the laws respecting Indians [Indian Act, 1876]* (the treaty process had begun that year), Canada also began passing laws designed to eliminate Indigenous peoples without their consent. In the later 1800s, Canadian parliamentarians began to view Indigenous peoples as an obstacle to complete control of the resources and territories in Canada and began to speak of "the Indian problem." The legislation and policies from this period of Canadian history have since been amended and altered, but the basic tenets remain.

CANADA'S RECORD IN THE UNITED NATIONS, 1948 TO 2009

In 1922, Cayuga Chief Deskaheh, then leader of Haudenosaunee Six Nations Confederacy, went to the League of Nations in Geneva to ask that Canada be prevented from taking over Haudenosaunee lands. Although The League of Nations did not agree to pursue the issue, supportive statements were made by Dutch, Panamanian, Estonian, and Persian delegations who administered sound rebukes to the United Kingdom and Canada for their treatment of Indigenous peoples.[6] In 1923, the Haudenosaunee applied to become members of the League of Nations, as did the Maori in 1925, but both claims were denied. The League categorized these claims of Indigenous nationhood as "domestic."[7]

Canada would find itself at odds with international standards for its treatment of Indigenous peoples several more times. When the UN was formed immediately after World War II, one of the fundamental purposes was to prevent what had happened to the Jewish people in Germany (the Holocaust) from happening to any other peoples of the world again. *Never Again.* This would be achieved by constructing a new international human rights regime to complement and support the ongoing body of international law. This human rights regime is now paramount and includes such prestigious United Nations documents as:

- *Convention on the Prevention and Punishment of the Crime of Genocide,* 1948

If it's "truth and reconciliation" we're after with regard to the residential schools, then the first truth we need to establish is that the Indian Residential Schools were not the result of a "misguided policy undertaken with the best of humanitarian intentions," as they're often described, but rather a pillar in the attempted genocide of Canada's indigenous peoples. The residential schools are often called a "tragedy," but they weren't a tragedy, they were a policy. They were conceived and run with genocidal intent, and from what I've seen on Main Street in Winnipeg and the lower east side of Vancouver and on the reserves, they are continuing to have a genocidal impact on Native societies.

Ward Churchill
Briarpatch Magazine
June/July 2008

- *Universal Declaration of Human Rights, 1948*
- *Geneva Conventions, 1949 (four protocols during wartime)*
- *Declaration of the Rights of the Child, 1959*
- *Declaration on the Elimination of Discrimination Against Women, 1967*
- *Declaration on the Elimination of All Forms of Racial Discrimination, 1963*
- *International Convenant on Civil and Political Rights, 1966*
- *Convention on the Law of the Sea, 1982*
- *Convention (No. 169) Concerning Indigenous and Tribal Peoples in Independent Countries, 1989*
- *Convention on Biological Diversity, 1993*
- *Convention on the Protection and Promotion of the Diversity of Cultural Expressions, 2005*
- *Declaration on the Rights of Indigenous Peoples, 2007*

From the start, Canada's treatment of Indigenous peoples was at odds with the UN human rights regime beginning with the *Convention on the Prevention and Punishment of the Crime of Genocide* and the *Universal Declaration of Human Rights*. The United Nations' *Convention on the Prevention and Punishment of the Crime of Genocide* states the following:

> The Contracting Parties confirm that genocide, whether committed in time of peace or in time of war, is a crime under international law …
>
> In the present Convention, genocide means any of the following acts committed with intent to destroy, in whole or in part, a national, ethnical, racial or religious group, as such:
>
> (a) Killing members of the group;
>
> (b) Causing serious bodily or mental harm to members of the group;
>
> (c) Deliberately inflicting on the group conditions of life calculated to bring about its physical destruction in whole or in part;
>
> (d) Imposing measures intended to prevent births within the group;
>
> (e) **Forcibly transferring children of the group to another group.**[8]

There is ample evidence that the residential school system clearly committed all acts of genocide listed above between 1831 and 1998, and more evidence is sure to emerge during the term of the Truth and Reconciliation Commission. Canada engaged in efforts to dodge the *Convention on the Prevention and Punishment of the Crime of Genocide* by presenting an illusion of acceptance. On 3 September 1952, Canada became a signatory to this convention. Meanwhile, Canada redefined genocide in its Criminal Code to omit any mention of policies or actions Canada was currently engaged in that would reflect genocidal acts as defined by the United Nations. The residential school system also stands in breech of the following articles of the *Universal Declaration of Human Rights*:

> Everyone has the right to freedom of thought, conscience and religion; this right includes freedom to change his religion or belief ...
> (1) Everyone has the right to education ...
> (2) Education shall be directed to the full development of the human personality and to the strengthening of respect for human rights and fundamental freedoms. It shall promote understanding, tolerance and friendship among all nations, racial or religious groups ...
> 3) Parents have a prior right to choose the kind of education that shall be given to their children.[9]

In 1978, Sandra Lovelace took her case of Indian Status removal and sexual discrimination under the *Indian Act* to the Human Rights Committee of the United Nations. The Committee asked for more information and allowed the Canadian government to defend its actions. The Canadian government claimed that it would like to change the law, but did not feel it could without the agreement of First Nations people, who were divided on the issue.[10] In 1981, the Committee found that Canada was in breach of Article 27 of the *International Convenant on Civil and Political Rights*.

REPORT OF THE UN SPECIAL RAPPORTEUR 2004

In 2004, The UN Commission on Human Rights mandated Special Rapporteur Rodolfo Stavenhagen to investigate the situation of human rights and fundamental freedoms of Indigenous people in Canada. He found that:

> Poverty, infant mortality, unemployment, morbidity, suicide, criminal detention, children on welfare, women victims of abuse, child prostitution, are all much higher among Aboriginal people than in any other sector of Canadian society, whereas educational attainment, health standards, housing conditions, family income, access to economic opportunity and to social services are generally lower.[11]

Stavenhagen's report states that Canada's interpretation and implementation of existing Aboriginal and treaty rights set out in the *Constitution Act* of 1982 has been slow. Also, the insufficient land base of First Nations reserves was in need of expansion to allow for future growth and development.

> While Aboriginal persons may eventually attain material standards of living commensurate with other Canadians, the full enjoyment of all their human rights, including the right of peoples to self-determination, can only be achieved within the framework of their reconstituted communities and nations, in the context of secure enjoyment of adequate lands and resources.[12]

Stavenhagen recommends:

> That special attention be paid to the nexus between the Residential Schools restitution process, the transgenerational loss of culture and its attendant social problems such as adolescent suicide rates and family disorganization ... That new legislation on Aboriginal rights be enacted by the Parliament of Canada, as well as provincial legislatures, in line with the proposals made by RCAP [Royal Commission on Aboriginal Peoples] ... and that it adopt an even more constructive leadership role in the process leading to the adoption of the Draft Declaration on the Rights of Indigenous Peoples, as demanded by numerous Canadian indigenous peoples' organizations and expected by many other organizations worldwide.[13]

THE UNITED NATIONS' DECLARATION ON THE RIGHTS OF INDIGENOUS PEOPLES

The Working Group on Indigenous Populations (WGIP) was established in 1982 as a subsidiary organ of the Sub-Commission on the Promotion and Protection of Human Rights. In 1985, WGIP began preparing a draft *Declaration on the Rights of Indigenous Peoples*, taking into account the comments and suggestions of participants in its sessions, particularly representatives of Indigenous peoples and governments. In 1993, the working group agreed on a final text for the *Declaration* and submitted it to the sub-commission.[14] The *Declaration* went through over a decade of redrafting and debate in WGIP and other rigorous and involved formal UN processes and forums. It was not until 2007 that the UN General Assembly adopted the *Declaration* by an overwhelming majority; however, it was opposed by the United States, Australia, New Zealand, and Canada.

The politics around the *Declaration* is an arduous struggle between Indigenous peoples and nation states in which a new paradigm for Indigenous peoples' integrity as international entities unto themselves will emerge.

The *Declaration* is on par with other UN human rights declarations and conventions listed previously. The *Declaration* contains all aspects of rights required for decolonization and the re-emergence of Indigenous nations. Indigenous peoples can no longer be viewed as cultural groups contained within the borders of nation states. Likewise, Indigenous peoples rights can no longer be regarded as the subjects of colonial nation states. The new, emergent consciousness displaces the familiar discriminatory models of imperialism and colonialism, based on racism.[15]

RECONCILIATION AND OPPOSING THE DECLARATION

Canada's proposed attempt at reconciliation against the background of its UN record and Stavenhagen's 2004 report is difficult to reconcile, especially when this report specifically recommended that Canada should take a leadership role in supporting the *Declaration*. How are Indigenous peoples in Canada supposed to comprehend this? Are we being asked not to make a connection between the country's domestic policies on

We have set the Indians apart as a race. We've set them apart in the ways the governments will deal with them. They have been set apart in law. They have been set apart in the relations with government and they've been set apart socially too.

Prime Minister Trudeau
From a speech on Indian, Aboriginal, and treaty rights Vancouver, British Columbia 8 August 1969

Indigenous peoples and its international ones? Are the *Indian Residential Schools Settlement Agreement* and the Apology supposed to overshadow the undoing of the *Kelowna Accord* and Canada's overt anti-Indigenous stance in the United Nations? To worsen the situation, of the four UN member states opposed to the *Declaration*, Canada is the only one who has not shown any movement since September 2007.

On 3 April 2009, The Government of Australia officially announced its support of the *Declaration on the Rights of Indigenous Peoples*.

> The Declaration on the Rights of Indigenous Peoples is the most comprehensive international tool to advance the rights of indigenous peoples. An overwhelming majority of the States voted for the Declaration in the General Assembly in 2007, and we are pleased to see that this support is today expanding further with Australia endorsing the Declaration.[16]

Debate has also taken place in New Zealand's Parliament, where Indigenous Members of Parliament, who knew of Australia's impending announcement of support for the *Declaration*, raised the issue and will continue to mount political pressure. There have also been strong statements from Barack Obama on Indigenous rights, such as the following message he made as a senator before he became the president of the United States:

> Indian nations have never asked much of the United States, only for what was promised by the treaty obligations made by their forebears. So let me be clear: I believe that treaty commitments are paramount law, I'll fulfill those commitments as president of the United States.[17]

There have also been some indications that the Obama administration may also reverse the United States' position on the *Declaration*.[18]

What may occur in New Zealand and in the United States regarding the *Declaration* is a matter of speculation at this point in time, but some potential for a change of positions appears to exist in the two countries. No such sign of potential change of position has yet been shown from Canada. The Apology of the current minority government and its purpose of supposedly paving the way for the Truth and Reconciliation Commission is not an isolated initiative. It must all be interpreted in the broader national and international context. The Government of Canada's position on the *Declaration on the Rights of Indigenous Peoples* puts the country out of line with the UN human rights regime and the aspirations of Indigenous peoples in Canada and elsewhere.

Neither a meaningful reconciliation with Indigenous peoples can occur under these circumstances nor a UN member state like Canada—which attempts to portray an image of respect for tolerance and human rights to its citizens and the world—can continue to uphold such a paradox in the face of international opinion and pressure. Such open hostility will continue to taint Canada's relationship with Indigenous peoples and act as an impediment to reconciliation. *Canada WILL sign the United Nations Declaration on the Rights of Indigenous Peoples.* It is only a matter of time, but history has already recorded the initial and ongoing opposition. This, too, will become another part of future generations of Canadians' inherited history and Indigenous peoples' blood memory.

NOTES

[1] Excerpt from The Tragically Hip's song *Now the Struggle has a Name* (2009). Retrieved 28 April 2009 from: http://www.thehip.com/albums/

[2] Warry, Wayne (2007:53). *Ending Denial: Understanding Aboriginal Issues.* Toronto, ON: University of Toronto Press.

[3] To see the full text of the *Royal Proclamation of 7 October 1763*, please visit the National Aboriginal Document Database: http://epe.lac-bac.gc.ca/100/205/301/ic/cdc/aboriginaldocs/m-stat.htm

[4] For full text, *see*: http://www.canlii.org/eliisa/highlight.do?text=british+north+america+act&language=en&searchTitle=Federal&path=/en/ca/const/const1867.html

[5] *See*: John Ralston Saul's article, "Reconciliation: Four Barriers to Paradigm Shifting," in this publication.

[6] Lâm, Maivân Clech (2004). Remembering the Country of their Birth: Indigenous Peoples and Territoriality. *Journal of International Affairs* 57(2):129–150.

[7] Henderson, James (Sa'ke'j) Youngblood (2008). *Indigenous Diplomacy and the Rights of Peoples: Achieving UN Recognition.* Saskatoon, SK: Purich Publishing.

The Government of Canada's position on the *Declaration on the Rights of Indigenous Peoples* puts the country out of line with the UN human rights regime and the aspirations of Indigenous peoples in Canada and elsewhere.

[8] United Nations' *Convention on the Prevention and Punishment of the Crime of Genocide*, 1948. Retrieved April 15 2009 from: http://www.un.org/millennium/law/iv-1.htm

[9] United Nations' *Universal Declaration of Human Rights*, 1948 [emphasis added]. Retrieved 15 April 2009 from: http://www.un.org/Overview/rights.html

[10] Sandra Lovelace biography (no date). Retrieved April 15 2009 from: www.mta.ca/about_canada/study_guide/famous_women/sandra_lovelace.html

[11] United Nations (2004:2–3). *Human rights and indigenous issues: Report of the Special Rapporteur on the situation of human rights and fundamental freedoms of indigenous people, Rodolfo Stavenhagen, on his mission to Canada* (21 May to 4 June 2004). Retrieved 15 April 2009 from: http://daccessdds.un.org/doc/UNDOC/GEN/G05/100/26/PDF/G0510026.pdf?OpenElement

[12] United Nations (2004:22).

[13] United Nations (2004:23–25).

[14] Posey, Darrell and Graham Dutfield (1996:29). *Beyond Intellectual Property: Toward Traditional Resource Rights for Indigenous Peoples and Local Communities.* Ottawa, ON: International Development Research Centre. Retrieved 15 April 2009 from http://www.idrc.ca/en/ev-9327-201-1-DO_TOPIC.html

[15] Henderson, James (Sa'ke'j) Youngblood (2008). *Indigenous Diplomacy and the Rights of Peoples: Achieving UN Recognition.* Saskatoon, SK: Purich Publishing.

[16] Australian government announcement on the UN *Declaration on the Rights of Indigenous Peoples*, 3 April 2009, Cited in the Statement by Michael Dodson – United Nations Permanent Forum on Indigenous Issues – Pacific community nominated member & Forum rapporteur. Retrieved 15 April 2009 from: http://www.un.org/esa/socdev/unpfii/documents/Australia_endorsement_UNDRIP_Michael_Dodson_statement.pdf

[17] Obama, Barack (no date) *Barack Obama's Commitment to Native Americans.* Retrieved 15 April 2009 http://www.democrats.org/a/2008/06/obama_native_americans.php

[18] Paul, Alexandra (2009). Chiefs hope Obama will listen: First Nations leaders meet with his advisers. *Winnipeg Free Press*, 9 January 2009. Retrieved 15 April 2009 from: http://www.winnipegfreepress.com/local/chiefs_hope_obama_will_listen.html

Courtesy of Legacy of Hope Foundation

CONCLUSION

WORK IN *PROGRESS*

From Truth to Reconciliation and *Response, Responsibility, and Renewal* present compelling arguments that the landscape of Canada has changed. The questions are *how* and *to what extent*.

Some may argue that Canada—the way we experience it, the way we perceive it—has changed for the better. Some may highlight recent words and actions and the impacts—positive or negative—on their lives. Others may argue that there have been changes for Aboriginal people—to whatever degree—but new words and actions have not rectified fundamental problems, and the sentiments and deeds are of little or no significance to non-Aboriginal Canadians. Others will and have argued that what we have seen is more of the same and, thus, not new and not *change* at all.

This last argument is a difficult one, both to make and, for some, to swallow. But, as some of the authors in the preceding pages have argued, issues like residential schools, child welfare, and various legislative, policy, and programmatic developments must be placed within a larger colonial context, and that context is in both history and present-day reality, with alarming possibilities for our future. Then, there is the fact that some people may have no idea what change we are talking about. However, we may be able to agree that there have, at the very least, been developments with regard to the relationship between Aboriginal people and Canada.

The *Indian Residential Schools Settlement Agreement*, a court-ordered settlement endorsed by Survivors' legal representatives, churches, and the federal government in 2006 and implemented as of September 2007, is an historic first. That is change. Within this larger historic first are other smaller changes: advance cash payments of $8,000 to all eligible former students who were 65 years of age or older on 30 May 2005; a common experience payment (CEP) of $10,000 for the first year and $3,000 for each subsequent year to Survivors living in 2005 or their estates if deceased; and an individual assessment process (IAP) for adjudication of cases of more serious abuse. These developments are *change*, most notably in the sense that CEP and IAP are responses to overwhelming criticism of the previous alternative dispute resolution process. Nonetheless, the compensation experience and, of course, the influx of tens of thousands of dollars into individual households and communities has meant impacts on individuals and communities—some positive, some neutral, and some negative.

The other components of the *Agreement* also signal change. The creation of a $20 million fund for commemoration of the legacy of residential schools, at both the national and with community-based events, and for the establishment of a Truth and Reconciliation Commission (TRC) with a five-year mandate consistent with many of the recommendations of the Royal Commission on Aboriginal Peoples (RCAP) is a response to Survivors' and communities' expressed desires to see the experiences of Survivors documented and shared and the effects nationally and internationally acknowledged. In commemoration, too, there is an opportunity to acknowledge and celebrate individual and collective Survivor and community resilience. The TRC has the potential, for some, to address many of the RCAP recommendations.

To what end?

This seems to be a question that remains afloat, without a definitive answer, beyond *reconciliation*. There are countless examples of individuals and organizations attempting to define what reconciliation is and what it means in context, philosophically and practically. This volume and its predecessor contain such examples. The five-year extension of funding for the Aboriginal Healing Foundation (AHF) to support community-based healing initiatives, the final component of the *Agreement*, has allowed the Foundation to engage in the reconciliation dialogue with others, and AHF has been privileged to work with many other parties in healing initiatives.

But to what end? So that "those affected by the legacy of Physical Abuse and Sexual Abuse experienced in Residential School ... [may address] the effects of unresolved trauma in meaningful terms, [break] ... the cycle of abuse, and ... [enhance] their capacity as individuals, families, communities and nations to sustain their well being and that of future generations."[1] Promoting reconciliation—whatever it means in the end—

is part of that commitment. So, too, is gauging the impacts on the healing journeys of individuals and communities for the purpose of better serving the needs of Survivors and of those affected intergenerationally. We see Aboriginal communities transformed, with healthier communities and individuals across and within Canada contributing to a transformed Canada, a *healthier* Canada.

Transformation is possible, as John Borrows, the renowned Indigenous lawyer and professor, writes:

> Canada is a work in progress. An unfinished national project that inspires hope, and an advanced federal state that bleeds along provincial seams. People in many countries would consider themselves fortunate to live in a country such as Canada. Others feel grateful to live in places that have a deeper sense of national purpose, historic legacy, and political cohesion … Nevertheless, Canada is a great place to live, for most. When you look at the alternatives, things could be much worse.[2]

For this transformation to succeed, all Canadians must become engaged in the effort. Reconciliation is not about residential schools alone; this long history did not exist in a vacuum and cannot be addressed as if it did.

To Indigenous nations with thousands of years of history and inherent rights in connection to this land, the new nation of Canada is a relatively recent development. When it became a British colony in 1867 through the *British North America Act* and then an independent nation in 1982 through the *Canada Act*, Canada took on the obligations to continue to uphold the honour of the British Crown where, Section 35 states, "The existing aboriginal and treaty rights of the aboriginal peoples of Canada are hereby recognized and affirmed."[3]

In the period of early contact between displaced Europeans and Indigenous nations, there was often a mutual respect and a harmonious sense of working together on many levels. How else would the fur trade and some treaties have been possible? Since that time, however, Canada has not done a very good job of upholding the honour of the Crown. Canada has often moved in an aggressive and intrusive manner, and this has created many problems on both sides. And Canada has a history of misinterpreting and misrepresenting what these problems are. It is not "the Indian problem" that some people *are* Indigenous. It is "the Canada problem," because Canada has failed to understand that Indigenous peoples are nations that developed on, and are linked to, their territories and, thus, possess distinct identities and rights that will never be legislated or schooled away.

Colonialism and assimilation clearly did not work and will not work. Indigenous peoples are still here asserting their identities and demanding rights. So what is the new course of action to accommodate this? As many authors have noted, Section 35 in 1982 and RCAP in 1994 articulated the new relationship that is needed, but words on paper are not enough. We are now 27 years into Section 35 and 15 years into RCAP's 20-year implementation plan.

The *Indian Residential Schools Settlement Agreement* is not the only landscape-changing development either. Since the failure of the conferences of First Ministers on Aboriginal Constitutional Matters mandated by Section 35, there have been a series of court cases further articulating Aboriginal rights in law; including, *Sparrow, Van der Peet, Delgamuukw, Gladstone,* and *Haida Taku,* but these judgments have thus far not been adequately reflected in policy and legislation at the grassroots level. So the question of change, posed above, can also be rephrased to reflect this movement: "When will there be significant change?" This question, too, can be hopeful and about all Canadians.

In 2007, the British Columbia Supreme Court released its decision in *Tsilhqot'in Nation v. British Columbia.* This decision is the most significant trial judgment on Aboriginal title and rights since the Supreme Court of Canada decided the *Delgamuukw* case in 1997.[4] In his 485-page judgment, the Honourable Mr. Justice Vickers spent the closing 18 pages on the issue of reconciliation. Justice Vickers states: "Throughout the course of the trial and over the long months of preparing this judgment, my consistent hope has been that, whatever the outcome, it would ultimately lead to an early and honourable reconciliation ... The time to reach an honourable resolution and reconciliation is with us today."[5] He refers to Black's Law Dictionary, eighth edition, defining reconciliation as: "Restoration of harmony between persons or things that had been in conflict."[6] Justice Vickers goes on to state:

> The relationship between Aboriginal and non-Aboriginal Canadians has a troubled history. Thus, there is a kindling of hope and expectation that a just and honourable reconciliation with First Nations people will be achieved by this generation of Canadians... Unfortunately, the initial reluctance of governments to acknowledge the full impact of s. 35(1) has placed the question of reconciliation in the courtroom – one of our most adversarial settings.[7]

The judge expressed the hope that his decision will assist the parties in finding a contemporary solution that balances Tsilhqot'in interests and needs with the interests and needs of the broader society. The Court's decision, he indicated, constituted one step in the process of reconciliation.[8] "Reconciliation," Justice Vickers says, "is a process. It is in the interests of all Canadians that we begin to engage in this process at the earliest possible date."[9] Justice Vickers' strong tone is speaking out beyond the judiciary to all of Canada, and hopefully Canadians can hear the message.

Like a growing child, a new nation makes mistakes and lessons are learned. Mistakes are to be corrected where possible and lessons, even hard lessons, are invaluable. Justice Vickers' statements, the Apology, and the Truth and Reconciliation Commission provide an encouragement for Indigenous peoples and Canada to correct the mistakes of the past and forge a new reality. The roadmap that RCAP laid out is available, and a legacy of inquiries, consultations, and legal judgments are also available to guide the way. There are also volumes of reports, books, essays, and other writings to draw upon, and the AHF hopes that this volume makes a valuable contribution to this research and discourse, leading us down the path to reconciliation.

As Borrows says,

> Canada is a work in progress and there is hope. Living here one gets the distinct sense that we are not yet finished forming our political, legal and social culture; the meaning of Canadian

citizenship is in a state of flux. Tomorrow might be different, even better than today. Despite much whining and complaining, there is a well-spring of public will to debate and reform our institutions and include an ever increasing circle of people within our nation.[10]

NOTES

[1] Aboriginal Healing Foundation (2001:9). *Aboriginal Healing Foundation Program Handbook, Third Edition.* Ottawa, ON: Aboriginal Healing Foundation. The vision, mission, and values can also be found on the AHF website at: http://www.ahf.ca/about-us/mission

[2] Borrows, John (2003:223). Measuring a Work in Progress: Canada, Constitutionalism, Citizenship and Aboriginal Peoples. In Ardith Walkem and Halie Bruce (eds.), *Box of Treasures or Empty Box? Twenty Years of Section 35.* Penticton, BC: Theytus Books Ltd: 223–262.

[3] *Canada Act 1982* (U.K.), 1982, Section 35.

[4] *Blakes Bulletin on Aboriginal Issues,* The Tsilhqot'in Nation Decision on Aboriginal Title and Rights, November 2007.

[5] *Tsilhqot'in Nation v. British Columbia* (2007:441), BCSC 1700.

[6] *Tsilhqot'in Nation v. British Columbia.*

[7] *Tsilhqot'in Nation v. British Columbia.*

[8] *Blakes Bulletin on Aboriginal Law,* The Tsilhqot'in Nation Decision on Aboriginal Title and Rights, November 2007.

[9] *Tsilhqot'in Nation v. British Columbia* (2007:458).

[10] Borrows (2003:224).

Postscript:

Within the Canadian context(s) discussed above, a new element has emerged as this volume goes to print. On 29 April 2009, Pope Benedict XVI met with a delegation led by Phil Fontaine, Grand Chief of the Assembly of First Nations, and the Most Reverend James Weisgerber, President of the Canadian Conference of Catholic Bishops, who delivered a statement to the Pope about the residential schools.

Due to the timing of this development, neither the contributors to this volume nor the editorial committee were able to discuss this historic occasion. We have, however, included the formal Communiqué of the Holy See Press Office released that day as Appendix 4.

Shirley Flowers and her brother about to depart for residential school. "My mother, because of her own experience [in residential school], she was really careful sending her children away. I guess she knew what could happen or kind of knew what to expect. Well, she made sure we were clean and no lice or nothing like that so that people wouldn't give us a hard time."

Photo: Courtesy of Shirley Flowers

(This photo can be found in the Legacy of Hope Foundation's *"We were so far away..."*: *The Inuit Experience of Residential Schools* exhibit)

Editorial Committee

Gregory Younging is a member of Opsakwayak Cree Nation in Northern Manitoba. He holds a Master of Arts degree from the Institute of Canadian Studies at Carleton University and a Master of Publishing degree from the Canadian Centre for Studies in Publishing at Simon Fraser University. He received his doctoral degree from the Department of Educational Studies at University of British Columbia.

Gregory has worked for the Royal Commission on Aboriginal Peoples, Assembly of First Nations, and Native Women's Association of Canada. From 1990 to 2003, he was Managing Editor of Theytus Books. He is now Coordinator of the Indigenous Studies Program at University of British Columbia Okanagan in Kelowna. Gregory is a former member of Canada Council's Aboriginal Arts Advisory Committee and the British Columbia Arts Council. He is currently Chair of the Indigenous Peoples Caucus of Creator's Rights Alliance.

Jonathan Dewar has served as Director of Research at the Aboriginal Healing Foundation since 2007 and is a past director of the Métis Centre at the National Aboriginal Health Organization. He has government and non-government research and policy experience on a variety of First Nations, Inuit, and Métis issues, including arts and wellness, language legislation and promotion, justice and crime prevention, youth social issues, education and literacy, and land claims. Jonathan was also the founding executive director of the Qaggiq Theatre Company in Iqaluit, Nunavut.

Born and raised in Ottawa, Ontario, Jonathan is proud of his mixed Canadian heritage, descended from Scottish, French, and Huron-Wendat ancestors. A wise man once told him that he should be sure to honour each of his grandparents, and Jonathan sees his work within the reconciliation effort as a fulfillment of that advice. Jonathan is the father of two beautiful girls and is presently completing his doctorate in Canadian Studies, focusing on art and reconciliation.

Mike DeGagné is founding Executive Director of the Aboriginal Healing Foundation, a national Aboriginal organization dedicated to addressing the legacy of Canada's Indian residential school system. He has worked in the field of addiction and mental health for the past 25 years, first as a community worker on-reserve in northern Ontario and later with the Addiction Research Foundation, the Canadian Centre on Substance Abuse, and the National Native Alcohol and Drug Abuse Program. With the federal government, he has been an executive manager in Aboriginal health and a land claims negotiator.

Mike lectures and teaches nationally and internationally on issues of Aboriginal health, residential schools, reconciliation, and governance. He is currently Vice-President of the Child Welfare League of Canada and past Chairman of the Queensway Carleton Hospital. He holds degrees in health and administration and a doctorate that focuses on Aboriginal post-secondary education.

ACKNOWLEDGEMENTS

The editorial committee gratefully acknowledges the many contributors to this collection and their willingness to accept our invitation in the midst of pressures and pressing deadlines in their own personal and professional lives. Each of them worked graciously with our editorial team, and we are touched by the depth of their engagement and commitment to serving the needs of community and communities in Canada.

We also express a deep gratitude for the outstanding efforts of Aboriginal Healing Foundation staff. Flora Kallies, senior research officer, managed all aspects of the project with great aplomb and provided the layout and design for the volume. She was ably assisted in fact-checking and copy-editing by research officer Jane Hubbard's similarly tireless efforts, with further assistance from Vanessa Stevens, research assistant. Jackie Brennan, executive assistant, handled the many pressing administrative details with her usual grace and efficiency. Working alongside each of them has been a pleasure.

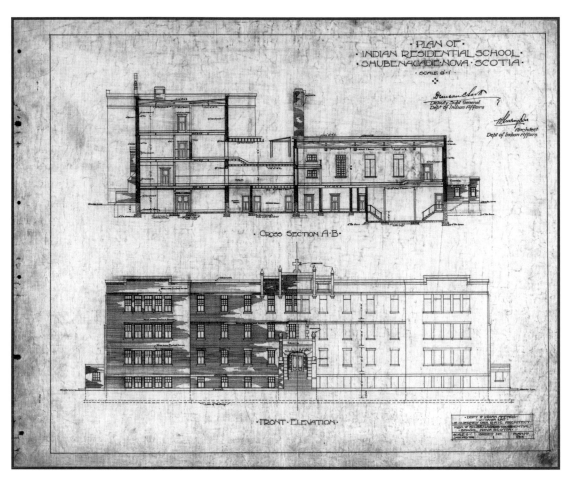

Courtesy of Legacy of Hope Foundation

(This photo can also be found, along with many other resources, at www.wherearethechildren.ca)

CANADA'S STATEMENT OF RECONCILIATION

LEARNING FROM THE PAST

As Aboriginal and non-Aboriginal Canadians seek to move forward together in a process of renewal, it is essential that we deal with the legacies of the past affecting the Aboriginal peoples of Canada, including the First Nations, Inuit and Métis. Our purpose is not to rewrite history but, rather, to learn from our past and to find ways to deal with the negative impacts that certain historical decisions continue to have in our society today.

The ancestors of First Nations, Inuit and Métis peoples lived on this continent long before explorers from other continents first came to North America. For thousands of years before this country was founded, they enjoyed their own forms of government. Diverse, vibrant Aboriginal nations had ways of life rooted in fundamental values concerning their relationships to the Creator, the environment, and each other, in the role of Elders as the living memory of their ancestors, and in their responsibilities as custodians of the lands, waters and resources of their homelands.

The assistance and spiritual values of the Aboriginal peoples who welcomed the newcomers to this continent too often have been forgotten. The contributions made by all Aboriginal peoples to Canada's development, and the contributions that they continue to make to our society today, have not been properly acknowledged. The Government of Canada today, on behalf of all Canadians, acknowledges those contributions.

Sadly, our history with respect to the treatment of Aboriginal people is not something in which we can take pride. Attitudes of racial and cultural superiority led to a suppression of Aboriginal culture and values. As a country, we are burdened by past actions that resulted in weakening the identity of Aboriginal peoples, suppressing their languages and cultures, and outlawing spiritual practices. We must recognize the impact of these actions on the once self-sustaining nations that were disaggregated, disrupted, limited or even destroyed by the dispossession of traditional territory, by the relocation of Aboriginal people, and by some provisions of the Indian Act. We must acknowledge that the result of these actions was the erosion of the political, economic and social systems of Aboriginal people and nations.

Against the backdrop of these historical legacies, it is a remarkable tribute to the strength and endurance of Aboriginal people that they have maintained their historic diversity and identity. The Government of Canada today formally expresses to all Aboriginal people in Canada our profound regret for past actions of the federal government which have contributed to these difficult pages in the history of our relationship together.

One aspect of our relationship with Aboriginal people over this period that requires particular attention is the Residential School system. This system separated many children from their families and communities and prevented them from speaking their own languages and from learning about their heritage and cultures. In the worst cases, it left legacies of personal pain and distress that continue to reverberate in Aboriginal communities to this day. Tragically, some children were the victims of physical and sexual abuse.

The Government of Canada acknowledges the role it played in the development and administration of these schools. Particularly to those individuals who experienced the tragedy of sexual and physical abuse at residential schools, and who have carried this burden believing that in some way they must be responsible, we wish to emphasize that what you experienced was not your fault and should never have happened. To those of you who suffered this tragedy at residential schools, we are deeply sorry.

In dealing with the legacies of the Residential School system, the Government of Canada proposes to work with First Nations, Inuit and Métis people, the Churches and other interested parties to resolve the longstanding issues that must be addressed. We need to work together on a healing strategy to assist individuals and communities in dealing with the consequences of this sad era of our history.

No attempt at reconciliation with Aboriginal people can be complete without reference to the sad events culminating in the death of Métis leader Louis Riel. These events cannot be undone; however, we can and will continue to look for ways of affirming the contributions of Métis people in Canada and of reflecting Louis Riel's proper place in Canada's history.

Reconciliation is an ongoing process. In renewing our partnership, we must ensure that the mistakes which marked our past relationship are not repeated. The Government of Canada recognizes that policies that sought to assimilate Aboriginal people, women and men, were not the way to build a strong country. We must instead continue to find ways in which Aboriginal people can participate fully in the economic, political, cultural and social life of Canada in a manner which preserves and enhances the collective identities of Aboriginal communities, and allows them to evolve and flourish in the future. Working together to achieve our shared goals will benefit all Canadians, Aboriginal and non-Aboriginal alike.

Retrieved 23 January 2008 from: http://www.ainc-inac.ca/gs/rec_e.html

CANADA'S STATEMENTS OF APOLOGY

PRIME MINISTER HARPER OFFERS FULL APOLOGY ON BEHALF OF CANADIANS FOR THE INDIAN RESIDENTIAL SCHOOLS SYSTEM

[On 11 June 2008, Canadian Prime Minister Stephen Harper offered a full apology on behalf of Canadians for the Indian Residential Schools system. Below is the text of his speech delivered in the House of Commons.]

The treatment of children in Indian Residential Schools is a sad chapter in our history.

For more than a century, Indian Residential Schools separated over 150,000 Aboriginal children from their families and communities. In the 1870's, the federal government, partly in order to meet its obligation to educate Aboriginal children, began to play a role in the development and administration of these schools. Two primary objectives of the Residential Schools system were to remove and isolate children from the influence of their homes, families, traditions and cultures, and to assimilate them into the dominant culture. These objectives were based on the assumption Aboriginal cultures and spiritual beliefs were inferior and unequal. Indeed, some sought, as it was infamously said, "to kill the Indian in the child". Today, we recognize that this policy of assimilation was wrong, has caused great harm, and has no place in our country.

One hundred and thirty-two federally-supported schools were located in every province and territory, except Newfoundland, New Brunswick and Prince Edward Island. Most schools were operated as "joint ventures" with Anglican, Catholic, Presbyterian or United Churches. The Government of Canada built an educational system in which very young children were often forcibly removed from their homes, often taken far from their communities. Many were inadequately fed, clothed and housed. All were deprived of the care and nurturing of their parents, grandparents and communities. First Nations, Inuit and Métis languages and cultural practices were prohibited in these schools. Tragically, some of these children died while attending residential schools and others never returned home.

The government now recognizes that the consequences of the Indian Residential Schools policy were profoundly negative and that this policy has had a lasting and damaging impact on Aboriginal culture, heritage and language. While some former students have spoken positively about their experiences at residential schools, these stories are far overshadowed by tragic accounts of the emotional, physical and sexual abuse and neglect of helpless children, and their separation from powerless families and communities.

The legacy of Indian Residential Schools has contributed to social problems that continue to exist in many communities today.

It has taken extraordinary courage for the thousands of survivors that have come forward to speak publicly about the abuse they suffered. It is a testament to their resilience as individuals and to the strength of their cultures. Regrettably, many former students are not with us today and died never having received a full apology from the Government of Canada.

The government recognizes that the absence of an apology has been an impediment to healing and reconciliation. Therefore, on behalf of the Government of Canada and all Canadians, I stand before you, in this Chamber so central to our life as a country, to apologize to Aboriginal Peoples for Canada's role in the Indian Residential Schools system.

To the approximately 80,000 living former students, and all family members and communities, the Government of Canada now recognizes that it was wrong to forcibly remove children from their homes and we apologize for having done this. We now recognize that it was wrong to separate children from rich and vibrant cultures and traditions that it created a void in many lives and communities, and we apologize for having done this. We now recognize that, in separating children from their families, we undermined the ability of many to adequately parent their own children and sowed the seeds for generations to follow, and we apologize for having done this. We now recognize that, far too often, these institutions gave rise to abuse or neglect and were inadequately controlled, and we apologize for failing to protect you. Not only did you suffer these abuses as children, but as you became parents, you were powerless to protect your own children from suffering the same experience, and for this we are sorry.

The burden of this experience has been on your shoulders for far too long. The burden is properly ours as a Government, and as a country. There is no place in Canada for the attitudes that inspired the Indian

Residential Schools system to ever prevail again. You have been working on recovering from this experience for a long time and in a very real sense, we are now joining you on this journey. The Government of Canada sincerely apologizes and asks the forgiveness of the Aboriginal Peoples of this country for failing them so profoundly.

Nous le regrettons

We are sorry

Nimitataynan

Niminchinowesamin

Mamiattugut

In moving towards healing, reconciliation and resolution of the sad legacy of Indian Residential Schools, implementation of the Indian Residential Schools Settlement Agreement began on September 19, 2007. Years of work by survivors, communities, and Aboriginal organizations culminated in an agreement that gives us a new beginning and an opportunity to move forward together in partnership.

A cornerstone of the Settlement Agreement is the Indian Residential Schools Truth and Reconciliation Commission. This Commission presents a unique opportunity to educate all Canadians on the Indian Residential Schools system. It will be a positive step in forging a new relationship between Aboriginal Peoples and other Canadians, a relationship based on the knowledge of our shared history, a respect for each other and a desire to move forward together with a renewed understanding that strong families, strong communities and vibrant cultures and traditions will contribute to a stronger Canada for all of us.

Retrieved 24 November 2008 from: http://pm.gc.ca/eng/media.asp?id=2149

HONOURABLE STÉPHANE DION
LEADER OF THE OFFICIAL OPPOSITION

Mr. Speaker, today, Canada comes face to face with some of the darkest chapters of its history: the forced assimilation of Aboriginal Peoples carried out through the residential schools system—a system, sadly, older than Confederation itself.

Schools aimed at "killing the Indian in the child" and eradicating aboriginal identity; schools built on the removal of children from their families and communities; schools designed to rip out of children their aboriginal identity, culture, beliefs and language.

A dehumanizing system that fostered the worst kinds of abuse.

Government policy destroyed the fabric of family in First Nations, Métis and Inuit communities. Parents and children were made to feel worthless. Parents and grandparents were given no choice. Their children were stolen from them.

And only now are we beginning to understand the terrible price of these policies.

Today we live in a reality created by the residential schools system, a present that is haunted by this tragic and painful heritage for those First Nations, Métis and Inuit children, for their families and their communities, a dark and painful heritage that all Canadians must accept as a part of our history.

For too long, Canadian governments chose denial over truth, and when confronted with the weight of truth, chose silence. For too long, Canadian governments refused to acknowledge their direct role in creating the residential schools system and perpetrating their dark and insidious goal of wiping out aboriginal identity and culture. For too long, Canadian governments chose to ignore the consequences of this tragedy instead of trying to understand them so that the suffering of First Nations, Métis and Inuit communities continues to this day.

Let me quote the damning verdict of the 1996 Royal Commission on Aboriginal Peoples:

> With very few exceptions, neither senior departmental officials nor churchmen nor members of Parliament raised their voices

against the assumptions that underlay the [residential schools] system or its abusive character. And, of course, the memory did not and has not faded. It has persisted, festered and become a sorrowful monument.

Today, we lay the first stone in building a new monument, a monument dedicated to truth, reconciliation and a better future.

Today, we representatives of the Canadian people apologize to those who survived residential schools and to those who died as a result of the laws enacted by previous governments and parliaments. By speaking directly to survivors and victims today on the floor of the House of Commons, we apologize to those who died waiting for these words to be spoken and these wrongs acknowledged.

Successive Canadian governments and various churches were complicit in the mental, physical and sexual abuse of thousands of aboriginal children through the residential schools system. As the leader of the Liberal Party of Canada, a party that was in government for more than 70 years in the 20th century, I acknowledge our role and our shared responsibility in this tragedy. I am deeply sorry. I apologize.

I am sorry that Canada attempted to wilfully eradicate your identity and culture by taking you away from your families when you were children and by building a system to punish you for who you were.

To First Nations, Inuit and Métis, mothers and fathers, I am so very sorry we took away your children. I am sorry we did not value you as parents. I am sorry we did not trust and respect you.

Today's apology is about a past that should have been completely different. But it must be also about the future. It must be about collective reconciliation and fundamental changes. It must be about moving forward together, Aboriginal and non-Aboriginal, into a future based on respect. It is about trying to find in each of us some of the immense courage that we see in the eyes of those who have survived.

It is about being inspired by the determination of survivors like National Chief Phil Fontaine and Willie Blackwater who had the courage to speak out and pursue justice. It is about building on the work of former First Nations Member of Parliament Gary Merasty, whose motion calling on the government to apologize to survivors of residential schools was unanimously adopted by members of Parliament on May 1, 2007.

If we are to succeed, we need to be firmly committed to the work of the Truth and Reconciliation Commission, chaired by Justice Harry LaForme, which is responsible for investigating all aspects of the residential school system in Canada.

This means listening to those who survived the physical, mental and sexual abuse that was inflicted on them. It means understanding how Canada allowed residential schools to spread so much illness and death through diseases such as tuberculosis and pneumonia. It also means finding out what happened to the many children who disappeared into unmarked graves.

It means giving a voice to those who Canada silenced. It means giving a name to those whose identities we destroyed. It means showing our respect to those whom we degraded. It means understanding the pain of those parents and families whom we injured, who we ripped apart through our actions.

We must listen carefully to the victims who testify before the Truth and Reconciliation Commission, and we must be prepared to hear reports from the Commission about our collective past that are truly shameful. We must together, as a nation, face the truth to ensure that we never have to apologize to another generation again, that the tragedy of forced assimilation of Aboriginal Peoples in Canada never happens again.

I say this thinking of the survivors I met last night. One woman remembers clearly her early days growing up in an isolated community with her family. At age seven, her father took her by canoe to a residential school. She has great memories of life with her parents and siblings up to that day. Yet, she has no memory of the years she spent at the residential school. She survived by erasing all memory of the harsh treatment she endured. Another survivor, Marion Ironquill-Meadmore, talked about the 10 years she spent in a church-run institution. The first lesson she was taught was that her parents were not worthy. After 10 years, students left the school feeling lost in both the aboriginal and non-aboriginal worlds, ill-equipped to return to the traditional lifestyle of their community, and yet never feeling at home elsewhere. Reconciliation will require a commitment from Canadian society for action. This means ensuring that all aboriginal Canadians, First Nations, Inuit and Métis alike, share in the bounty and opportunity of this country. This means ensuring that we hear the voices of First Nations, Métis and Inuit people in their own languages, and that these aboriginal voices and languages continue to enrich the cultural heritage of the world.

We cannot be intimidated by the scale of the challenge or discouraged by the failures of the past. We owe it to all our children to pass along an even better country than we inherited from our parents and we will not do so as long as aboriginal Peoples continue to be left behind.

Four years after the conclusion of the five-year Truth and Reconciliation Commission, Canada will mark the 150th anniversary of Confederation. On that anniversary, it is my sincere hope that Aboriginal and non-Aboriginal Peoples in this country will fulfill the dream voiced in this very building 60 years ago by decorated Aboriginal veteran Thomas Prince, a dream of First Nations, Inuit and Métis people and non-Aboriginal Canadians forging a new and lasting relationship.

In his own words: "so that they can trust each other and...can walk side by side and face this world having faith and confidence in one another."

Until that day, we humbly offer our apology as the first step on the path to reconciliation and healing.

Merci. Thank you. *Meegwetch. Ekosi. Nakurmiik.*

Bloc Québécois Leader Gilles Duceppe

Mr. Speaker, I am very pleased to be here to witness—at last—the Canadian government's apology to the First Nations, Métis and Inuit people who were victims of federally funded residential schools.

Nearly 150,000 people have waited their whole lives for this day of truth and reconciliation; 90,000 of them are still with us. These 90,000 are true survivors. Over 100 years ago, the Bryce Report revealed that the mortality rate in residential schools was close to 25%. In the Old Sun residential school in Alberta, the death rate was as high as 47%. That is why I consider these former students to be survivors.

These 150,000 people were abducted from their mothers and fathers. They were separated from their sisters and brothers. They were forcibly uprooted from their communities and their traditional cultures.

For those who cannot imagine the impact that residential schools had on Aboriginal Peoples, picture a small village, a small community. Now picture all of its children, gone. No more children between 7 and 16 playing in the lanes or the woods, filling the hearts of their elders with their laughter and joy. Imagine the ever-present fear of watching their children disappear when they reached school age.

Rumours abounded about what happened to the children. All these years later, it is still horrifying to think of these things. Children were torn from their parents' arms to be assimilated. They were taken away and raised by people who had but one goal: to "kill the Indian in the child". Forced to unlearn their languages, these children could no longer communicate with their own parents. All of these things really happened, and they are a part of our collective history.

Between 1934 and 1962, six residential schools were established in Quebec: two in Cree territory, one in Algonquin territory, one in Atikamekw territory and two in Innu territory. Just like residential schools everywhere, these ones left wounds caused by abuse, ill-treatment and neglect.

Roméo Saganash, himself a survivor of residential schools, told me the story of his brother, who died within a year of entering the school. His family never found out why he died, and it took 40 years—40 long years—for his mother to find the place where he had been buried. It is impossible to erase these indelible scars, impossible to heal the souls shattered by these memories.

Yet this apology is necessary. Necessary, but not sufficient. As Roméo Saganash says, "An apology, once made, is only as good as the actions that come after it." For those who lost their childhood in the residential schools, the best apology consists of real action that will allow their children and grandchildren to hope in the future. This means that the government must take real action now. For example, the government is not spending enough to help aboriginal children reach their full potential. When problems occur that affect children, the government recommends that the children be taken out of their community for their own protection. In a way, the government is repeating the mistakes of the past.

For more than a year, we and the First Nations of Quebec have been calling for more money for First Nations so that children can remain in their communities.

Does the government not think that enough aboriginal children were removed from their communities in the past?

Here is another example. The Assembly of First Nations of Quebec and Labrador has been waiting for over a year and a half for a response from the government so that it can implement its "10,000 possibilities" project.

This 10-year plan is aimed at building 10,000 housing units, helping 10,000 young people graduate from high school and creating 10,000 jobs. If the Prime Minister's apology is sincere, let him take real action. We will support him.

Finally, there is this disgrace: the government's refusal to endorse the United Nations Declaration on the Rights of Indigenous Peoples. I am very proud that the Bloc Québécois has given clear support to this draft declaration. By agreeing to endorse the declaration, the Prime Minister can send a clear message to Aboriginal people that he has learned from past mistakes and is making a solemn promise to the victims that their children and grandchildren will have respect and dignity.

I am speaking to you, the Aboriginal representatives present on the floor of the House and watching from the gallery. All the members of the Bloc Québécois join me in reaching out to you so that, together, we can build a better future for our children and grandchildren.

That requires a relationship of mutual respect that can only be forged between nations.

On behalf of the Bloc Québécois, I extend a sincere apology for the past, and I invite us to build the future together, as nations.

Retrieved 26 November 2008 from: http://www.blocquebecois.org/archivage/discours_duceppe_pardonautochtones_anglais_080611.pdf

NEW DEMOCRATIC PARTY LEADER JACK LAYTON

Mr. Speaker, today, I rise in this House to add the voice of the New Democratic Party to the profound apology being offered humbly to first nations, Métis and Inuit on behalf of the Canadian people.

I wish to acknowledge and honour the elders who are with us here today and are participating in this ceremony, the length and breadth of this land at this very moment.

I wish to pay tribute to the First Nations, Métis and Inuit leaders who are here with us and to all of those who are guiding their communities through this difficult, emotional, momentous and hope-filled day.

I wish to recognize the children, here in this chamber today and watching at home in gatherings across the land, who also bear witness to the legacy of the residential schools.

Most importantly, I want to say to the survivors of the residential schools, some of whom have joined us here today, we are sorry for what has taken place.

Today we mark a very significant moment for Canada. It is the moment when we, as a Parliament, as a country, take responsibility for one of the most shameful periods in our history. It is the moment for us to finally apologize. It is the moment when we will start to build a shared future, a future based on equality and built on mutual respect and truth. It was this Parliament that enacted, 151 years ago, the racist legislation that established the residential schools. This Parliament chose to treat First Nations, Métis and Inuit people as not equally human. It set out to kill the Indian in the child. That choice was horribly wrong. It led to incredible suffering. It denied First Nations, Métis and Inuit the basic freedom to choose how to live their lives. For those wrongs that we have committed, we are truly sorry.

Our choice denied their children the love and nurturing of their own families and communities. It denied children the pride and self-esteem that come from learning one's heritage, language, culture and traditions. In addition to these wounds, they experienced our neglect, inadequate health care, mistreatment, and sexual abuse, all of which harmed so many children and even killed some.

Because of Canada's policies, those who survived learned to be ashamed of who they are. For these terrible actions, we are sorry.

The legacy of residential schools casts a shadow over our country. It tore apart families and communities for generations, and this continues to be felt, and felt very personally.

Nearly every First Nations person of my age that I have met is a survivor. Many are also the children of survivors.

One of those children told me about her mother, a Cree from northern Quebec, who had 12 of her 14 children taken from her. Her brother died in a residential school, but their mother was never told why or how. She was never told where her son was buried. She did not have the right to pay tribute to his life or his death. She could not mourn or say her final goodbyes to her child, as every mother should. Many years later, her daughter was working in northern Ontario and she happened to mention the story of her brother to a local. He said, "I know where your brother is buried". They went to the graveyard and he pointed to a spot beside a headstone, and said, "Your brother is buried here, unmarked". The pain inflicted by the residential schools is deeply felt by these children, who were forced to attend, and by the parents who had their children stolen from them. It is still felt in First Nations, Métis and Inuit communities across the country. The destruction of family and community ties, the psychological wounds, the loss of language and culture, and substandard education all led to widespread poverty, which remains rampant in First Nations, Métis and Inuit communities today.

The horrors of the residential schools continue to harm even those who never experienced them personally.

There can be no equivocation. The laws consciously enacted in this House put the residential schools into place and kept them going for many years.

It is in this House that we must start the process of reconciliation. That is why we are here together today and why we are here together to say we are sorry. This is a crucial first step.

However, reconciliation must be built through positive steps that show respect and restore trust. This apology must not be an end; it must be a beginning.

What is needed is a commitment to never again allow such a travesty of justice and transgression against equality to occur.

It begins with officially recognizing the rights and cultures of First Nations, Métis and Inuit Peoples by signing the UN Declaration on the Rights of Indigenous Peoples.

But reconciliation also means that, as a Parliament and as a country, we must take action to address the terrible inequality faced by First Nations, Métis and Inuit communities. We can start by restoring the nation-to-nation relationship between the Government of Canada and First Nations, Métis and the Inuit.

Even as we speak here today, thousands of aboriginal children are without proper schools or clean water, adequate food, their own bed, good health care, safety, comfort, land and rights. We can no longer throw up our hands and say, "There's nothing we can do". Taking responsibility and working toward reconciliation means saying, "We must act together to resolve this". Let us reverse the horrific and shameful statistics afflicting aboriginal populations, now: the high rates of poverty, suicide, the poor or having no education, overcrowding, crumbling housing, and unsafe drinking water. Let us make sure that all survivors of the residential schools receive the recognition and compensation that is due to them.

We must make a serious, collective commitment. All of us together—First Nations, Métis and Inuit, Canadians who have been here for generations and new Canadians as well—must build a future based on fairness, equality and respect.

This must be our deep collective commitment.

Let us all, First Nations, Métis, Inuit, Canadians who have been here for generations, and new Canadians, build a fair, equal and respectful Canada for all.

Meegwetch. Ekosi. Nakurmiik.

Retrieved 26 November 2008 from: http://archive.ndp.ca/page/6525/print

CHURCH APOLOGIES

THE UNITED CHURCH OF CANADA
APOLOGY TO FIRST NATIONS PEOPLES (1986)

Long before my people journeyed to this land your people were here, and you received from your Elders an understanding of creation and of the Mystery that surrounds us all that was deep, and rich, and to be treasured.

We did not hear you when you shared your vision. In our zeal to tell you of the good news of Jesus Christ we were closed to the value of your spirituality.

We confused Western ways and culture with the depth and breadth and length and height of the gospel of Christ. We imposed our civilization as a condition for accepting the gospel.

We tried to make you be like us and in so doing we helped to destroy the vision that made you what you were. As a result you, and we, are poorer and the image of the Creator in us is twisted, blurred, and we are not what we are meant by God to be.

We ask you to forgive us and to walk together with us in the Spirit of Christ so that our Peoples may be blessed and God's creation healed.

Right Reverend Robert Smith

Retrieved 26 November 2008 from: http://www.united-church.ca/beliefs/policies/1986/a651

THE UNITED CHURCH OF CANADA
APOLOGY TO FIRST NATIONS (1998)

To Former Students of United Church Indian Residential Schools, and to Their Families and Communities:

From the deepest reaches of your memories, you have shared with us your stories of suffering from our church's involvement in the operation of Indian Residential Schools. You have shared the personal and historic pain that you still bear, and you have been vulnerable yet again. You have also shared with us your strength and wisdom born of the life-giving dignity of your communities and traditions and your stories of survival.

In response to our church's commitment to repentance, I spoke these words of apology on behalf of the General Council Executive on Tuesday, October 27, 1998:

> "As Moderator of The United Church of Canada, I wish to speak the words that many people have wanted to hear for a very long time. On behalf of The United Church of Canada, I apologize for the pain and suffering that our church's involvement in the Indian Residential School system has caused. We are aware of some of the damage that this cruel and ill-conceived system of assimilation has perpetrated on Canada's First Nations Peoples. For this we are truly and most humbly sorry.

> "To those individuals who were physically, sexually, and mentally abused as students of the Indian Residential Schools in which The United Church of Canada was involved, I offer you our most sincere apology. You did nothing wrong. You were and are the victims of evil acts that cannot under any circumstances be justified or excused.

> "We know that many within our church will still not understand why each of us must bear the scar, the blame for this horrendous period in Canadian history. But the truth is, we are the bearers of many blessings from our ancestors, and therefore, we must also bear their burdens." Our burdens include dishonouring the depths of the struggles of First Nations Peoples and the richness of your gifts. We seek God's forgiveness and healing grace as we take steps toward building respectful, compassionate, and loving relationships with First Nations Peoples.

We are in the midst of a long and painful journey as we reflect on the cries that we did not or would not hear, and how we have behaved as a church. As we travel this difficult road of repentance, reconciliation, and healing, we commit ourselves to work toward ensuring that we will never again use our power as a church to hurt others with attitudes of racial and spiritual superiority.

"We pray that you will hear the sincerity of our words today and that you will witness the living out of our apology in our actions in the future."

The Right Reverend Bill Phipps
Moderator of The United Church of Canada

Retrieved 26 November 2008 from: http://www.united-church.ca/beliefs/policies/1998/a623

THE MISSIONARY OBLATES OF MARY IMMACULATE

An Apology to the First Nations of Canada by The Oblate Conference of Canada

The Missionary Oblates of Mary Immaculate in Canada wish, after one hundred and fifty years of being with and ministering to the Native Peoples of Canada, to offer an an apology for certain aspects of that presence and ministry.

A number of historical circumstances make this moment in history most opportune for this.

First, there is a symbolic reason. Next year, 1992, marks the five hundredth anniversary of the arrival of Europeans on the shores of America. As large scale celebrations are being prepared to mark this occasion, the Oblates of Canada wish, through this apology, to show solidarity with many Native people in Canada whose history has been adversely affected by this event. Anthropological and sociological insights of the late 20th century have shown how deep, unchallenged, and damaging was the naive cultural, ethnic, linguistic, and religious superiority complex of Christian Europe when its Peoples met and interrelated with the aboriginal Peoples of North America.

As well, recent criticisms of Indian residential schools and the exposure of instances of physical and sexual abuse within these schools call for such an apology.

Given this history, Native Peoples and other groups alike are realizing that a certain healing needs to take place before a new and more truly cooperative phase of history can occur. This healing cannot however happen until some very complex, long-standing, and deep historical issues have been addressed.

It is in this context, and with a renewed pledge to be in solidarity with Native Peoples in a common struggle for justice, that we, the Oblates of Canada, offer this apology:

We apologize for the part we played in the cultural, ethnic, linguistic, and religious imperialism that was part of the mentality with which the Peoples of Europe first met the aboriginal Peoples and which consistently has lurked behind the way the Native Peoples of Canada have been treated by civil governments and by the churches. We were, naively, part of this mentality and were, in fact, often a key player in its implementation. We recognize that this mentality has, from the beginning, and ever since, continually threatened the cultural, linguistic, and religious traditions of the Native Peoples.

We recognize that many of the problems that beset Native communities today - high unemployment, alcoholism, family breakdown, domestic violence, spiraling suicide rates, lack of healthy self-esteem - are not so much the result of personal failure as they are the result of centuries of systemic imperialism. Any people stripped of its traditions as well as of its pride falls victim to precisely these social ills. For the part that we played, however inadvertent and naive that participation, might have been, in the setting up and maintaining of a system that stripped others of not only their lands but also of their cultural, linguistic, and religious traditions we sincerely apologize.

Beyond this regret for having been part of a system which, because of its historical privilege and assumed superiority did great damage to the Native Peoples of Canada, we wish to apologize more specifically for the following:

In sympathy with recent criticisms of Native Residential Schools, we wish to apologize for the part we played in the setting up and the maintaining of those schools. We apologize for the **existence of the schools themselves**, recognizing that the biggest abuse was not what happened in the schools, but that the schools themselves happened ... that the primal bond inherent within families was violated as a matter of policy, that children were usurped from their natural communities, and that, implicitly and explicitly, these schools operated out of the premise that European languages, traditions, and religious practices were superior to Native languages, traditions, and religious practices. The residential schools were an attempt to assimilate aboriginal Peoples and we played an important role in the unfolding of this design. For this we sincerely apologize.

We wish to apologize in a very particular way for the instances of physical and sexual abuse that occurred in those schools. We reiterate that the bigger issue of abuse was the existence of the schools themselves but we wish to publicly acknowledge that there were instances of individual physical and sexual abuse. Far from attempting to defend or rationalize these cases of abuse in any way, we wish to state publicly that we acknowledge that they were inexcusable, intolerable, and a betrayal of trust in one of its most serious forms. We deeply, and very specifically, apologize to every victim of such abuse and we seek help in searching for means to bring about healing.

Finally, we wish to apologize as well for our past dismissal of many of the riches of Native religious tradition. We broke some of your peace pipes and we considered some of your sacred practices, and we considered some of your sacred practices as pagan and superstitious. This too had its origins in the colonial mentality, our European superiorly complex, which was grounded in a particular view of history. We apologize for this blindness and disrespect.

One qualification is, however, in order. As we publicly acknowledge a certain blindness in our past, we wish, too, to publicly point to some of the salient reasons for this. We do this, not as a way of subtly excusing ourselves or of rationalizing in any way so as to denigrate this apology, but as a way of more fully exposing the reasons for our past blindness and, especially, as a way of honoring, despite their mistakes, those many men and women, Native and white alike, who gave their lives and their very blood in a dedication that was most sincere and heroic.

Hindsight makes for 20-20 vision and judging the past from the insights of the present is an exact and often cruel science. When Christopher Columbus set sail for the Americas, with the blessing of the Christian Church, Western civilization lacked the insights it needed to appreciate what Columbus met upon the shores of America. The cultural, linguistic, and ethical traditions of Europe were caught up in the naive belief that they were inherently superior to those found in other parts of the world. Without excusing this superiority complex, it is necessary to name it. Sincerity alone does not set people above their place in history. Thousands of persons operated out of this mentality and gave their lives in dedication to an ideal that, while sincere in its intent, was, at one point, naively linked to a certain cultural, religious, linguistic, and ethnic superiority complex. These men and women sincerely believed that their vocations and actions were serving both God and the best interests of the Native Peoples to whom they were ministering. History has, partially, rendered a cruel judgment on their efforts, showing how, despite much sincerity and genuine dedication, their actions were sometimes naive and disrespectful in that they violated the sacred and cherished traditions of others. Hence, even as we apologize for some of the effects of their actions, we want at the same time to affirm their sincerity, the goodness of their intent, and the goodness, in many cases, of their actions.

Recognizing that within every sincere apology there is implicit the promise of conversion to a new way of acting. We, the Oblates of Canada, wish to pledge ourselves to a renewed relationship with Native Peoples which, while very much in line with the sincerity and intent of our past relationship, seeks to move beyond past mistakes to a new level of respect and mutuality. Hence ...

We renew the commitment we made 150 years ago to work with and for Native Peoples. In the spirit of our founder, Blessed Eugene De Mazenod, and the many dedicated missionaries who have served in Native communities during these 150 years, we again pledge to Native Peoples our service. We ask help in more judiciously discerning what forms that service might take today.

More specifically, we pledge ourselves to the following:

♦ We want to support an effective process of disclosure visa-vis Residential Schools. We offer to collaborate in any way we can so that the full story of the Indian Residential Schools may be written, that their positive and negative features may be recognized, and that an effective healing process might take place.

♦ We want to proclaim as inviolable the natural rights of Indian families, parents and children, so that never again will Indian communities and Indian parents see their children forcibly removed from them by other authorities.

♦ We want to denounce imperialism in all its forms and, concomitantly, pledge ourselves to work with Native Peoples in their efforts to recover their lands, their languages, their sacred traditions, and their rightful pride.

♦ We want, as Oblates, to meet with Native Peoples and together help forge a template for a renewed covenant of solidarity. Despite past mistakes and many present tensions, the Oblates have felt all along as if the Native Peoples and we belonged to the same family. As members of the same family it is imperative that we come again to that deep trust and solidarity that constitutes family. We recognize that the road beyond past hurt may be long and steep but we pledge ourselves anew to journey with Native Peoples on that road.

Reverend Doug Crosby
OMI President of the Oblate Conference of Canada
On behalf of the 1200 Missionary Oblates of Mary Immaculate
living and ministering in Canada

Retrieved 25 November 2008 from: http://www.cccb.ca/site/images/stories/pdf/oblate_apology_english.pdf

THE ANGLICAN CHURCH OF CANADA

A message from the Primate, Archbishop Michael Peers, to the National Native Convocation Minaki, Ontario, Friday, August 6, 1993

My Brothers and Sisters:

Together here with you I have listened as you have told your stories of the residential schools. I have heard the voices that have spoken of pain and hurt experienced in the schools, and of the scars which endure to this day.

I have felt shame and humiliation as I have heard of suffering inflicted by my people, and as I think of the part our church played in that suffering.

I am deeply conscious of the sacredness of the stories that you have told and I hold in the highest honour those who have told them.

I have heard with admiration the stories of people and communities who have worked at healing, and I am aware of how much healing is needed.

I also know that I am in need of healing, and my own people are in need of healing, and our church is in need of healing. Without that healing, we will continue the same attitudes that have done such damage in the past.

I also know that healing takes a long time, both for people and for communities.

I also know that it is God who heals, and that God can begin to heal when we open ourselves, our wounds, our failures and our shame to God. I want to take one step along that path here and now.

I accept and I confess before God and you, our failures in the residential schools. We failed you. We failed ourselves. We failed God. I am sorry, more than I can say, that we were part of a system which took you and your children from home and family.

I am sorry, more than I can say, that we tried to remake you in our image, taking from you your language and the signs of your identity.

I am sorry, more than I can say, that in our schools so many were abused physically, sexually, culturally and emotionally.

On behalf of the Anglican Church of Canada, I present our apology.

I do this at the desire of those in the Church like the National Executive Council, who know some of your stories and have asked me to apologize.

I do this in the name of many who do not know these stories.

And I do this even though there are those in the church who cannot accept the fact that these things were done in our name.

As soon as I am home, I shall tell all the bishops what I have said, and ask them to co-operate with me and with the National Executive Council in helping this healing at the local level. Some bishops have already begun this work.

I know how often you have heard words which have been empty because they have not been accompanied by actions. I pledge to you my best efforts, and the efforts of our church at the national level, to walk with you along the path of God's healing.

The work of the Residential Schools Working Group, the video, the commitment and the effort of the Special Assistants to the Primate for this work, the grants available for healing conferences, are some signs of that pledge, and we shall work for others.

This is Friday, the day of Jesus' suffering and death. It is the anniversary of the first atomic bomb at Hiroshima, one of the most terrible injuries ever inflicted by one people on another.

But even atomic bombs and Good Friday are not the last word. God raised Jesus from the dead as a sign that life and wholeness are the everlasting and unquenchable purpose of God.

Thank you for listening to me.

Michael Peers
Archbishop and Primate

Retrieved 11 November 2008 from: http://www.anglican.ca/Residential-Schools/resources/ apology.htm

THE PRESBYTERIAN CHURCH IN CANADA

Confessions and Apologies

"It is with deep humility and in great sorrow that we come before God and our Aboriginal brothers and sisters with our confession..."

Our Confession:

The Holy Spirit, speaking in and through Scripture, calls The Presbyterian Church in Canada to confession. This confession is our response to the word of God. We understand our mission and ministry in new ways, in part because of the testimony of Aboriginal Peoples.

We, the 120th General Assembly of The Presbyterian Church in Canada, seeking the guidance of the Spirit of God, and aware of our own sin and shortcomings, are called to speak to the Church we love. We do this, out of new understandings of our past, not out of any sense of being superior to those who have gone before us, nor out of any sense that we would have done things differently in the same context. It is with deep humility and in great sorrow that we come before God and our Aboriginal brothers and sisters with our confession.

We acknowledge that the stated policy of the Government of Canada was to assimilate Aboriginal Peoples to the dominant culture, and that The Presbyterian Church in Canada co-operated in this policy. We acknowledge that the roots of the harm we have done are found in the attitudes and values of western European colonialism, and the assumption that what was not yet molded in our image was to be discovered and exploited. As part of that policy we, with other churches, encouraged the Government to ban some important spiritual practices through which Aboriginal Peoples experienced the presence of the creator God. For the Church's complicity in this policy we ask forgiveness.

We recognize that there were many members of The Presbyterian Church in Canada who, in good faith, gave unstintingly of themselves in love and compassion for their aboriginal brothers and sisters. We acknowledge their devotion and commend them for their work. We recognize that there were some who, with prophetic insight, were aware of the damage that was being done and protested, but their efforts were thwarted. We acknowledge their insight. For the times we did not support them adequately nor hear their cries for justice, we ask forgiveness.

We confess that The Presbyterian Church in Canada presumed to know better than Aboriginal Peoples what was needed for life. The Church said of our Aboriginal brothers and sisters, "If they could be like us, if they could think like us, talk like us, worship like us, sing like us, work like us, they would know God as we know God and therefore would have life abundant". In our cultural arrogance we have been blind to the ways in which our own understanding of the Gospel has been culturally conditioned, and because of our insensitivity to aboriginal cultures, we have demanded more of Aboriginal Peoples than the gospel requires, and have thus misrepresented Jesus Christ who loves all Peoples with compassionate, suffering love that all may come to God through him. For the Church's presumption we ask forgiveness.

We confess that, with the encouragement and assistance of the Government of Canada, The Presbyterian Church in Canada agreed to take the children of Aboriginal Peoples from their own homes and place them in Residential Schools. In these schools, children were deprived of their traditional ways, which were replaced with Euro-Canadian customs that were helpful in the process of assimilation. To carry out this process, The Presbyterian Church in Canada used disciplinary practices which were foreign to Aboriginal Peoples, and open to exploitation in physical and psychological punishment beyond any Christian maxim of care and discipline. In a setting of obedience and acquiescence there was opportunity for sexual abuse, and some were so abused. The effect of all this, for Aboriginal Peoples, was the loss of cultural identity and the loss of a secure sense of self. For the Church's insensitivity we ask forgiveness.

We regret that there are those whose lives have been deeply scarred by the effects of the mission and ministry of The Presbyterian Church in Canada. For our Church we ask forgiveness of God. It is our prayer that God, who is merciful, will guide us in compassionate ways towards helping them to heal.

We ask, also, for forgiveness from Aboriginal Peoples. What we have heard we acknowledge. It is our hope that those whom we have wronged with a hurt too deep for telling will accept what we have to say. With God's guidance our Church will seek opportunities to walk with Aboriginal Peoples to find healing and wholeness together as God's people.

"God not only calls the church to confession, but to a ministry of reconciliation, walking together, seeking to restore justice in relationships where it is lacking. Our church is called to commit itself to support processes for healing of the wounds inflicted on aboriginal people."

Retrieved 25 November 2008 from: http://www.presbyterian.ca/ministry/canada/ nativeministries/confessions

COMMUNIQUÉ OF THE HOLY SEE PRESS OFFICE

At the end of the General Audience, the Holy Father met with Mr. Phil Fontaine, the Grand Chief of the Assembly of First Nations of Canada, and the Most Reverend James Weisgerber, President of the Canadian Conference of Catholic Bishops, together with those accompanying them, and he listened to their stories and concerns.

His Holiness recalled that since the earliest days of her presence in Canada, the Church, particularly through her missionary personnel, has closely accompanied the indigenous peoples. Given the sufferings that some indigenous children experienced in the Canadian Residential School system, the Holy Father expressed his sorrow at the anguish caused by the deplorable conduct of some members of the Church and he offered his sympathy and prayerful solidarity. His Holiness emphasized that acts of abuse cannot be tolerated in society. He prayed that all those affected would experience healing, and he encouraged First Nations Peoples to continue to move forward with renewed hope.

29 April 2009

Government of Newfoundland Apology

Statement of Apology to Inuit of the former Communities of Nutak and Hebron

Premier Danny Williams, on behalf of the Government of Newfoundland and Labrador, delivered a statement of apology to the Inuit of the former communities of Nutak and Hebron.

Newfoundlanders and Labradorians value a society of equality and justice. The Government of Newfoundland and Labrador, on behalf of the citizens of the province, recognizes that, in the past, it made mistakes in its treatment of the Inuit of Labrador. It is willing to learn from the past and to find ways to heal the negative impact that historical decisions and actions continue to have for certain Labrador Inuit today.

In 1956 and 1959, the Government of Newfoundland closed the communities of Nutak and Hebron.

Looking back, the closures were made without consultation with the Inuit of Nutak and Hebron. As a result of the closures, and the way they were carried out, the Inuit of Nutak and Hebron experienced a variety of personal hardships and social, family and economic problems. Some of those Inuit and their descendants continue to suffer difficulties.

The Government of Newfoundland and Labrador, on behalf of the citizens of the province, apologizes to the Inuit of Nutak and Hebron for the way in which the decision to close those communities was made and for the difficulties experienced by them and their descendants as a result of the closures.

What happened at Nutak and Hebron serves as an example of the need for governments to respect and carefully consider the needs and aspirations of the people affected by its decisions.

As a symbol of reconciliation, the Government of Newfoundland and Labrador will assist the Labrador Inuit Association in erecting an appropriate monument to remember those relocated from Nutak and Hebron, upon which this apology will be inscribed.

Andrea Webb, on behalf of the Hebron Committee, accepted the statement of apology

Mr. Premier:

On behalf of the Inuit of Nutak and Hebron, I would like to accept your apology.

We accept your apology—for ourselves, our ancestors and our descendants.

We have waited over 45 painful years for this apology, and we accept it because we want the pain and the hurting to stop. Hearing your apology helps us to move on.

We see this as a moment of recognition and truth. And we now have reason to hope that all our governments will always recognize our humanity, and will be truthful to us.

Today, the surviving Inuit of Nutak and Hebron remember all those people who are no longer with us and who have passed on without the reconciliation of this day.

To our children and grandchildren, I say to you that we recognize, with love in our hearts, that you want lives of joy, hope and opportunity. By accepting this apology, we are saying that we believe in you, and that we want to stop passing on the loss and the pain that we have carried with us.

On behalf of the Hebron Committee, I want to acknowledge the confidence and support that we have had from the Inuit of Nutak and Hebron since they elected us at our reunion in 1999. It is our wish that no ill feelings arise because we have accepted this apology. But, our job will not be over until we have received the compensation that was promised to us. We expect LIA to keep that promise as soon as possible.

When we, the Inuit of Nutak and Hebron, were evicted from our homes, we carried with us much that is precious and good: the spirit of our ancestors, the beauty of our land, the treasure of our language and the love of our God who gave us hope for our future. These are the things that we want to pass on to our children and grandchildren in a spirit of humility and forgiveness.

It is in that spirit that I say to all those who had a hand in the closing of Nutak and Hebron, and who promised that this was done for our benefit:

We forgive you.

AUSTRALIA'S APOLOGY

APOLOGY TO AUSTRALIA'S INDIGENOUS PEOPLES
HOUSE OF REPRESENTATIVES
PARLIAMENT HOUSE, CANBERRA
13 FEBRUARY 2008

I move:

> That today we honour the Indigenous Peoples of this land, the oldest continuing cultures in human history.
>
> We reflect on their past mistreatment.
>
> We reflect in particular on the mistreatment of those who were Stolen Generations—this blemished chapter in our nation's history.
>
> The time has now come for the nation to turn a new page in Australia's history by righting the wrongs of the past and so moving forward with confidence to the future.
>
> We apologise for the laws and policies of successive Parliaments and governments that have inflicted profound grief, suffering and loss on these our fellow Australians.
>
> We apologise especially for the removal of Aboriginal and Torres Strait Islander children from their families, their communities and their country.
>
> For the pain, suffering and hurt of these Stolen Generations, their descendants and for their families left behind, we say sorry.
>
> To the mothers and the fathers, the brothers and the sisters, for the breaking up of families and communities, we say sorry.
>
> And for the indignity and degradation thus inflicted on a proud people and a proud culture, we say sorry.
>
> We the Parliament of Australia respectfully request that this apology be received in the spirit in which it is offered as part of the healing of the nation.
>
> For the future we take heart; resolving that this new page in the history of our great continent can now be written.
>
> We today take this first step by acknowledging the past and laying claim to a future that embraces all Australians.
>
> A future where this Parliament resolves that the injustices of the past must never, never happen again.
>
> A future where we harness the determination of all Australians, Indigenous and non-Indigenous, to close the gap that lies between us in

life expectancy, educational achievement and economic opportunity.
A future where we embrace the possibility of new solutions to
enduring problems where old approaches have failed.
A future based on mutual respect, mutual resolve and mutual responsibility.
A future where all Australians, whatever their origins, are truly equal
partners, with equal opportunities and with an equal stake in shaping
the next chapter in the history of this great country, Australia.

There comes a time in the history of nations when their Peoples must
become fully reconciled to their past if they are to go forward with
confidence to embrace their future. Our nation, Australia, has reached
such a time. And that is why the parliament is today here assembled: to
deal with this unfinished business of the nation, to remove a great stain
from the nation's soul and, in a true spirit of reconciliation, to open a new
chapter in the history of this great land, Australia.

Last year I made a commitment to the Australian people that if we formed
the next government of the Commonwealth we would in parliament say
sorry to the Stolen Generations. Today I honour that commitment. I said
we would do so early in the life of the new parliament. Again, today I
honour that commitment by doing so at the commencement of this the
42nd parliament of the Commonwealth. Because the time has come, well
and truly come, for all Peoples of our great country, for all citizens of
our great Commonwealth, for all Australians—those who are Indigenous
and those who are not—to come together to reconcile and together build
a new future for our nation.

Some have asked, 'Why apologise?' Let me begin to answer by telling the
parliament just a little of one person's story—an elegant, eloquent and
wonderful woman in her 80s, full of life, full of funny stories, despite
what has happened in her life's journey. A woman who has travelled a long
way to be with us today, a member of the Stolen Generation who shared
some of her story with me when I called around to see her just a few days
ago. Nungala Fejo, as she prefers to be called, was born in the late 1920s.
She remembers her earliest childhood days living with her family and her
community in a bush camp just outside Tennant Creek. She remembers
the love and the warmth and the kinship of those days long ago, including
traditional dancing around the camp fire at night. She loved the dancing.
She remembers once getting into strife when, as a four-year-old girl, she
insisted on dancing with the male tribal elders rather than just sitting and
watching the men, as the girls were supposed to do.

But then, sometime around 1932, when she was about four, she remembers the coming of the welfare men. Her family had feared that day and had dug holes in the creek bank where the children could run and hide. What they had not expected was that the white welfare men did not come alone. They brought a truck, they brought two white men and an Aboriginal stockman on horseback cracking his stockwhip. The kids were found; they ran for their mothers, screaming, but they could not get away. They were herded and piled onto the back of the truck. Tears flowing, her mum tried clinging to the sides of the truck as her children were taken away to the Bungalow in Alice, all in the name of protection.

A few years later, government policy changed. Now the children would be handed over to the missions to be cared for by the churches. But which church would care for them? The kids were simply told to line up in three lines. Nanna Fejo and her sister stood in the middle line, her older brother and cousin on her left. Those on the left were told that they had become Catholics, those in the middle Methodists and those on the right Church of England. That is how the complex questions of post-reformation theology were resolved in the Australian outback in the 1930s. It was as crude as that. She and her sister were sent to a Methodist mission on Goulburn Island and then Croker Island. Her Catholic brother was sent to work at a cattle station and her cousin to a Catholic mission.

Nanna Fejo's family had been broken up for a second time. She stayed at the mission until after the war, when she was allowed to leave for a prearranged job as a domestic in Darwin. She was 16. Nanna Fejo never saw her mum again. After she left the mission, her brother let her know that her mum had died years before, a broken woman fretting for the children that had literally been ripped away from her.

I asked Nanna Fejo what she would have me say today about her story. She thought for a few moments then said that what I should say today was that all mothers are important. And she added: 'Families—keeping them together is very important. It's a good thing that you are surrounded by love and that love is passed down the generations. That's what gives you happiness.' As I left, later on, Nanna Fejo took one of my staff aside, wanting to make sure that I was not too hard on the Aboriginal stockman who had hunted those kids down all those years ago. The stockman had found her again decades later, this time himself to say, 'Sorry.' And remarkably, extraordinarily, she had forgiven him.

Nanna Fejo's is just one story. There are thousands, tens of thousands of them: stories of forced separation of Aboriginal and Torres Strait Islander children from their mums and dads over the better part of a century. Some of these stories are graphically told in Bringing Them Home, the report commissioned in 1995 by Prime Minister Keating and received in 1997 by Prime Minister Howard. There is something terribly primal about these firsthand accounts. The pain is searing; it screams from the pages. The hurt, the humiliation, the degradation and the sheer brutality of the act of physically separating a mother from her children is a deep assault on our senses and on our most elemental humanity.

These stories cry out to be heard; they cry out for an apology. Instead, from the nation's parliament there has been a stony and stubborn and deafening silence for more than a decade. A view that somehow we, the parliament, should suspend our most basic instincts of what is right and what is wrong. A view that, instead, we should look for any pretext to push this great wrong to one side, to leave it languishing with the historians, the academics and the cultural warriors, as if the Stolen Generations are little more than an interesting sociological phenomenon. But the Stolen Generations are not intellectual curiosities. They are human beings, human beings who have been damaged deeply by the decisions of parliaments and governments. But, as of today, the time for denial, the time for delay, has at last come to an end.

The nation is demanding of its political leadership to take us forward. Decency, human decency, universal human decency, demands that the nation now steps forward to right a historical wrong. That is what we are doing in this place today. But should there still be doubts as to why we must now act. Let the parliament reflect for a moment on the following facts: that, between 1910 and 1970, between 10 and 30 per cent of Indigenous children were forcibly taken from their mothers and fathers. That, as a result, up to 50,000 children were forcibly taken from their families. That this was the product of the deliberate, calculated policies of the state as reflected in the explicit powers given to them under statute. That this policy was taken to such extremes by some in administrative authority that the forced extractions of children of so-called 'mixed lineage' were seen as part of a broader policy of dealing with 'the problem of the Aboriginal population'.

One of the most notorious examples of this approach was from the Northern Territory Protector of Natives, who stated, and I quote:

Generally by the fifth and invariably by the sixth generation, all Native characteristics of the Australian aborigine are eradicated. The problem of our half-castes to quote the protector—will quickly be eliminated by the complete disappearance of the black race, and the swift submergence of their progeny in the white ...

The Western Australian Protector of Natives expressed not dissimilar views, expounding them at length in Canberra in 1937 at the first national conference on Indigenous affairs that brought together the Commonwealth and state protectors of Natives. These are uncomfortable things to be brought out into the light. They are not pleasant. They are profoundly disturbing. But we must acknowledge these facts if we are to deal once and for all with the argument that the policy of generic forced separation was somehow well motivated, justified by its historical context and, as a result, unworthy of any apology today.

Then we come to the argument of intergenerational responsibility, also used by some to argue against giving an apology today. But let us remember the fact that the forced removal of Aboriginal children was happening as late as the early 1970s. The 1970s is not exactly a point in remote antiquity. There are still serving members of this parliament who were first elected to this place in the early 1970s. It is well within the adult memory span of many of us. The uncomfortable truth for us all is that the parliaments of the nation, individually and collectively, enacted statutes and delegated authority under those statutes that made the forced removal of children on racial grounds fully lawful.

There is a further reason for an apology as well: it is that reconciliation is in fact an expression of a core value of our nation—and that value is a fair go for all. There is a deep and abiding belief in the Australian community that, for the Stolen Generations, there was no fair go at all. And there is a pretty basic Aussie belief that says it is time to put right this most outrageous of wrongs. It is for these reasons, quite apart from concerns of fundamental human decency, that the governments and parliaments of this nation must make this apology. Because, put simply, the laws that our parliaments enacted made the Stolen Generations possible. We, the parliaments of the nation, are ultimately responsible, not those who gave effect to our laws, the problem lay with the laws themselves. As has been said of settler societies elsewhere, we are the bearers of many blessings from our ancestors and therefore we must also be the bearer of their burdens as well. Therefore, for our nation, the course of action is clear. Therefore for our people, the course of action is clear. And that is, to deal now with what has become one of the darkest chapters in Australia's history. In doing so, we are doing more than contending with the facts, the evidence and the often rancorous public debate. In doing so, we are also wrestling with our own soul. This is not, as some would argue, a black-armband view of history; it is just the truth: the cold, confronting, uncomfortable truth. Facing with it, dealing with it, moving on from it. And until we fully confront that truth, there will always be a shadow hanging over us and our future as a fully united and fully reconciled people. It is time to reconcile. It is time to recognise the injustices of the past. It is time to say sorry. It is time to move forward together.

To the Stolen Generations, I say the following: as Prime Minister of Australia, I am sorry. On behalf of the Government of Australia, I am sorry. On behalf of the Parliament of Australia, I am sorry. And I offer you this apology without qualification. We apologise for the hurt, the pain and suffering we, the parliament, have caused you by the laws that previous parliaments have enacted. We apologise for the indignity, the degradation and the humiliation these laws embodied. We offer this apology to the mothers, the fathers, the brothers, the sisters, the families and the communities whose lives were ripped apart by the actions of successive governments under successive parliaments. In making this apology, I would also like to speak personally to the members of the Stolen Generation and their families: to those here today, so many of you; to those listening across the nation—from Yuendumu, in the central west of the Northern Territory, to Yabara, in North Queensland, and to Pitjantjatjara in South Australia.

I know that, in offering this apology on behalf of the government and the parliament, there is nothing I can say today that can take away the pain you have suffered personally. Whatever words I speak today, I cannot undo that. Words alone are not that powerful. Grief is a very personal thing. I say to non-Indigenous Australians listening today who may not fully understand why what we are doing is so important, I ask those non-Indigenous Australians to imagine for a moment if this had happened to you. I say to honourable members here present: imagine if this had happened to us. Imagine the crippling effect. Imagine how hard it would be to forgive. But my proposal is this: if the apology we extend today is accepted in the spirit of reconciliation, in which it is offered, we can today resolve together that there be a new beginning for Australia. And it is to such a new beginning that I believe the nation is now calling us.

Australians are a passionate lot. We are also a very practical lot. For us, symbolism is important but, unless the great symbolism of reconciliation is accompanied by an even greater substance, it is little more than a clanging gong. It is not sentiment that makes history; it is our actions that make history. Today's apology, however inadequate, is aimed at righting past wrongs. It is also aimed at building a bridge between Indigenous and non-Indigenous Australians—a bridge based on a real respect rather than a thinly veiled contempt. Our challenge for the future is now to cross that bridge and, in so doing, embrace a new partnership between Indigenous and non-Indigenous Australians. Embracing, as part of that partnership, expanded link-up and other critical services to help the Stolen Generations to trace their families, if at all possible, and to provide dignity to their lives. But the core of this partnership for the future is to closing the gap between Indigenous and non-Indigenous Australians on life expectancy, educational achievement and employment opportunities. This new partnership on closing the gap will set concrete targets for the future: within a decade to halve the widening gap in literacy, numeracy and employment outcomes and opportunities for Indigenous children, within a decade to halve the appalling gap in infant mortality rates between Indigenous and non-Indigenous children and, within a generation, to close the equally appalling 17-year life gap between Indigenous and non-Indigenous when it comes when it comes to overall life expectancy.

The truth is: a business as usual approach towards Indigenous Australians is not working. Most old approaches are not working. We need a new beginning. A new beginning which contains real measures of policy success or policy failure. A new beginning, a new partnership, on closing the gap with sufficient flexibility not to insist on a one-size-fits-all approach for each of the hundreds of remote and regional Indigenous communities across the country but instead allows flexible, tailored, local approaches to achieve commonly-agreed national objectives that lie at the core of our proposed new partnership. And a new beginning that draws intelligently on the experiences of new policy settings across the nation. However, unless we as a parliament set a destination for the nation, we have no clear point to guide our policy, our programs or our purpose; no centralised organising principle.

So let us resolve today to begin with the little children—a fitting place to start on this day of apology for the Stolen Generations. Let us resolve over the next five years to have every Indigenous four-year-old in a remote Aboriginal community enrolled and attending a proper early childhood education centre or opportunity and engaged in proper preliteracy and prenumeracy programs. Let us resolve to build new educational opportunities for these little ones, year by year, step by step, following the completion of their crucial preschool year. Let us resolve to use this systematic approach to building future educational opportunities for Indigenous children to provide proper primary and preventive health care for the same children, to begin the task of rolling back the obscenity that we find today in infant mortality rates in remote Indigenous communities— up to four times higher than in other communities.

None of this will be easy. Most of it will be hard—very hard. But none of it, none of it, is impossible, and all of it is achievable with clear goals, clear thinking, and by placing an absolute premium on respect, cooperation and mutual responsibility as the guiding principles of this new partnership on closing the gap. The mood of the nation is for reconciliation now, between Indigenous and non-Indigenous Australians. The mood of the nation on Indigenous policy and politics is now very simple. The nation is calling on us, the politicians, to move beyond our infantile bickering, our point-scoring and our mindlessly partisan politics and elevate at least this one core area of national responsibility to a rare position beyond the partisan divide. Surely this is the spirit, the unfulfilled spirit, of the 1967 referendum. Surely, at least from this day forward, we should give it a go.

So let me take this one step further to take what some may see as a piece of political posturing and make a practical proposal to the opposition on this day, the first full sitting day of the new parliament. I said before the election the nation needed a kind of war cabinet on parts of Indigenous policy, because the challenges are too great and the consequences too great to just allow it all to become a political football, as it has been so often in the past. I therefore propose a joint policy commission, to be led by the Leader of the Opposition and myself and, with a mandate to develop and implement—to begin with—an effective housing strategy for remote communities over the next five years. It will be consistent with the government's policy framework, a new partnership for closing the gap. If this commission operates well, I then propose that it work on the further task of constitutional recognition of the first Australians, consistent with the longstanding platform commitments of my party and the pre-election position of the opposition. This would probably be desirable in any event because, unless such a proposition were absolutely bipartisan, it would fail at a referendum. As I have said before, the time has come for new approaches to enduring problems. And working constructively together on such defined projects, I believe, would meet with the support of the nation. It is time for fresh ideas to fashion the nation's future.

Today the parliament has come together to right a great wrong. We have come together to deal with the past so that we might fully embrace the future. And we have had sufficient audacity of faith to advance a pathway to that future, with arms extended rather than with fists still clenched. So let us seize the day. Let it not become a moment of mere sentimental reflection. Let us take it with both hands and allow this day, this day of national reconciliation, to become one of those rare moments in which we might just be able to transform the way in which the nation thinks about itself, whereby the injustice administered to these Stolen Generations in the name of these, our parliaments, causes all of us to reappraise, at the deepest level of our beliefs, the real possibility of reconciliation writ large. Reconciliation across all Indigenous Australia. Reconciliation across the entire history of the often bloody encounter between those who emerged from the Dreamtime a thousand generations ago and those who, like me, came across the seas only yesterday. Reconciliation which opens up whole new possibilities for the future.

For the nation to bring the first two centuries of our settled history to a close, as we begin a new chapter and which we embrace with pride, admiration and awe these great and ancient cultures we are blessed, truly blessed, to have among us. Cultures that provide a unique, uninterrupted human thread linking our Australian continent to the most ancient prehistory of our planet. And growing from this new respect, to see our Indigenous brothers and sisters with fresh eyes, with new eyes, and with our minds wide open as to how we might tackle, together, the great practical challenges that Indigenous Australia faces in the future.

So let us turn this page together: Indigenous and non-Indigenous Australians, Government and Opposition, Commonwealth and State, and write this new chapter in our nation's story together. First Australians, First Fleeters, and those who first took the Oath of Allegiance just a few weeks ago. Let's grasp this opportunity to craft a new future for this great land: Australia. I commend the motion to the House.

Kevin Rudd
Prime Minister of Australia

Retrieved 6 April 2009 from: http://www.pm.gov.au/media/speech/2008/speech_0073.cfm

United States of America's Proposed Apology

S. J. Res. 4
[Report No. 110-83]

To acknowledge a long history of official depredations and ill-conceived policies by the United States government regarding Indian tribes and offer an apology to all Native Peoples on behalf of the United States.

In the Senate of the United States

March 1, 2007

Mr. Brownback, (for himself, Mr. Inouye, Ms. Cantwell, Mr. Dodd, Ms. Landrieu, Mr. Crapo, Mr. Dorgan, Mrs. Boxer, Mr. Lieberman, and Mr. Akaka) introduced the following joint resolution; which was read twice and referred to the Committee on Indian Affairs

June 18, 2007
reported by Mr. Dorgan, without amendment

Joint Resolution

To acknowledge a long history of official depredations and ill-conceived policies by the United States government regarding Indian tribes and offer an apology to all Native Peoples on behalf of the United States.

Whereas the ancestors of today's Native Peoples inhabited the land of the present-day United States since time immemorial and for thousands of years before the arrival of Peoples of European descent;

Whereas the Native Peoples have for millennia honored, protected, and stewarded this land we cherish;

Whereas the Native Peoples are spiritual Peoples with a deep and abiding belief in the creator, and for millennia their Peoples have maintained a powerful spiritual connection to this land, as is evidenced by their customs and legends; whereas the arrival of europeans in north america opened a new chapter in the histories of the Native Peoples; Whereas, while establishment of permanent european settlements in North America did stir conflict with nearby Indian tribes, peaceful and mutually beneficial interactions also took place;

Whereas the foundational english settlements in Jamestown, Virginia, and Plymouth, Massachusetts, owed their survival in large measure to the compassion and aid of the Native Peoples in their vicinities;

Whereas in the infancy of the United States, the founders of the republic expressed their desire for a just relationship with the Indian tribes, as evidenced by the northwest ordinance enacted by congress in 1787, which begins with the phrase, "the utmost good faith shall always be observed toward the Indians";

Whereas Indian tribes provided great assistance to the fledgling Republic as it strengthened and grew, including invaluable help to Meriwether Lewis and William Clark on their epic journey from St. Louis, Missouri, to the Pacific Coast;

Whereas Native Peoples and non-Native settlers engaged in numerous armed conflicts;

Whereas the United States Government violated many of the treaties ratified by congress and other diplomatic agreements with Indian tribes;

Whereas this nation should address the broken treaties and many of the more ill-conceived federal policies that followed, such as extermination, termination, forced removal and relocation, the outlawing of traditional religions, and the destruction of sacred places;

Whereas the United States forced Indian tribes and their citizens to move away from their traditional homelands and onto federally established and controlled reservations, in accordance with such acts as the Indian Removal Act of 1830;

Whereas many Native Peoples suffered and perished—
(1) during the execution of the official United States government policy of forced removal, including the infamous rail of tears and long walk;
(2) during bloody armed confrontations and massacres, such as the sand creek massacre in 1864 and the wounded knee massacre in 1890; and
(3) on numerous Indian reservations;

Whereas the United States government condemned the traditions, beliefs, and customs of the Native Peoples and endeavored to assimilate them by such policies as the redistribution of land under the general allotment act of 1887 and the forcible removal of Native children from their families to faraway boarding schools where their Native practices and languages were degraded and forbidden;

Whereas officials of the United States government and private United States citizens harmed Native Peoples by the unlawful acquisition of recognized tribal land and the theft of tribal resources and assets from recognized tribal land;

Whereas the policies of the United States government toward Indian tribes and the breaking of covenants with Indian tribes have contributed to the severe social ills and economic troubles in many Native communities today;

Whereas, despite the wrongs committed against Native Peoples by the United States, the Native Peoples have remained committed to the protection of this great land, as evidenced by the fact that, on a per capita basis, more Native people have served in the United States armed forces and placed themselves in harm's way in defense of the United States in every major military conflict than any other ethnic group;

Whereas Indian tribes have actively influenced the public life of the United States by continued cooperation with congress and the department of the interior, through the involvement of Native individuals in official United States government positions, and by leadership of their own sovereign Indian tribes; whereas Indian tribes are resilient and determined to preserve, develop, and transmit to future generations their unique cultural identities;

Whereas the national museum of the american Indian was established within the smithsonian institution as a living memorial to the Native Peoples and their traditions; and

Whereas Native Peoples are endowed by their creator with certain unalienable rights, and that among those are life, liberty, and the pursuit of happiness: now, therefore, be it Resolved by the Senate and House of Representatives of the United States of America in Congress assembled,

SECTION 1. ACKNOWLEDGMENT AND APOLOGY.

The United States, acting through congress—

(1) recognizes the special legal and political relationship the Indian tribes have with the United States and the solemn covenant with the land we share;

(2) commends and honors the Native Peoples for the thousands of years that they have stewarded and protected this land;

(3) recognizes that there have been years of official depredations, ill-conceived policies, and the breaking of covenants by the United States Government regarding Indian tribes;

(4) apologizes on behalf of the people of the United States to all Native Peoples for the many instances of violence, maltreatment, and neglect inflicted on Native Peoples by citizens of the United States;

(5) expresses its regret for the ramifications of former wrongs and its commitment to build on the positive relationships of the past and present to move toward a brighter future where all the people of this land live reconciled as brothers and sisters, and harmoniously steward and protect this land together;

(6) urges the President to acknowledge the wrongs of the United States against Indian tribes in the history of the United States in order to bring healing to this land by providing a proper foundation for reconciliation between the United States and Indian tribes; and

(7) commends the state governments that have begun reconciliation efforts with recognized Indian tribes located in their boundaries and encourages all State governments similarly to work toward reconciling relationships with Indian tribes within their boundaries.

SEC. 2. DISCLAIMER.

Nothing in this joint resolution—

(1) authorizes or supports any claim against the United States; or

(2) serves as a settlement of any claim against the United States.

Retrieved 6 April 2009 from: http://www.govtrack.us/congress/billtext.xpd?bill=sj110-4

PRESIDENT BARACK OBAMA'S MESSAGE FOR FIRST AMERICANS

The truth is few have been ignored by Washington as much as the American Indians... That will change when I am President of the United States... We need a Nation-to-Nation relationship... I understand the tragic history between the United States and Tribal Nations. And we've got to acknowledge that truth if we are going to move forward in a fair and honest way. Indian Nations have never asked much of the United States. Only for what was promised by Treaty obligations made to their forbearers. So let me be absolutely clear: I believe Treaty commitments are paramount law, and I will fulfill those commitments when I am President of the United States. That means working with tribal governments to ensure that all American Indians receive accessible and affordable health care services. That's why I co-sponsored the Indian Health Care Improvement Act in the United States Senate. And that's why I fought to ensure full funding of the Indian health service so that it has the resources it needs. It also means guarantying a world class education for all our children. I'll work with tribal nations to reform No Child Left Behind. I'll create opportunities for tribal citizens to become teachers, so you can be free to teach your children the way you know best. I'll increase funding to tribal colleges. And I will make Native language education and preservation a priority... And I will never forget the services and sacrifices that generation of American Indians have given to this country. We have to keep our sacred trust with Indian veterans by making sure that no veteran falls into homelessness... The American Indians that I have met across this country will be on my mind each day that I am in the Whitehouse. You deserve a President who is committed to being a full partner with you, to respecting you, honouring you, working with you every day. That is the commitment I will make to you as President of the United States.

Retrieved and transcribed on 8 April 2009 from: http://www.youtube.com/watch?v=OWocEgu3bPk